The Dialects of Basque

Center for Basque Studies
Occasional Papers Series, No. 21

The Dialects of Basque

Koldo Zuazo

Translated by Aritz Branton

Center for Basque Studies
University of Nevada, Reno
Reno, Nevada

This book was published with generous financial support from the Basque government.

Center for Basque Studies
Occasional Papers Series, No. 21
Series Editors: Joseba Zulaika and Cameron J. Watson

Center for Basque Studies
University of Nevada, Reno
Reno, Nevada 89557
http://basque.unr.edu

Originally published as *Euskalkiak: Euskararen dialektoak* by Elkar (Donostia-San Sebastián, 2008)

Map and book design by John Coleman
Cover photo: "Reds at San Fermin, Pamplona" by rusticus80 from Wikimedia Commons, edited by Daniel Montero and John Coleman
Cover dictionary text: modified from *CBS-Morris English-Basque/Basque-English Dictionary* by Michael Morris

Library of Congress Cataloging-in-Publication Data

Zuazo, Koldo.
[Euskalkiak. English]
The Dialects of Basque / Koldo Zuazo ; Translated by Aritz Branton.
pages cm. -- (Occasional papers ; no. 21)
Originally published as: Euskalkiak, Euskararen Dialektoak (Basque Dialects) in 2008."
ISBN 978-1-935709-42-8 (pbk.)
1. Basque language--Dialects. I. Branton, Aritz, translator. II. Title.

PH5187.Z82913 2013
499'.927--dc23

2013030066

Gasteizko Filologia Fakultateko ikasleei,
berez ikasle soil zirenak
irakasle bikain gertatu direlako maiz.
Eskerrik zintzoena denei.

To the students at the Philology Faculty in Gasteiz.
Many who were once just students
have become excellent teachers.
My most sincere thanks to all of you.

Contents

Basque Dialects and Sub-Dialects

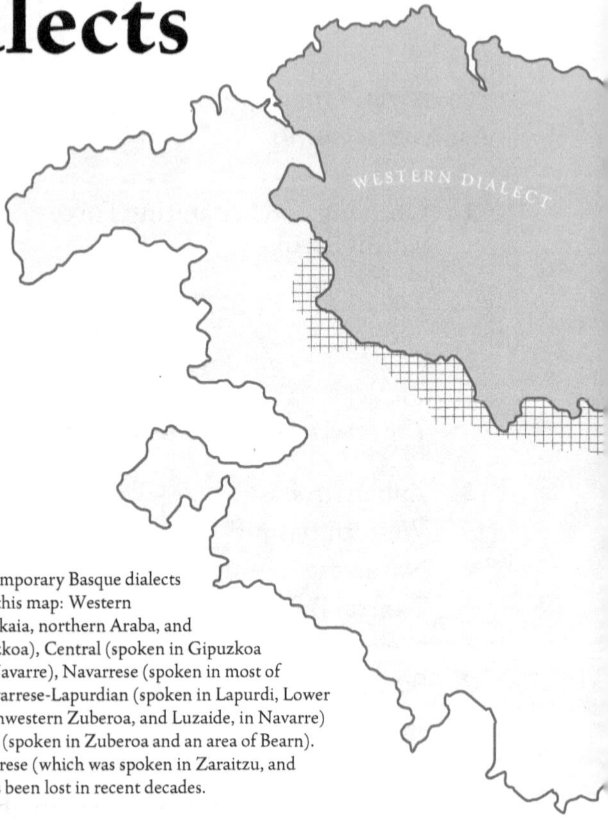

WESTERN DIALECT

Zuberoan

Western

Central

Navarrese

Navarrese-Lapurdian

The five contemporary Basque dialects are shown on this map: Western (spoken in Bizkaia, northern Araba, and western Gipuzkoa), Central (spoken in Gipuzkoa and western Navarre), Navarrese (spoken in most of Navarre), Navarrese-Lapurdian (spoken in Lapurdi, Lower Navarre, northwestern Zuberoa, and Luzaide, in Navarre) and Zuberoan (spoken in Zuberoa and an area of Bearn). Eastern Navarrese (which was spoken in Zaraitzu, and Erronkari) has been lost in recent decades.

Eleven sub-dialects are shown on the following maps with different tones: two of these are Western, three Central, two Navarrese-Lapurdian, and four Navarrese. Zuberoan is highly homogeneous. Lined areas are used to shown intermediate ways of speech, which combine features from two or more dialects: those from Aezkoa and Burunda, both in Navarre, are the most particular, combining three dialects as they do.

Basque is a very unusual language, being neither Latin-based nor Indo-European. It is astonishing that it still exists, being a small language compared with its two very large neighbors, French and Spanish. Furthermore, the latter two have been the official state languages of France and Spain, respectively, since the eighteenth century, having completely marginalized the other languages spoken in their respective territories: Catalan, Breton, German, Occitan, and so on. As far as Basque is concerned, the Spanish Civil War (1936–39) was particularly hard, as was Franco's subsequent military dictatorship: the language almost disappeared. It has reinforced itself in recent years, although it is still in a critical state in Navarre and in the three provinces under French administra-tion (Lapurdi, Lower Navarre, and Zuberoa).

Compared with Louis Lucien Bonaparte's map (1850–70) Basque's geographical withdrawal is clear, and that is shown with dotted areas on this map.

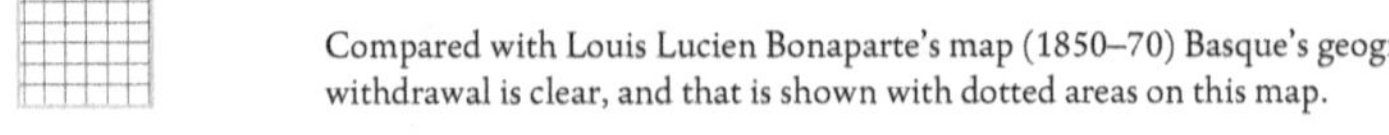

The frontiers of Basque 1850-1870 (L-L Bonaparte)

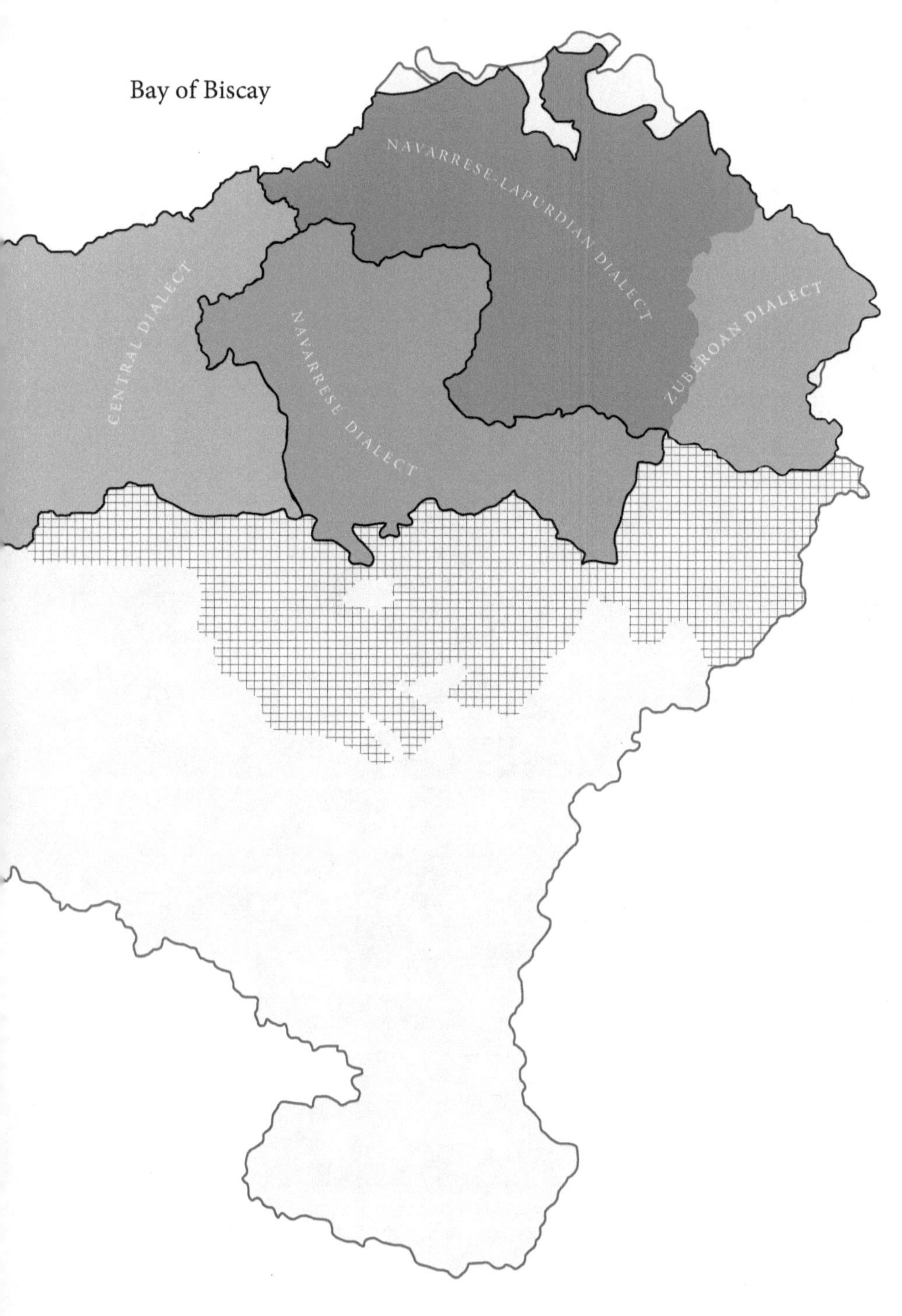
Bay of Biscay
NAVARRESE-LAPURDIAN DIALECT
CENTRAL DIALECT
NAVARRESE DIALECT
ZUBEROAN DIALECT

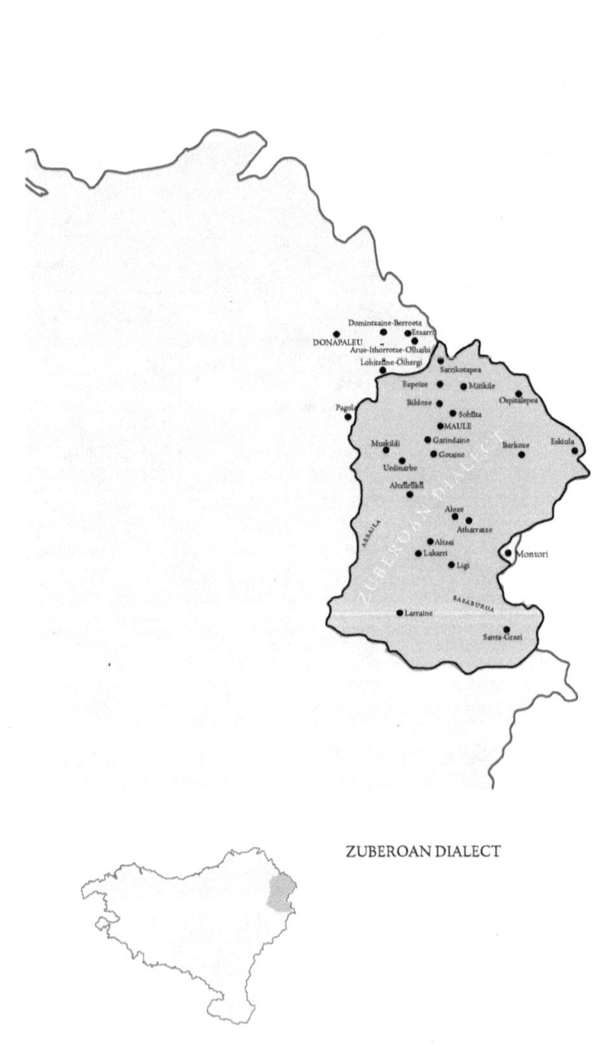

ZUBEROAN DIALECT

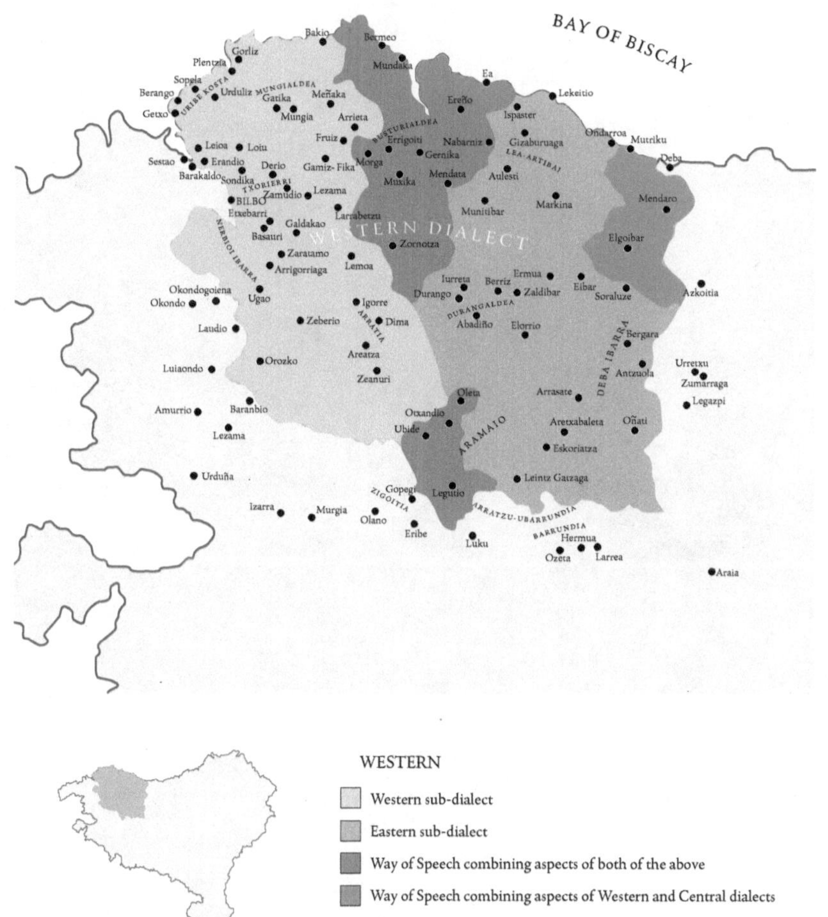
BAY OF BISCAY
WESTERN DIALECT
URIBE KOSTA
MUNGIALDEA
BUSTURIALDEA
LEA-ARTIBAI
TXORIERRI
NERBIOI IBARRA
ARRATIA
DURANGALDEA
DEBA IBARRA
ARAMAIO
ZIGOITIA
ARRATZU-UBARRUNDIA
BARRUNDIA
Bakio
Bermeo
Mundaka
Gorliz
Plentzia
Sopela
Berango
Getxo
Urduliz
Gatika
Meñaka
Mungia
Arrieta
Fruiz
Leioa
Loiu
Sestao
Erandio
Barakaldo
Derio
Sondika
Zamudio
Lezama
Gamiz-Fika
Morga
Errigoiti
Gernika
Muxika
Ea
Ereño
Nabarniz
Mendata
Ispaster
Lekeitio
Gizaburuaga
Aulesti
Ondarroa
Mutriku
Deba
Munitibar
Markina
Mendaro
Elgoibar
BILBO
Etxebarri
Basauri
Galdakao
Larrabetzu
Zornotza
Zaratamo
Arrigorriaga
Lemoa
Okondogoiena
Okondo
Ugao
Igorre
Laudio
Zeberio
Dima
Areatza
Orozko
Luiaondo
Zeanuri
Iurreta
Durango
Berriz
Ermua
Zaldibar
Eibar
Soraluze
Azkoitia
Abadiño
Elorrio
Bergara
Antzuola
Urretxu
Zumarraga
Legazpi
Arrasate
Amurrio
Baranbio
Lezama
Oleta
Otxandio
Ubide
Aretxabaleta
Oñati
Eskoriatza
Urduña
Leintz Gatzaga
Legutio
Gopegi
Izarra
Murgia
Olano
Eribe
Luku
Hermua
Ozeta
Larrea
Araia
WESTERN
Western sub-dialect
Eastern sub-dialect
Way of Speech combining aspects of both of the above
Way of Speech combining aspects of Western and Central dialects

BAY OF BISCAY
NAVARRESE DIALECT
BAZTAN
ULTZAMA
ANUE
ODIETA
ESTERIBAR
ERROIBAR
AEZKOA
BASABURUA
IMOTZ
Oiartzun
Sara
Ainhoa
Urdazubi
Bidarrai
Baigorri
Banka
Amaiur
Errazu
Arizkun
Elizondo
Irurita
Almandoz
Aldude
Urepele
Goizueta
Ezkurra
Eratsun
Beruete
Jauntsarats
Etxaleku
Oskotz
Irurtzun
Senosiain
Arteta
Goñi
Amunarriz
Altsasu
Bakaiku
Urdiain
Elzaburu
Alkotz
Arraitz
Iraizotz
Lizaso
Olague
Ziaurritz
Ostitz
Eritze
Iragi
Usetxi
Eugi
Zilbeti
Zubiri
Aurizberri
Mezkiritz
Orbaizeta
Garralda
Aribe
Orotz-Betelu
Abaurreagaina

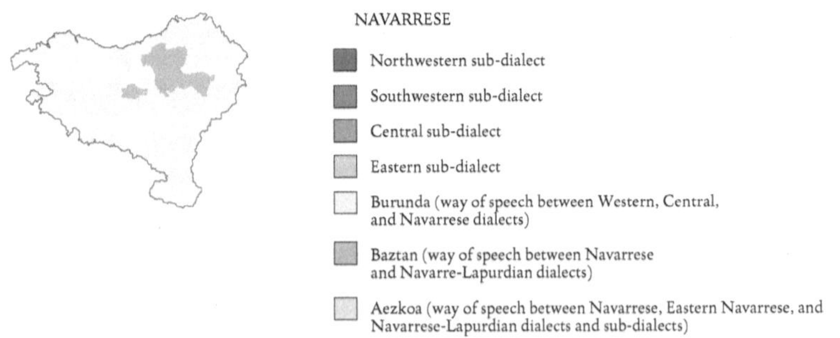

NAVARRESE
Northwestern sub-dialect
Southwestern sub-dialect
Central sub-dialect
Eastern sub-dialect
Burunda (way of speech between Western, Central, and Navarrese dialects)
Baztan (way of speech between Navarrese and Navarre-Lapurdian dialects)
Aezkoa (way of speech between Navarrese, Eastern Navarrese, and Navarrese-Lapurdian dialects and sub-dialects)

Bay of Biscay

Mutriku
Deba
Mendaro
Elgoibar
Getaria
Zumaia
Zarautz
Orio
Aizarnazabal
Zestoa
UROLALDEA
Azpeitia
Azkoitia
Aia
CENTRAL DIALECT
DONOSTIA
Usurbil
Lasarte-Oria
BETERRI
Hernani
Urnieta
Astigarraga
Andoain
Asteasu
Larraul
Villabona
Errezil
Alkiza
Bidania-Goiatz
TOLOSALDEA
Tolosa
Beizama
Albiztur
Berastegi
Hondarribia
Hendaia
Biriatu
Irun
Lezo
Pasaia
Errenteria
Oiartzun
Bera
Goizueta
Bergara
Antzuola
Urretxu
Zumarraga
Legazpi
Oñati
Ikaztegieta
Alegia
Legorreta
Orendain
Baliarrain
Ordizia
Gaintza
Abaltzisketa
Beasain
Amezketa
Lazkao
Zaldibia
Idiazabal
Segura
Ataun
GOIERRI
Zegama
ARAITZ
Betelu
Leitza
Areso
Gorriti
Uitzi
Azpirotz
LARRAUN
Errazkin
Lekunberri
Ezkurra
Eratsun
BASABURUA
Beruete
Eltzaburu
Alkotz
Jauntsarats
Larraintzar
Etxaleku
Oskotz
Beuntza
Muskitz
Eritze
IMOTZ
Irurtzun
Irañeta
Uharte Arakil
Lakuntza
Arbizu
Arruazu
Etxarri Aranatz
Bakaiku
Altsasu
Urdiain
SAKANA
BURUNDA
Araia
Ziordia
ERGOIENA

CENTRAL

Western sub-dialect

Central sub-dialect

Way of speech combining aspects of the Western and Central sub-dialects

Eastern sub-dialect (way of speech combining aspects of Central and Navarrese dialects)

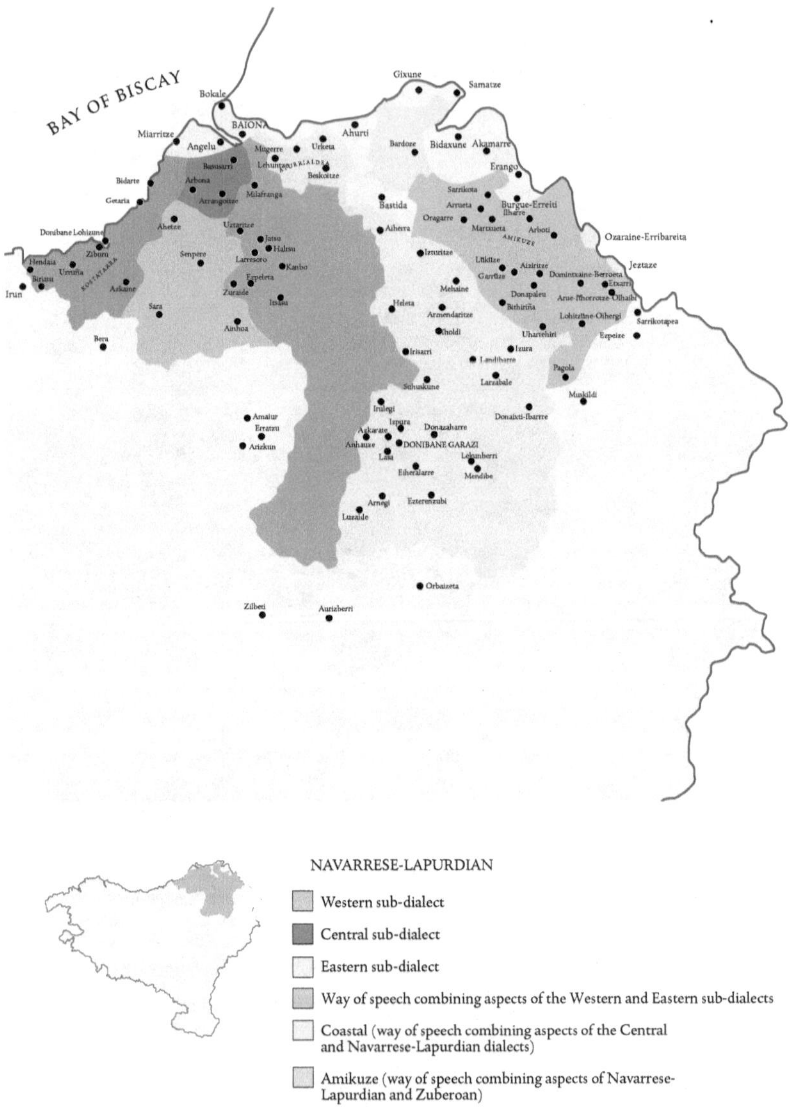

BAY OF BISCAY
Bokale
BAIONA
Gixune
Samatze
Miarritze
Angelu
Ahurti
Bardoze
Bidaxune
Akamarre
Bidarte
Getaria
Arbona
Basusarri
Arrangoitze
Mugerre
Urketa
Lehuntze
Beskoitze
Milafranga
Erango
Sarrikota
Arrueta
Burgue-Erreiti
Ilharre
Bastida
Oragarre
Martxueta
Arboti
Donibane Lohizune
Ahetze
Uztaritze
Aiherra
AMIKUZE
Ozaraine-Erribareita
Ziburu
Jatsu
Haltsu
Izturitze
Hendaia
Urruña
Senpere
Larresoro
Kanbo
Luhuso
Garrüze
Aiziritze
Domintxaine-Berroeta
Jeztaze
Biriatu
KOSTALDEA
Azkaine
Ezpeleta
Mehaine
Etxarri
Irun
Zuraide
Itsasu
Donapaleu
Arue-Ithorrotze-Olhaibi
Sara
Heleta
Armendaritze
Bithiriña
Lohitzüne-Oihergi
Sarrikotapea
Ainhoa
Iholdi
Uhartehiri
Ezpeize
Bera
Izura
Irisarri
Landibarre
Pagola
Suhuskune
Larzabale
Muskildi
Irulegi
Donaixti-Ibarre
Amaiur
Erratzu
Ispura
Azkarate
Donazaharre
Arizkun
Anhauze
DONIBANE GARAZI
Lasa
Lekunberri
Eiheralarre
Mendibe
Arnegi
Ezterenzubi
Luzaide
Orbaizeta
Zilbeti
Aurizberri

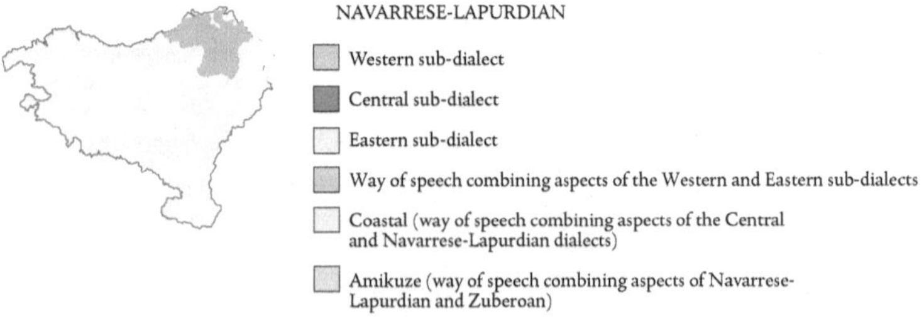

Acknowledgments

I published the book *Euskalkiak: Herriaren lekukoak* (Basque Dialects: Witnesses to a People) in 2003. The second print followed shortly and when that too sold out, I wondered whether to run a third print or to rewrite the book. In the end, I decided to rewrite, update, and add new contents in order to publish a new book. That new book, published in 2008, has become the edition that is being translated into English.

In 2003, I was afraid that the book would not be received enthusiastically, and, for that reason, I gave only a brief description of the Basque dialects. In 2008, however, having seen that many readers are interested in the subject, I offered a more complete, detailed description. Furthermore, while my original objective was to present a new point of view about the Basque dialects, and having seen that this aim was achieved to an extent, I believed that the time had come to take a step further.

I included many of the original contents in the new Basque edition, but also made significant changes. For example, some sections were removed and new sections added. The sections about the dialects of Araba (Álava), Zaraitzu (Salazar), and Erronkari (Roncal) were removed and precedence given to dialects that are still in use. I included further explanations about contemporary Basque and tried to make these explanations clearer and more exact. On the other hand, the section about Basque spoken in the Americas was the most eye-catching of all because of it being a subject that has not been mentioned or written about in this way. The very nature of the book having changed, I decided to change its title to *Euskalkiak: Euskararen dialektoak (The Dialects of Basque)*, and as I have said this more complete book is now appearing in English.

I would like to thank the many friends and colleagues who read the previous book and the Basque draft of this book for the corrections and observations that they made: Xabier Artiagoitia, Xabier Bilbao, Jean-Baptiste Coyos, Jean-Louis Davant, Irantzu Epelde, Jose Ignazio Hualde, Leire Mendiboure, Txipi Ormaetxea, Ernesto Pastor Diaz de Garaio, Txomin Sagarzazu, Patxi Salaberri Zaratiegi, and, of course, Xabier Mendiguren Elizegi, the editor of the original edition in Basque. The publication of this book in Basque was possible thanks to all of their help and for that reason I thank them again here at the occasion of the publishing of the English translation.

For the preparation of the English edition, I would first like to thank the editorial board of the Center for Basque Studies for their belief in the value of this book. I would like to thank senior editor Cameron Watson for his championing of the book and for his manuscript editing and for striving to make this subject appeal to an English readership. I would like to thank the staff at the Center for their assistance, especially Daniel Montero for managing publication, Kimberly Daggett for her editing and manuscript preparation, John Coleman for the re-creation of the maps and for designing this edition, and AnnElise Hatjakes-Bowman for her careful proofreading. My final and deep thanks go to the translator, Aritz Branton, for his dedication to this translation and for his invaluable and skillful assistance in bringing my work into English. Thank you.

– Koldo Zuazo
The Basque Country, Fall 2013

1
Unifying and Separating Forces within Basque

As the Swiss linguist Ferdinand de Saussure wrote in his book *Cours de Linguistique générale*, there are two forces that coexist within languages at the same time.[1] Some of these forces are unifying, supporting each language's unity and uniformity, while others separate languages into dialects.

In living languages, these two forces are normally balanced, but things are very different in the Basque Country, where the separating forces are much stronger. In fact, the existence of so very many different areas in such a small territory, with considerable differences between them, reveals a language that has been destructured and broken down.

However, the same characteristics also appear within Basque itself. A district or a valley is sometimes the area in which the same characteristics can be found. In other cases, the areas are more extensive, with the boundaries of a whole region encompassing a form of speech. There are also characteristics that can be found in more than one region, as well as those that can be found throughout the Basque Country – furthermore, the latter are much more numerous than is often thought. The unity between the different areas in a destructured, broken down language demonstrates that there are also unifying forces.

It is not difficult to understand the fundamental reasons for these contradictory factors; one only has to take a look at the course of events over recent years. The Basque Country is divided between two large states, and each of them has imposed its powerful means on each side of the frontier: administrative structures, school networks, means of communication, among others, and the Spanish and French languages have been the axis for all of this. Therefore the country in which Basque is spoken is divided, broken up, and the official status of Basque is negligible – in some places inexistent – on each side of the border. At the end of the day, these are the two main reasons for the existence of so many and such varied dialects of Basque: the administrative division of the Basque Country and Basque's lack of official status.

Yet at the same time, Basque-speaking people have also worked to support their language. The *ikastolas* (schools in which all instruction is carried out in Basque) were founded around 1960, the *euskaltegis* (evening schools for teaching Basque to adults) around 1965, the contribution of small magazines and radios increased enormously in 1982 (when the public radio and television stations in Basque were established) and in 1990 when a daily newspaper in Basque was published for the first time. In literature, too, there has been enormous progress since Jose Antonio Loidi published his novel *Amabost egun Urgainen* (Fifteen days in Urgain) in 1955. Many other steps have been taken as well and Euskara Batua (Standard or Unified Basque) has been the basis for all of them. In fact, the result of all this work is that Basque has become more unified or standardized since 1960.

I would like to briefly explain what Unified Basque is.

Writers used to have many different options in terms of models for writing in Basque rather than just a single choice. Four dialects formed the basic models for writing literature: Lapurdian, Zuberoan, Gipuzkoan, and Bizkaian Basque. Indeed, there were moreover two different subgroups within written Bizkaian Basque. In the 1960s, however, with the impact of the *ikastolas* and a flourishing of Basque-language literature, it became impossible to carry on in the same vein: creating a single model for all Basques was indispensable.

After much debate, Gipuzkoan Basque was chosen as the basis for this unification. This decision was taken for the following reasons: geographically speaking, Gipuzkoa is in the center of the Basque Country and its Basque thus easily understandable for all Basques; there was more widespread knowledge and use of Basque in Gipuzkoa than any other province; since the eighteenth century, Gipuzkoan Basque has been the most widely used in churches and in literature, and because of that it remained the most prestigious dialect; and finally, there were a number of fairly large towns in Gipuzkoa where Basque was spoken and that, too, would help to spread the new standard form of Basque.

But let us return to our story and look at some events and factors from the past. For example, one should highlight the influence of markets held weekly or bi-weekly. The main marketplaces were: Bilbo (also spelled Bilbao),† Mungia (Munguía), Gernika (Guernica), Durango, and Markina (Marquina), in the Basque-speaking part of Bizkaia (Vizcaya); Arrasate (Mondragón), Elgoibar, Azpeitia, Ordizia, Tolosa, Donostia (San Sebastián), and Irun in Gipuzkoa (Guipúzcoa); Baiona (Bayonne), Hazparne (Hasparren), Donibane Lohizune (Saint-Jean-de-Luz), and Ezpeleta (Espelette) in Lapurdi (Labourd); Donibane Garazi (Saint-Jean-Pied-de-Port), Donapaleu (Saint-Palais), and Irisarri (Irissarry) in Lower Navarre; Atharratze (Tardets) and Maule (Mauléon) in

† Editor's note: For the most part, place names will be rendered in Basque with Spanish or French equivalents in parentheses on first mention.

Zuberoa (Soule); and Lesaka, Doneztebe (Santesteban), Elizondo, Irurtzun (Irurzun), Auritz (Burguete), and Aribe (Arive) in the Basque-speaking area of Navarre. Young people, on the other hand, got together at popular festivals. And one of the effects of these markets and festivities was the unification of Basque in each valley or district.

In addition to weekly markets and popular festivities, markets held annually on particular dates and during major festivals were also meeting places. The markets included those held in Baiona and Ezpeleta in Lapurdi; in Donibane Garazi, Donapaleu, Heleta (Hélette), and Garruze (Garris) in Lower Navarre; and in Maule and Atharratze in Zuberoa. The best-known of these markets were those held in Zumarraga (Gipuzkoa) on Saint Lucy's Day, in Abadiño (Bizkaia) on Saint Blaise's Day, and, most importantly of all, in Iruñea (Pamplona), on Saint Fermin's Day. Meanwhile, the best known festivals were those held at Urkiola in Bizkaia, at Ernio in Gipuzkoa, the Saint Michael of Aralar shrine in Navarre (on the border with Gipuzkoa), at Orreaga (Roncesvalles) in the Basque-speaking area of Navarre, and at Maidalena in Zuberoa – all of these mountain settings with important religious sites that were (and in some cases still are) visited by people from surrounding towns and villages on specific dates once or twice every year. Basques are also sports and competition enthusiasts, and events such as Basque pelota, racing, rowing, woodchopping competitions, stonelifting, and many other sports have been very important over the centuries. On other occasions, there were livestock competitions, with people meeting for example to hold ox and ram competitions. Of course, no linguistic changes took place during the one or two days during which these meetings were held, but at least people were able to familiarize themselves with each other's ways of speaking.

These exchanges were often long-lasting, particularly when they centered on work issues. Until very recently, for instance, herding families took their livestock to far-off places for winter pasturing. For example, some went from the Aezkoa Valley in Navarre to the plains of Lower Navarre and Lapurdi, others from the Goierri region of central Gipuzkoa (including, among others, the towns of Beasain, Ordizia, Lazkao, Idiazabal, Ataun, and Ormaiztegi) in Gipuzkoa to various parts of Bizkaia: the Txorierri Valley (Derio, Sondika, Zamudio, Lezama, Loiu, and Larrabetzu), the Mungialdea area (including Mungia, Bakio, Gatika, and Gamiz-Fika), and the Busturialdea area spanning the Urdaibai Estuary (including Gernika, Bermeo, Mundaka, Muxika, Ea, Elantxobe, and Morga).[2] There were also continuous exchanges between fishing villages and similarly, among farmers, people went from one area to another at harvest time to bring in the crops. As Orreaga Ibarra shows,[3] people used to go from the Ebro Valley to Erroibar (the Erro Valley), from one end of Navarre to another, to thresh their wheat. Similarly, it seems that the people of Erroibar used to go to Urrotz (Urroz) to plough the land.

Of course, smaller groups of people also traveled between places: stonemasons, roofers, forestry workers, charcoal burners, servants, wet nurses, and many others who moved around to fill temporary posts. One well-known example of this flow of people, for instance, is that of the women of Erronkari in Navarre who used to travel to Zuberoa to make espadrilles. There is no doubt that these exchanges had a deep effect on the language, and Iñaki Camino finds a good example of this in the Aezkoa Valley of Navarre, where the herders of Orbaizeta used to speak in the Basque dialect of the Garazi area (Cize, in Lower Navarre) while they worked.[4]

However, this centuries-old way of life has completely changed in recent years, and mostly from 1960 onward. Thanks to today's infrastructures and means of transport, we can easily and often go anywhere where we want, and, thanks to contemporary means of communication, without even leaving home we can hear the way Basque is spoken in all areas. These times of change have definitely led to the unification of Basque.

On the other hand, the mountainous nature of the Basque Country has often been quoted as a reason for the diversity of Basque dialects, and evidently mountains are an obstacle to such linguistic exchange. However, these obstacles have always been quickly overcome when there has been work, markets, or other beneficial things on the other side of the mountains in question. Here are two examples of this:

Two towns in Gipuzkoa, Oñati and Legazpi, are very close to one another geographically, yet their ways of speaking are quite different. This is in all probability due to the mountains that stand between the two towns. But, on the other hand, although there are also mountains between Oñati and Vitoria-Gasteiz (Araba), and although Vitoria-Gasteiz is farther away than Legazpi, there has been a continual long-standing relationship between Oñati and the capital of Araba, and, apparently, the Basque that used to be spoken in Vitoria-Gasteiz was similar to that spoken in Oñati. Of course, Vitoria-Gasteiz was always a large city compared with Legazpi and had a much larger market, a fact that encouraged ties between Oñati and the capital of Araba.

I previously mentioned the example of the espadrille makers who used to travel from Erronkari in Navarre to Zuberoa. The highest mountains in the Basque Country, with a height of about two thousand meters (approximately six and half thousand feet), are in that area, but, even so, they were not a decisive obstacle and, as well as people going from Erronkari to Zuberoa, others made the opposite journey from Zuberoa to Erronkari to make cheese during the sheep milk season. As a result, the Basque of Erronkari was similar to that of Zuberoa.

Furthermore, there have been routes crossing mountains and linking different areas together for a long time; those connecting Iruñea with Baiona and Iruñea with the Gipuzkoan coast, via Tolosa, have been the most significant. As can be seen, then, the Navarrese capital Iruñea was the most important axis for the Basque Country in the past.

Literature has also had an influence on these connections. It should always be taken into account that, while Unified Basque is very recent, there have long been local ways of speaking and writing; spoken language was rendered into written form in the Lapurdian dialect of Basque in the seventeenth century; in Gipuzkoan in the eighteenth century; in both forms of Bizkaian and Zuberoan in the nineteenth century; and in Navarrese-Lapurdian in the twentieth century. It is clear that these ways of speaking were based around regions. In addition, writers, priests, and friars also made use of them, and, thanks to their influence, ordinary people also came to know them and then take them as their own. In fact, these ways of speaking are the main uniting force in the Basque language.

At the end of the day, Basque speakers have taken advantage of cracks in the strong networks imposed by the non-Basque states they live in and created their own small networks down the centuries. Indeed, thanks to these small networks, Basque has maintained some form of unity.

In my opinion, this is the main reason for publishing this book in English. It is astonishing that Basque has survived up to the twenty-first century. It is a language with a small number of speakers and has always had to compete with much larger languages – centuries ago with Latin and now with French and Spanish. But while it has survived, it is divided into several dialects. In fact, it is also split into many sub-dialects as well as different ways of speaking the language. In fact, this old language's essence is to be found in these smaller units, and for this reason it is worth examining their structures.

The Subject of This Study

The objective of this study is to examine the characteristics of Basque as a contemporary living language. The aim is not to give precise, in-depth descriptions of every dialect and sub-dialect; the study limits itself to describing the fundamental and most significant characteristics spread throughout the dialects of Basque. Given that, the area in which each characteristic exists has to be carefully taken into account. Features that are exclusive to small areas have been completely left out, and I have focused on characteristics that are to be found in relatively wide areas. In the author's local area, for instance, the linking word *barren* is often used: *nora zoiaz hain goiz, seirak be eztira barren!* ("Where are you going to so early, it isn't even six o'clock yet!" in the local dialect of the Debabarrena or Lower Deba Valley) would, in Unified Basque, be *nora zoaz hain goiz, seiak ere ez dira eta!* This structure, much appreciated and identified with by the author, is not included in this study because it is used in no more than a dozen towns in the whole of the Basque Country. And even though some of those towns are quite large (Eibar, Elgoibar, Azkoitia, and so on), the word clearly does not fit in the with the study's criteria.

This is not the way Basque dialects are usually studied. In the Basque Country, and globally as well, peculiar ways of speaking fascinate and amaze people. But if we allow special, small details to take up our time and enthusiasm, we will never be able to take a scholarly approach to the subject. When a particular town or region is under study, there is a place for examining small features, but when the whole of the Basque Country is the field of study each characteristic's area of usage must be carefully taken into account.

Apart from that, leaving the characteristics common to many areas to one side, this study tries to show the whole of the language: phonology, morphology, and syntax. Vocabulary (*atera/irten/jalgi* "to take/go out," *jin/etorri* "to come," *bidali/igorri* "to send") and lexical variants (*beldur/bildur* "fear," *esan/erran* "to say," *gazta/gaztai/gasna* "cheese") have been examined, although studying those aspects of the language is exceptionally difficult.† In itself, it is difficult to demarcate the boundaries between words and variants in words, and, furthermore, very little lexicographical work has been done on the dialects of Basque: in other words, there are very few studies available into the words of specific towns or areas. Even so, this study looks into this subject; you cannot always turn a blind eye to things just because they are difficult. The study explains the information found, and in the future the inevitable gaps in our understanding will be filled and any mistakes will be corrected.

Methodological Criteria

The historian Esteban Garibai included the saying "*Bardin Burgos eta Markina*" ("Burgos is the same as Markina") in a collection of proverbs he compiled in the sixteenth century. The proverb implies that putting large and small things on the same level involves a risk, and this often happens in the study of dialects. In fact, there are many different options when you want to say something. The same thing is said in many different ways in a single town, and sometimes a single speaker says a single thing in many different ways. However, those many different options should not all be measured equally, and it is worth separating substantial and less substantial features. In order to avoid

† Editor's note: Translations of Basque vocabulary into English are included to give the nonexpert reader some notion of the meanings. The translations do not attempt to be exhaustive and may only represent one of several different renderings.

this potential danger, I have identified four groups for use in this study: rules, undeveloped rules, variants, and irrelevant features. These four groups can be briefly described as follows:

Rules

These are features that are always or often found. In Zuberoa, for example, *u* becomes *ü* (*laguna* → *lagüna* "friend"), and this happens in an infinite number of words. In many places in the Basque Country, similarly, there is a tendency to pronounce *i* + *n* as *iñ* and *i* + *l* as *ill* (*mina* → *miña* "pain," *ile* → *ille* "hair"), and that, too, happens in a countless number of words. These are rules and take priority when explaining a language.

Furthermore, rules tend to be either productive or fossilized. "Living" rules – the rules applied to new words that come either from Basque itself or from foreign languages – are productive. For instance, the rule of *i* + *n* becoming *iñ* and *i* + *l* becoming *ill* is fairly productive: thus, "marketing" has become *marketiña* and "e-mail" has become *emailla* in many areas. Some other rules, on the other hand, are fossilized. In Western Basque, for example, the vowel *i* used to change *z* into *x* and *tz* into *tx*: *goiz* → *gox* "morning" or "early," *haitz* → *atx* "rock." But this is no longer productive. Recently, the first names Alaitz and Arkaitz, for instance, have become popular and they are pronounced in this way in the western Basque Country and do not become *Alatx or *Arkatx. The nature of each rule must be taken into account and, naturally, productive rules take priority.

Some fossilized rules, in fact, have been completely abandoned. There used to be a well-known tendency for *f* to become *p* in Gipuzkoa and surrounding areas. The sisters Ainhoa and Idoia Fraile, for example, found examples such as *afizio* → *apiziyo* ("fondness" or "liking"), *fallo* → *pallo* ("mistake" or "fault"), and *fundamentu* → *pulamentu* ("foundation" or "reason"), in Oiartzun, Gipuzkoa. It also seems that this rule is still in force among speakers of a certain age, and an example of this is the loanword *footing* ("jogging"), taken from Spanish, which has become the rather peculiar *putiñ* as pronounced by some people in Oiartzun.[5] However, with the exception of a few speakers, most people in Oiartzun and throughout Gipuzkoa have no difficulty in pronouncing /*f*/, and the previous rule has become completely fossilized. Because of this, /*f*/ becoming /*p*/ will not be mentioned in this study.

Undeveloped Rules

Compared with the rules mentioned above, here there are two differences: these rules are seldom or at least not always applied, and they are not productive. Here are some examples.

Many words with the consonant cluster *-rtz-* in one part of the Basque Country have the cluster *-st-* in other areas. This can be seen with the words *beste/bertze* ("other"), *bost/bortz* ("five"), and *heste/hertze* ("intestine"), and in compound words including the cluster *ost-/ortz-* (*ostegun/ortzegun* "Thursday," *ostiral/ortziral* "Friday," *ostadar/ortzadar* "rainbow," and *ostots/ortots* "thunder"). But that is the complete list of words in which this happens; there are no further examples of this. For example, *hartza* ("bear") and *hortza* ("tooth") are words used throughout the Basque Country; they do not become *hartza/hasta*, *hortza/hosta* depending on different areas. Furthermore, there is no doubling up like this with new words. The Spanish word *cárcel* ("prison"), for instance, has only become *kartzela* in Basque; it has not become **kastela* anywhere. In contrast, the old loanword from Spanish *merced* ("mercy" or "favor") led to both *mertxede* and *mesede*.

Here is another example. In the western Basque Country, certain words start with *u-*, while in other parts of the Basque Country they start with *i-*; examples of this are *hiri/huri* ("city"), *igel/ugaraxo* ("frog"), *ile/ule* ("hair"), *iltze/untza* ("nail" or "clove"), *irin/urun* ("flour"), *irten/urten* ("to go out"), and *izain/uzen* ("leech"). Furthermore, in most of Bizkaia *igeri* ("to swim") is *uger*, and *izen* ("name") is *uzen* in a few towns near Bilbao; but that is all. This conversion, furthermore, is no longer productive. The loanword *intifada*, for example, is pronounced as such in the western Basque Country; it has not become **untifada*.

Throughout Navarre, similarly, *g-* is added to four words that start with the consonant cluster *oa-*: *goartu* comes from *ohartu* "to realize," *goatze* from *ohatze* (*ohea* in Unified Basque†) "bed," *guai* from *orain* "now" and, in some forms of speech, *goa/goaye* from (*hi*) *hoa* "you are going" (in the familiar *hika* form). But these are the only examples of this and they have no influence on new words. The loanword *oasi*, meaning a humid area in a desert, for instance, is pronounced that way in Navarre and has not become **guasi*. *Oharra* ("note"), which has been introduced by Unified Basque, is pronounced as such in Navarre and not **guarra*.

These undeveloped rules are of significance, naturally, but can by no means be given the same importance as complete, decisive rules. They are taken into secondary consideration throughout this study, separately from real rules.

Variants

These are evolutions that can only be found in various specific words: *aipatu/aitatu* ("to mention"), *apaiz/apez* ("priest"), *ardo/ardau/arno/ardú* ("wine"),

† Editor's note: Throughout the text, where a significant difference is evident, the Euskara Batua or Unified Basque equivalents of words mentioned will be given.

behor/bohor ("mare"), *belarri/beharri* ("ear"), *beldur/bildur* ("fear"), *beltz/baltz* ("black"), *borroka/burruka* ("fight"), *eman/emon/emun* ("to give"), *esan/erran* ("to say"), *guzti/guzi* ("everything" or "all"), *hezur/hazur* ("bone"), *hogei/hogoi* ("twenty"), *negar/nigar* ("tear" or "crying"), *txiki/ttiki/ttipi* ("small"), *zein/zoin/zuin* ("which"), and so on. There are many of them and they, too, have their own significance, but they are individual and not recent, and thus this study only mentions those that are widely used. Likewise, these are taken into secondary consideration.

Irrelevant Features

As with the variants mentioned above, the variants in this group only affect some individual words, but in most cases have appeared recently and do not form widely used, precise models. They are only used in a few, scattered places. Thus, from a linguistic and dialectical point of view, they are of scarce importance. In many cases, they have appeared due to assimilation: *atera* → *atara* ("to take out"), *hurrengo* → *hurrungo* ("next" or "following"), *irakin* → *irikin* ("to boil" or "to ferment"), *ireki* → *iriki* ("to open"), *itsaso* → *itxoso* ("sea" or "ocean"), *omen* → *emen* ("reportedly"), *oren* or *ordua* → *oron* ("hour" or "time"), and so forth. In other cases, they have been created by metathesis: for example, *alor* < — > *arlo* ("field"), *atera* → *etara* ("to take out" or "to go/come out"), *gabe* < — > *bage* ("without"), *hodei* → *hedoi* ("cloud"), and *irudi* → *iduri* ("image"). In other cases, diphthong simplification has been the cause of this: *bezain* → *bezin* ("as … as"), *orain* → *oin* ("now"), *bait-* → *bit-* (prefix meaning "since," "as," "for," or "that"), *aulki* → *alki* ("chair"), *aurpegi* → *arpegi* ("face"), *arraultza* → *arrutza/arrotza* ("egg"), *basaurde* → *basurde* ("wild boar"), and so on. New diphthongs also appear on occasion: *azken* → *aizken* ("last" or "end"), *laster* → *laister* ("soon" or "fast"), *handi* → *haundi* ("big"), *paso* → *pauso* ("step"), and so forth.

Nor are changes in stop consonants at the start of words (*p-*, *t-*, *k-*, *b-*, *d-*, *g-*) meaningful in terms of the study of dialect: *bago/pago* ("beech tree"), *bekatu/pekatu* ("sin"), *biztu/piztu* ("to revive," "to light," and "to turn on," among other meanings) , *dorre/torre* ("tower"), *garrasi/karrasi* ("shriek" or "scream"), *gartzela/kartzela* ("prison"), *gastatu/kastatu* ("to spend" or "to wear (off)"), *gonbidatu/konbidatu* ("to invite"), *gorosti/korosti* ("holly"), *gorotz/korotz* ("manure"), and so on. This feature can be found in various different places, with no particular pattern, and is not mentioned in this study. However, when this distinguishes one particular area, it is taken into account. For instance, *biper* instead of *piper* (Unified Basque for "pepper") in Navarrese-Lapurdian Basque; *gatu* instead of *katu* ("cat") in Eastern Basque; *dermio* (from the Spanish, *término*) instead of *eremua* ("domain," "extension," or "area") in Navarrese Basque; *pake* instead of *bake* ("peace") and *parre* instead of *barre* ("laugh" or "laughter") in Central Basque; *keixa* instead of *gerezia* ("cherry") and *kipula* instead of *tipula* ("onion") in Western Basque, and so forth.

Nor are features to be found in all dialects relevant from a dialectical point of view. For instance, it is common to mix up stop consonants: *iguzki/iduzki* for *eguzkia* ("sun"), *gurdi/burdi* ("cart"), *gurpil/burpil* ("wheel"), *ogi/obi* ("bread"), and *suge/sube* ("snake"). It is also common for stop consonants and the letter *r* to disappear between vowels: for example, in *egin* → *ein* → *in* ("to do"), *ezagutu* → *ezautu* ("to know" or "to meet"), *dabiltza* → *dailtza* ("they are walking"), *aditu* → *aitu* ("to listen" or "to perceive"), *eduki* → *euki* ("to have"), *etorri da* → *etorri'a* ("he/she/it has come"), *etxera* → *etxea* ("to the house"), *etxerik* → *etxeik* ("from the house"), and *egon delarik* → *eon delaik* ("while he/she/it was" – a circumstance clause). And it is common for the particle *ez* to merge with certain verb forms: *ez* + *d-* → *t* (*ez dabil* → *eztabil* "it is not working"), *ez* + *b-* → *p* (*ez bada* → *ezpada* "if it is not"), *ez* + *g-* → *k* (*ez ginen* → *ezkinen* "we were not"), *ez* + *n-* → *ø* (*ez nituen* → *enituen* "I did not have" with a plural object), and *ez* + *l-* → *ø* (*ez luke* → *eluke* "he/she/it would not have"). From a dialectical point of view, these features are irrelevant and will not be taken into account in this study.

Contemporary Basque Dialect Areas

This study also aims to update the approach taken by Louis-Lucien Bonaparte toward Basque dialects in the mid-nineteenth century and to offer a new point of view. In fact, work has already been carried out to correct Bonaparte's approach, but these corrections have not been presented in an appropriate way and, among other reasons, it is precisely because of this that they have not been taken into consideration.

Before going any further, it must be said that Bonaparte himself admitted that separating two Navarrese dialects and two Lower Navarrese dialects might not have been the correct decision, and that it might instead have been most appropriate to have classified these four dialects as two.[6] Some of his successors have agreed with this and at present, furthermore, it seems even more necessary because these ways of speaking have unified further. Above all, the move toward unification has been very strong in the Northern Basque Country, with the ways of speaking in Lapurdian and Lower Navarrese becoming very similar; despite some differences, a single dialect is spoken in these two regions nowadays.

In Navarre, on the other hand, there have been two significant changes. People from the northern valleys of Navarre used to share close ties with the Northern Basque Country, and that is how Bonaparte classified them; he linked the Basque of Erronkari with Zuberoan; the Basque of Zaraitzu with Eastern Lower Navarrese; the Basque of the Aezkoa and the Luzaide (Valcarlos) Valleys with Western Lower Navarrese; and the Basque of the Baztan Valley, Urdazubi (Urdax), and Zugarramurdi with Lapurdian. Bonaparte was probably not entirely right about this, and, in addition, things have changed considerably since then: all of those valleys have for a long time now been more closely connected with Navarre and with the Southern Basque Country in general than with the Northern Basque Country.

In western Navarre, meanwhile, a different type of change has taken place: in short, the Basque there has increasingly come to resemble that of neighboring Gipuzkoa. This transformation has been strengthened over recent decades due to Unified Basque being based on Gipuzkoan and this new standardized language being introduced into many important fields such as education, public administration, and the media.

For these reasons, it has become necessary to update the classification of Basque dialects that Bonaparte drew up in 1869. Almost a century and a half has gone by since then and Basque, like the languages around it, has changed considerably during this long period. We also know Basque itself much better now, and the criteria for classifying dialects are not the same as before. With regard to these criteria, I should state that I have based my study on the direction normally taken by the renewal of the language in order to classify particular areas as part of one Basque dialect or another.

In order to explain what is meant by renewal, we will take as an example the Burunda area of Navarre, whose main town is Altsasu (Alsasua).

In that area, for example, when an article is added to words ending in *-a*, this becomes *-e* and then *-i*: *taberna + a → tabernea → tabernia* ("bar"). This new form comes from the western Basque Country, which demonstrates that the Burunda area has been in increasing contact with that area.

As in the western Basque Country, similarly, *j-* is characteristic of the absolutive case in *hitano* (a form of address used by speakers on close personal terms, by workmates, or by older people when speaking with younger people: this form of address is not used by all Basque speakers) verbs: for example, *hitano* people in the Burunda area say *jituk* for *ditik*, *jok* for *zagok*, *jeilek* for *zabilek*, *juek* for *zoak*, *jukak* for *zaukak*, and *jakik* for *zakik*.

Several words originally from Western Basque are also used in Burunda, such as *domeka* instead of *igandea* ("Sunday"), *izara* instead of *maindirea* ("bedsheet"), *pits* instead of *aparra* ("foam"), and *ubaraxa* instead of *igela* ("frog"). In addition to this, a few other Western variants are also used: *gaztai* instead of *gazta* ("cheese"), *eskutur* instead of *eskumutur* ("wrist"), *kaixa* instead of *gerezia* ("cherry"), *narru* instead of *larru* ("skin"), *txixa* instead of *pixa* ("pee"), and so on. All of this demonstrates that the way of speaking in Burunda is linked to Western Basque.

In contrast, the *-r-* (> *-d-* > *ø*) variants (*bear* instead of *belar* "grass," *irar* instead of *ilar* "pea," *irargi* instead of *ilargi* "moon," and *zidar* instead of *zilar* "silver") do not demonstrate any connection with Western Basque because they are not new forms that emerged in the Western Basque area but rather old variants that have also been kept in use in this area, and coincidences in using old forms of words is not enough to show a connection between two different areas. It seems, for instance, that *burar* instead of *bular* ("breast") and *zirar* instead of *zilar* were also used in Erronkari.

I would like to underline a further factor with regard to classifying areas. Bonaparte used a single approach for classifying dialects, sub-dialects, and areas, and naturally things are not always that straightforward. It is often difficult to decide which dialect a particular area belongs to and which is the most appropriate, and therefore the correct criterion in these cases is to define an "intermediate way of speaking." This concept is often used internationally, but it has yet to be used in the Basque Country because Bonaparte has been followed with blind faith until now. In this study, however, this concept is often used and describes the areas in the north of the Deba Valley (Elgoibar, Mendaro, and Mutriku); the area around Oiartzun, Hondarribia (Fuenterrabía), and Irun; the Basaburua, Araitz (Araiz), and the Imotz (Imoz) valleys of Navarre; the Burunda, Baztan Valley, and Urdazubi-Zugarramurdi areas of Navarre; the Aezkoa Valley, also in Navarre; the Lapurdi coastal area; and the Amikuze (Pays de Mixe) area of Lower Navarre. On the maps, this has been shown using shading.

The Names of Basque Dialects

The fact that Basque dialect areas have changed means that the names used for some dialects up to now have to be changed as well. The issue with this is that the names of dialects were based on the names of the regions, even though the two did not always coincide. The terms "Zuberoan Basque" and "Navarrese Basque," however, have been left untouched as they do not go beyond their regional boundaries.

In contrast I used the term "Navarrese-Lapurdian Basque" to describe the dialect spoken in Lapurdi and in Lower Navarre, although this is not original. Pierre Lafitte first mentioned it in 1944 in his *Grammaire basque (navarro-labourdin littéraire)* (Basque grammar [Literary Navarrese-Lapurdian]).[7]

The Basque forms in Erronkari and in Zaraitzu have been grouped together. Those two valleys used to be influenced from both the north and the south, but for a long time now their main source of influence has been Navarre, to the south. However, they retained their own special character and did not become completely assimilated into the other areas of Navarre, and, because of that, I decided to call this dialect "Eastern Navarrese" Basque. However, this dialect was completely lost during the twentieth century and has not been included in this study.

Basque with the same structure is spoken in Bizkaia, the Deba Valley in Gipuzkoa, and in Aramaio (Aramayona) and Legutio (Villareal) in Araba. This type of Basque has some other differentiating characteristics that are also to be found in a wider area, including the Urolaldea and the Goierri areas in Gipuzkoa and Burunda in Navarre. This is true, for instance, of the main differentiating phonological characteristic: the rule *alaba* + *a* → *alabea*/*alabia*/*alabie* ("daughter"). Until now, this rule has been classified as part of Bizkaian Basque, which is by no means accurate. It is far more accurate to describe it as Western Basque. Furthermore, it seems that many of the characteristics of Western Basque were created in Araba, and more precisely in Vitoria-Gasteiz, and I do not think it is judicious to term a dialect that emerged in Araba "Bizkaian Basque."

As regards the fourth and final new term, since the eighteenth century Gipuzkoa has formed the core of the Basque-speaking territory and its Basque has grown in both reputation and influence. Its influence is particularly noticeable in western Navarre; there, because Basque had disappeared in the provincial capital Iruñea, it had no dialect to offer and turning toward Gipuzkoa to stay alive was the best option. Bearing this in mind, it seems to me that "Central Basque" is a more appropriate term than Gipuzkoan Basque.

Final Observations

To conclude this introduction, I would like to state that the publication of this study is not intended to be exclusively for experts in the field. In order for anybody interested in the subject to be able to read and use it, I have tried to avoid technical terms and specialized linguistic phonetic symbols. In this way, experts in the subject will have no difficulty understanding the study and it will be easier for non-experts as well.

With regard to the structure of the work, it is divided into two main parts. The first part addresses the characteristics of each dialect, while the second examines the characteristics that have spread beyond a single dialect into a wider area. This second section is original in that this topic has not been previously explored and it is my hope that its conclusions will lead to further examinations in this field.

In addition to these two sections, I also look into two specific geographical areas in order to show how I approached this study: the Baztan Valley in Navarre and the area around Irun and Errenteria (Rentería) in Gipuzkoa. This also allows me to explain what intermediary dialects are.

Lastly, I must make a further observation: I have researched the dialects of Basque as they stand at the start of the twenty-first century. Great attention is usually paid to the Basque spoken by older people. I have also taken their speech into account, as well as that of young people, giving priority to the Basque spoken by both old and young people. When their two ways of speaking differ, I have tried to sieve through them in order to discover what has been created recently. With regard to linguistic matters in the Basque Country, there is one factor that must be taken into account at all times. I have already noted this, but I will now mention it again because I want to underscore its importance: Basque has changed completely since 1960 and that is why testimonies dating from that year and beyond are indispensable.

Part I
Basque Dialects

The Structure of Basque Dialects

There are five dialects of Basque in the Basque Country at present: the Western, Central, Navarrese, Navarrese-Lapurdian, and Zuberoan dialects. However, when the structures of these five dialects are compared with Basque spoken in the center of the Basque Country, one can see that the differences between them are slight; indeed, the Central, Navarrese, and Navarrese-Lapurdian dialects share the same structures. It is the dialects on the edges of the Basque Country that are the most distinctive: in other words, the Western, Zuberoan, and (now extinct) Eastern Navarrese dialects.

This feature questions a belief that is deeply rooted in the Basque Country: namely, that the Basque dialects were formed long ago. Arnaut Oihenart advanced this hypothesis in the seventeenth century when he connected these dialects to ancient lineages;[1] and the idea was thoroughly communicated and accepted down to the twentieth century when Julio Caro Baroja linked them not only to ancient lineages but also to ancient dioceses, linking all three elements together.[2] Clearly, if the Basque dialects were as ancient as that, they would be considerably more differentiated, and not just on the fringes of the Basque territory.

Furthermore, there are reasons for particular characteristics being found at the peripheries of the Basque Country. On the one hand, old characteristics tend to survive near boundaries, moving away from central dialects. This is why, in fact, there are similarities between the Basque spoken in Bizkaia and in Zuberoa. Clearly these similarities were not caused by the same innovations being introduced in both places, but rather because the same archaic forms survive in both places. In addition, the dialects on the peripheries are in constant contact with foreign languages and the loanwords they have taken on separate them from other dialects. This has happened in Basque, with areas in Araba, Bizkaia, Erronkari, and Zuberoa having taken on many words from the foreign languages bordering them.

On studying each Basque dialect in itself, it can also be seen that some dialects are more homogeneous than others. In fact, the Zuberoan dialect is the most homogeneous of all because it has no sub-dialects or distinctive, separate areas.

The Navarrese-Lapurdian dialect has also become considerably more homogeneous in recent times, although Western Lapurdian still keeps some of its own characteristics. Because of this, there are two sub-dialects within Lapurdian: Western and Eastern.

The Basque in Gipuzkoa has also become more homogeneous, but the influence of Western Basque has not entirely disappeared from the Goierri and Urolaldea areas. The old Eastern Basque characteristics can also be found around Oiartzun, Hondarribia, and Irun (Gipuzkoa) and in Larraun, Basaburua, and Imotz (Navarre). So within this dialect there are three sub-dialects: Western, Central, and Eastern.

There are two sub-dialects in Western Basque, and they are both clearly demarcated: Western and Eastern. Furthermore, in the Deba Valley the influence of Gipuzkoan Basque has been considerable, yet the innovations that have appeared in central Bizkaia have not extended that far.

The Navarrese dialect is the most splintered of all. As Basque disappeared from Iruñea long ago, there has been no strong unifying force, and four sub-dialects have appeared: Northwestern (in the Bortziriak [Cinco Villas] area, the Malerreka [High Bidasoa] area, the Bertizarana Valley, and several surrounding towns); Southwestern (in Sakana); Central; and Eastern (in Esteribar and Erroibar).

This, in short, is what is to be seen on the surface of the Basque dialects; the substance within each dialect will be studied in the following sections. As well as these five dialects, the Basque spoken by emigrants to the Americas will also be examined, for the first time, in this study. Joseba Etxarri is quite right when he writes that "we realized very clearly that being Basque is not only for those of us who have grown up on the slopes of the Pyrenees, it is also a part of the United States,"[3] and that being so it seemed fair and necessary to include information about this in the present study. Furthermore, it has often been said that the Basques who went to the Americas created a special type of Basque, combining all the Basque dialects and mixing them together. I have investigated whether this is true or not and will include testimonies I have found on this subject.

2
Zuberoan Basque

Zuberoan Basque has two main characteristics. On the one hand, it is quite distinct compared to the other dialects, and, on the other, it is highly unified and homogeneous. Its distinctive nature comes as the result of it being located geographically on the edge of the Basque Country. While Basque in Zuberoa is unlike other Basque dialects, it is not completely different. In fact, it has had strong connections to Erronkari and Zaraitzu in Navarre, and even more so to Lower Navarre as a whole.

In fact, despite an inevitable and continual relationship with neighboring Basque communities, there have been few institutions historically (and any such bodies as did exist only did so for very short periods of time) with the kind of authority needed to unify these areas. The church, for example, separated Zuberoa from other Basque territories and combined it with Béarn (in Occitania) under the Diocese of Oloron.

With regard to public administration, the period after the French Revolution of 1789 was the most significant exception; Zuberoa and Lower Navarre were grouped together in the same *arrondisement* or district (an administrative division larger than a *canton* but smaller than a *département*), with the *canton* of Maule (Zuberoa) as its administrative center, and this situation lasted until 1926. Since then, Zuberoa has been grouped with Béarn in a single *arrondissement* and separated from Lapurdi and Lower Navarre. Moreover, the administrative center of this district was moved from Maule to Oloron in Béarn, which limited Maule's potential growth.

The consequences of being fairly separate are noticeable in every way, but here I will mention just one of them; the people of Zuberoa call all other people from the Northern Basque Country *manex*, and the boundary between the two groups is not just a matter of names. In the language atlas that Euskaltzaindia (the Academy of the Basque Language) is currently working on, for instance, it states that the people of Zuberoa use the term *manex aizia* to describe a westerly wind, and a source from Zuberoa itself adds: *manexetik eztela aide hunik ez gizun hunik jiten* (nothing good comes from a *manex*, neither the air nor the man).[1] So beware anything coming from a "*manex*"!

Zuberoan Basque Territory/Area

Province boundary
Dialect Boundary
Overlapping Dialects

Obviously being isolated has helped make Zuberoan Basque unified and homogeneous, but other reasons should also be taken into account. Maule and Atharratze are the main towns and marketplaces in Zuberoa, and those two towns have been the principal meeting places for the people of Zuberoa.

Zuberoan has enjoyed a rich popular literature and this has also acted as a unifying force. Writers of drama, songs, and *bertsos* (oral improvised poetry) have used the same way of speaking, as have priests. The model for this usage, however, was laid down by language regulators (grammarians and linguists) and many people have carried out work in this field. In this regard, the first Zuberoan Basque grammar book was published in 1836 by Antoine Abbadie and Augustin Xaho, although Oihenart had already written several notes about the subject in his 1638 work.[2] This was followed by Emmanuel Intxauspere's grammar book in 1858 and Louis Gèze's grammar book in 1873.[3] Meanwhile, Jean-Baptiste Arxu published his teaching method in 1852.[4] Many other works were published during the twentieth century, and have been widely available for anyone wanting to satisfy their curiosity about Zuberoan Basque.

The Sub-Dialects of Zuberoan

Zuberoan Basque is highly homogeneous, although one should also qualify this statement. On the one hand, it is clear from the first recorded data existing on this subject that the people of Zuberoa themselves have always made a distinction between two different areas in their province: the mountainous Basabürü area (Haute Soule or Upper Zuberoa) and the lowland Pettarra area (Basse Soule or Lower Zuberoa). This distinction is to be seen, for example, in the glossary that Arnaut Oihenart provided at the end of his collection of poetry in 1657.[5] Likewise, in northwestern Zuberoa there is an area in which the Basque spoken there resembles more that of Lower Navarre: Domintxaine-Berroeta (Domezain-Berraute), Arüe-Ithorrotze-Olhaibi (Aroue-Ithorots-Olhaïby), Lohitzüne-Oihergi (Lohitzun-Oyhercq), Etxarri (Etcharry), and Pagola (Pagolle). Let us address this second issue first.

The villages listed are close to the boundary with Lower Navarre, and the Lower Navarrese town of Donapaleu is their nearest urban center as well as the administrative center of their canton. It is therefore hardly surprising that this connection should have an influence on the spoken language.

If we look at matters within Zuberoa, however, things are not so clear. It seems that there are variations in accent between Basabürü and Pettarra, and it also seems, similarly, that all types of contractions are more common in the Pettarra area than they are in the Basabürü area. It also seems, lastly, that different words have existed in the two different areas. However, be that as it may, the local people there have easily and quickly realized that the nuances between the two areas are not numerous or extreme when it comes to looking at the language as a whole, and it is also clear, furthermore, that Zuberoan Basque has become more homogeneous in recent times. At present, in fact, there are no sub-dialects or particular ways of speaking within Zuberoa Basque. However, I would like to make some observations about the previously mentioned distinctive features.

Variations in accent and intonation are habitual occurrences. This frequently happens, in fact, between neighboring towns. It is not surprising, then, that such differences should exist from one end of Zuberoa to another. Contractions, on the other hand, are a matter of priority and speediness: they were first used in the Pettarra area and then spread to Basabürü. To put it another way, Pettarra, on the plains, has been innovative while the mountainous area has been more conservative in its language evolution, a phenomenon that has been observed in many places all over the world. Txomin Peillen gives an example of this:[6] Throughout Zuberoa, the words *jun* ("to go") and *mendin* ("on the mountain") are used, whereas in Santa-Grazi (Sainte-Engrâce) – an isolated village high up in the mountains in the southeast of the province – they are *joan* and *mendian*.

Questions about words, at the end of the day, are always superficial, but words are also witnesses to language evolution. In the case of Zuberoa, in fact, relationships with various neighboring areas have brought in many different words: Basabürü has had exchanges with Erronkari and Zaraitzu in Navarre, while the Pettarra area has historically looked more toward Gascony.

In fact, Gascon has been the main source of innovation in Zuberoan Basque, and Gascon was the official administrative language used in Zuberoa from the fourteenth through to the sixteenth century. Since then, it has also been frequently used in daily life, particularly in market negotiations, and many young people used to go to Béarn to work as servants, where they also learned Gascon. This continued until the mid-twentieth century, when Gascon became marginalized in favor of French.

One should also note that three towns in Zuberoa have had majority Gascon-speaking populations: Montori (Montory), Jeztaze (Gestas), and Ozaraine (Osserain). Similarly, Basque has made inroads into Béarn. As well as sixteen districts where Basque is spoken in Béarn, there is also one full Basque-speaking town, Eskiula (Esquiule). Its proximity to Barkoxe (Barcus), the nearest large town, is probably the reason for Basque surviving there.[7]

Features of Zuberoan Basque

Two features stand out in the explanations given to now: the people of Zuberoa have been relatively isolated from other Basque speakers and they have had a close relationship with Béarn. The consequences of these two factors very quickly come to light when Zuberoan Basque is studied. On the one hand, many innovations that have appeared in other parts of the Basque Country have not reached Zuberoa, while on the other, in contrast, Zuberoan Basque has taken on many Gascon characteristics. Of course, there are also innovations introduced by the people of Zuberoa themselves.

Phonology

It is mainly phonology that makes Zuberoan Basque so distinct. Phonology is comprised of vowels, consonants, and accent.

Vowels

The most significant innovation in Zuberoan Basque, and one influenced directly by Gascon, is the transformation *u* → *ü*. The vowel *ü* is now used throughout the Northern Basque Country because of the influence of French: for example, in words like *faktüra* ("invoice"), *kandidatüra* ("candidature"), *nümero* ("number"), and so on. In Zuberoa, however, this also affects Basque words such as *bürü* (> bü) ("head"), *ezágün* ("acquaintance"), *négü* ("winter"), and *txákür* ("dog"), which people there always pronounce that way.

However, there are limits to this rule. With single letter *rs*, *rd*, and *rth* the letter *u* is normally pronounced as such, even though in this case as well the transformation *u* → *ü* can be heard on occasion. Here are some examples of when the letter *u* is kept as such:

- Before single *rs*: thus *axuria* (instead of *arkumea* or "lamb" in Unified Basque) is pronounced *axúi*, *barau* ("fast) is *báu* (< *barur*), *gure* ("our") is *gúe* and *guri* ("to us") is *gúi*, hiru ("three") is *híu* (< from the old *hirur*), *hura* (the demonstrative "that") is *húa*, while *ura* ("water") is *húra isuri* ("slope" or "flow) is *ixúi*, *urina* ("fat" or "lard") is *úin*, *zuria* ("white") is *xúi*, *zure* ("your") is *zúe* and *zuri* ("to you") is *zúi*, and *zura* ("wood") is *zur*. However, the transformation *u* → *ü* takes place with loanwords ending in *-üra*: *arenküa* instead of *arrangura* or *kezka* in Unified Basque ("complaint"), *fresküa* instead of *freskura* ("coolness"), *itxüa* instead of *itxura* ("shape" or "image"), *mentü(a)z* instead of *menturaz* or *beharbada* in Unified Basque ("maybe"), and so on. This also happens with the participle *-türik*, for example in the cases of *aitzinatüik* instead of *aitzinaturik* or *aurreraturik* ("advanced"), *eskolatüik* instead of *eskolaturik* ("schooled"), and *opeatüik* instead of *operaturik* ("operated [on]"). The letter *ü* is also used before the future suffix *-ren* in, for example, *ausartüen* instead of *ausartuko* ("[will] dare"), *hartüen* instead of *hartuko* ("[will] take"), and *sorthüen* instead of *sortuko* ("[will] create").
- Before *rd* and *rth*: *úrde* ("pig"), *úrdin* ("blue"), Urdiñárbe (a town in

Zuberoa, Ordiarp in French), *urthấil* instead of *urtarrila* in Unified Basque ("January"), *úrthe* instead of *urtea* ("year"), *urthúki* instead of *jaurti* or *bota* ("to throw"),and so on.

- Before *s*: for example, in *bústi* ("wet"), *ikhúsi* instead of *ikusi* ("to see") and *eákutsi* instead of *erakutsi* ("to show" or "to teach"), *itxúsi* instead of *itsusi* ("ugly"), *gustátü* ("to like"), *náusi* instead of *nagusi* ("boss"), *phúsa* instead of *bultza* ("push"), and *úste* ("opinion").
- Naturally, if a *u* was originally an *o*, it does not become *ü*. For instance, the transformation *non* → *nun* ("where") took place, but that *nun* has not led to **nün* being used.

However, due to being before an *r* or an *s*, *u*s that should remain so have become *ü*s when they are in the following syllables. The following are examples of this assimilation: *buru* → *burü* → *bürü* (→ bü) ("head"), *haiduru* instead of *zain* in Unified Basque → *haidurü* → *haidürü* (→ *haidü*) ("waiting"), and *usu* instead of *maiz* → *usü* → *üsü* ("often").

The influence of Gascon has led to a further innovation: *o* has transformed into *u*. There are examples of this shift throughout the Northern Basque Country and in northwestern Navarre (including the Bortziriak area and the Baztan Valley), but it is most frequent and strongest in Zuberoa. As well as before nasal consonants (*m*, *n*, *ñ*), it also occurs in other cases in Zuberoa. Here are a few examples: *ezkontü* or *ezkondu* in Unified Basque → *ezkúntü* ("to marry"), *ohoin* or *lapurra* → *uhúñ* ("thief"), *oin* → *huñ* ("foot"), *on* → *hun* ("good"), and *soin* → *suñ* ("body"). It is the rule with regard to pronouns, question words, and words derived from them: for example, *noiz* → *nuiz* ("when"), *nola* → *núla* ("how"), *nor* → *nur* ("who"), *zoin* or *zein* in Unified Basque→ *zuñ* ("which"), *zonbait* or *zenbait* → *zumáit* ("how much/many"), *inor* → *ihúr* ("anyone/someone/no one"), and *norbait* → *nurbáit* ("someone"). It is also frequent in loanwords: *kontatu* → *khuntátü* ("to count"), *kontent* or *pozik* → *kuntént* ("happy"), *kontra* → *kúntre* ("against"), *kontserbatu* → *kuntserbátü* ("to keep/preserve"), *laborari* or *nekazaria* → *labuái* ("farmer"), *moda* → *múda* ("fashion"), *moldatu* → *muldátü* ("to arrange"or "to adapt (to)"), *motz* → *mutz* ("short"), *ohore* → *uhúe* ("honor"), *oignon* or *tipula* → *uñhú* ("onion"), *pastorala* → *phastuála* ("pastorale"), *tronpatu* or *erratu* → *trunpátü* ("to make a mistake"), and so on.

The assimilation *i* - *u* → *u* - *u* → *ü* - *ü* is used in Zuberoa: for example, *aingiru* or *aingeru* in Unified Basque → *ainguru* → *aingürü* → *aingü* ("angel"). Similar steps have been taken with the following words: *bihurtu* → *bühürtü* ("to turn into"), *higuin* → *hügün* ("disgust"), *iduri* or *irudi* → *üdüi* ("image"), *ikhuzi* or *garbitu* → *ükhüzi* ("to clean"), *ilhun* or *ilun* → *ülhün* ("dark"), *inguru* → *üngü* ("surroundings" or "around"), *inhurri* or *inurri* → *üñhüri* ("ant"), *ithurri* or *iturri* → *üthüri* ("spring" or "source"), *itsu* → *ütsü* ("blind"), *itzuli* → *ützüli* ("to return"), and *zintzur* → *züntzür* ("throat" or "ravine"). It also takes place with absolutive-ergative auxiliary verbs: *gitu* or *gaitu* → *gütü*, *zitu* or *zaitu* → *zütü*, *ninduzun* → *nündüzün*, and *gintuzun* → *güntüzün*. In Erronkari, too, the first step of this evolution was used, in other words *i* - *u* → *u* - *u*, but not the second. On occasion, this goes in the other direction: *u* - *i* → *u* - *u* → *ü* - *ü*. For example, in *burdina* → *burduña* → *bürdüña* ("iron"), and *hurritz* → *urrutx* → *ürütx* ("hazelnut tree").

In Zuberoa (and this used to be the case in Erronkari as well), the *-au-* diphthong tends to become *-ai-*: for example, in *auzo* → *áizo* ("neighborhood"), *belhaun* → *belhain* → *belháñ* ("knee"), *gau* → *gai* ("night"), *gauza* → *gáiza* ("thing"), *hautatu* → *haitátü* ("to choose/select/elect"), *irauli* → *iraili* → *iálli* ("to turn over"), and *iraun* → *irain* → *iáñ* ("to endure"). This also happens with the *zuka* (the more formal and commonly used "you" form) absolutive-ergative auxiliary verbs: *nau* → *nái*, *naue* or *naute* → *náie*, *haugu* → *háigü*, *haue* or *haute* → *haié*, and so on. The *-au-* → *-ü-* transformation in both *zuka* (common/formal) and *hika* (intimate) should also be mentioned: *nauzu* → *nüzü*, and *nauk*/*naun* → *nük*/*nün*.

There are also exceptions to this rule, mostly before the consonants *r*/*rr* and *s*/*ts* and after *j-*. Here are a few examples of where *-au-* has been kept:

- Before r/rr: *aurhíde* instead of *anaia-arrebak* ("sibling"), *áurthen* instead of *aurten* ("this year"), *gaur*, the demonstrative *hau* (formerly < *haur*) ("this"), *haur* instead of *umea* ("child"), *intzáur* instead of *intxaur* ("walnut"), and the quantifier *lau* (formerly < *laur*) ("four"). It is also used in emphatic pronouns: *niháu* instead of *neu* ("I myself"), *ziháu* instead of *zeu* ("you yourself"), and *giháu* instead of *geu* ("we ourselves").
- Before *s*/*ts*: *ausártü* ("to dare"), *háutse* instead of *hautsi* ("to break"), *káusa* ("cause"), *khausítü* instead of *aurkitu* ("to find"), *phausátü* instead of *atseden hartu* ("to rest"), and so on.
- At the beginning of words starting with *j-*: *jaun* ("mister"), *jáuntsi* instead of *jantzi* ("to wear"), *jáuzi* ("to jump"), and so forth.
- Naturally, when the origin of the diphthong *-au-* is *-ao-*, there are no further modifications to it. For instance, *aroa* ("time," "age," or "period") becomes *aua*, but does not go on to become **aia*.

Nasal vowels have survived in Zuberoa, but recently they have begun to disappear there as well in young people's speech. They are mostly pronounced beside aspirations and nasal consonants. Here are a few examples:

- Beside aspirations: *âhâl* for *ahal* in Unified Basque ("capacity"), *âhâtze* for *ahantzi* ("to forget"), *âhâi* for *ahari* ("ram"), *mêhê* for *mehe* ("thin" or "lean"), *ûhûñ* for *ohoin* or *lapurra* ("thief"), and so on.

- Beside nasal consonants: *gízôn* for *gizon* ("man"), *hândi* for *handi* ("big"), *lântháe* for *landare* ("plant"), *mêndi* for *mendi* ("mountain"), *ûntzi* for *ontzi* ("container" or "boat"), and so on.
- They are also sometimes pronounced after nasal consonants, but this is not frequent in this area: *âmâ* for *ama* ("mother"), *aranû* for *arrano* ("eagle"), and so on.

Consonants

There are many sibilant consonants in Basque, with *z*, *s*, *x*, *tz*, *ts*, and *tx* being standard, while a further two are used in Zuberoa. These are not expressed in writing, but the sibilant sounds */z/* and */z/* can frequently be heard in speech there. These are most frequently used in loanwords and above all between vowels and before sonorous consonants (*l*, *m*, *n*, *ñ*, *b*, *d*, *g*). Let us examine a few examples of this:

- Between vowels: for example, *ara[z]ú* instead of *arrazoi* in Unified Basque ("reason"), *baliú[z]a* instead of *baliotsua* ("valuable"), *de[z]égin* instead of *desegin* ("to undo" or "to come apart"), *ko[z]ía* instead of *lehengusua* ("cousin"), *bede[z]í* instead of *sendagilea* ("doctor"), *sa[z]ú* instead of *sasoia* ("season"), and *só[z]a* instead of *sosa* or *dirua* ("money").
- Before sonorous consonants: for example, *bo[z]ná* instead of *bosna* ("five each"), *bo[z]gía* instead of *bost gara* ("there are five of us"), *ga[z]ná* instead of *gazta* ("cheese"), *ha[z] bédi* for *has bedi* ("let it begin"), *heo[z]dün* instead of *herosdun* or *zaratatsua* ("noisy"), and *ikhá[z]le* for *ikasle* ("student").

In several loanwords, furthermore, there are the sibilant, sonorous, fricative consonants [*d*] and [*dz*]: *aren[d]átzen* instead of *konpontzen* ("mending"), *bulan[d]eiá* instead of *okindegia* ("bakery"), *e[dz]ênplía* for *etsenplua* or *adibidea* ("example"), *e[dz]aména* for *etsamina* or *azterketa* ("examination"), *espún[d]a* instead of *belakia* ("sponge"), *jân[d]á* instead of *laranja* ("orange"), *lân[d]éa/lân[d]éia* for *lanjerra* or *arriskua* ("danger"), and so on.

The pronunciation of *j-* is distinctive and resembles that of French. This is normally written as <*dx*> and pronounced similarly at the start and in the middle of words: for example, *dxákin* for *jakin* ("to know"), *dxan* for *jan* ("to eat"), *dxun* for *joan* ("to go"), *eredxêntá* for *errejenta* or *irakaslea* in Unified Basque ("teacher"), *eidxéra* for *ederra* ("beautiful"), and *garádxe* for *garaje* ("garage").

Zuberoan Basque is also special in its use of vibrant syllables. Other Basque speakers have almost completely lost the use of single vibrant syllables, and, because of that, there have been transformations such as *eroririk* → *ióyik*, *haragi* → *ági* ("meat"), Iruri (the town name, Trois-Villes in French) → Iúi. The sound pronounced by other Basque speakers with three or four vibrations, in contrast, are said with a single vibration: *harri* → *hári* ("stone"), *haurrer* or *haurrei* in Unified Basque → *haurér* ("to the children"), *herri* → *héri* ("town" or "people"). Nowadays, the single vibration is most heard in loanwords: *aperitíva* ("aperitif"), *garáje* ("garage"), *jeneralín* instead of *jeneralean* ("in general"), *natüra* ("nature"), *tra(k)türa* for *traktora* (tractor"), *turísta* ("tourist"), and so on.

Aspirations have been kept in use in Zuberoan with greater strength and liveliness than any other Basque dialect. As well as appearing at the start of words and between vowels, they are also used after the sonorous consonants *l*, *n*, and *r*, and the occlusive aspirations *ph*, *th*, and *kh* are also often heard, and are also used by young people. The following are examples of this:

- After sonorous consonants: *bélhar* for *belar* ("grass"), *élhür* for *elur* ("snow"), *lanhú* for *laino* ("fog" or "cloud"), *sénhar* for *senar* ("husband"), *ürháts* for *urrats* ("step"), and *ürhéntü* for *urrentu* or *amaitu* in Unified Basque ("to finish").
- Occlusive aspirations: *aiphátü* for *aipatu* ("to mention"), *phíztü* for *piztu* ("to light" or "to switch on"), *béthi* for *beti* ("always"), *úrthe* for *urte* ("year"), *ékhi* for *eguzki* ("sun"), *ikhúsi* for *ikusi* ("to see"), and so on. Occlusive aspirations are also common in loanwords: for example, *khanbiátü* ("to change"), *khexátü* ("to complain"), *khuntátü* ("to count"), *phála* ("racket," "bat," or "shovel"), *pharkátü* ("to forgive"), *phausátü* ("to pause"), *phenátü* ("to tire" or "to punish"), *phentsátü* ("to think"), and *thapátü* ("to cover"). There are also aspirations after sonorous consonants: for example, *manhátü* instead of *agindu* ("to order"), and *uñhú* instead of *tipula* ("onion"). And they also exist in words that come from Unified Basque: *ikhastolá* for *ikastola* (Basque-language medium school).

In Zuberoa (and this was also the case in Erronkari), it is more common than anywhere else to hear the letters *t* and *k* after the consonants *n* and *l*: for example, in *álte* for *alde* ("place" or "side") and *etxálte* for *baserria* ("farmstead") as well as *sükhálte* for *sukaldea* ("kitchen"), *galthátü* for *galdetu* ("to ask [for]"), *igánte* for *igande* ("Sunday"), and *ménte* for *mende* ("century"). Loanwords have also been adapted to this model, such as *abéntü* or *abendu* in Unified Basque ("December"), *bontháte* or *borondate* ("will"), *jénte* or *jende* ("people"), *lantháe* or *landare* ("plant"), and *zánkho* or *zango* ("leg" or "calf"). This is the rule for the benefactive suffix *-entako* (*lagünentáko* or *lagunendako*, "for the friends"), the ablative and local-genitive suffixes *nondik* and *nongo* (*hebénti* or *hemendik* "from here," *hánko* or *hango* "from there"), the suffixes *-mentü* and *-tár* (*kuntentaméntü* "contentment," *larraintár* "an inhabitant of Larraine"), and in most *-tü* participle suffixes (*héltü* or *heldu* "to arrive," *lagünthü* or *la-*

gundu "to help"); although not in the cases of *bíldü* ("to meet" or "to gather"), *gáldü* ("to lose"), and *sáldü* ("to sell").

Accent

This is another of Zuberoan Basque's significant features. It has a very strong accent, and syllables with and without emphasis are easily differentiated. It is easy, however, to work out where the emphasis goes: normally, on the penultimate syllable. Basque speakers from other areas find it strange to hear pronunciations such as *bezaláko* for *bezalako* in Unified Basque ("as" or "like"), *izigaríko* for *izugarrizko* ("tremendous"), and *lagünáen* for *lagunaren* ("of or pertaining to a friend") in Zuberoan Basque.

Often, however, the emphasis moves to the last syllable, and this new positioning shows that a contraction was made at some time in the past. This is clearly seen, for example, in words ending in the letter *-a* to which the article *a* is added; in Zuberoan Basque, this gives *-a + a* → *-áa* → -á. As a result, *alhabá* (or *alaba* "daughter" in Unified Basque) is the singular and *alhába* the indefinite.

In past tense auxiliary verbs, likewise, the emphasis goes on the last syllable and there is as well a type of contraction. Examples of this are words such as *ginén* and *zinén*, which may have originally been **gináen* and **zináen*, respectively.

There have also been contractions in some cases in plural words, and, in Zuberoan, singular and plural are differentiated by emphasis: *lagü'nak* and *lagünék*, *lagünái* and *lagünér*, *lagünáen* and *lagünén*, and so on. As can be seen, the emphasis is on the last syllable in plural words and on the penultimate syllable in singular words. The absolutive is the exception to this, with emphasis going in the same place in both singular and plural: *lagü'na* and also *lagü'nak*.

Contractions from long ago can also be seen in some other words with the emphasis on the last syllable: for example, in *ardú* (< **ardano*) or *ardoa* in Unified Basque ("wine"), *gazná* (< **gaztana*) *gazta* ("cheese"), and *orgá* (< **organa*) *orga* or *gurdia* ("cart"). Of course, there are also some quite recent contractions. On the one hand, the rule in Zuberoan Basque is that in words that end with a vowel the article is assimilated and combined with that vowel, for instance in words such as *itsasóak* → *itxasúak* → *itxasúk*, *itsasóan* → *itxasúan* → *itxasún*. On the other hand, /r/ between vowels has been almost completely lost: *ogírik* → *ogík*, *igáran* → *igán*.

With loanwords, naturally, if the emphasis in the original language was on the last syllable, it remains so in Zuberoan Basque: for example, in *bedezí* instead of *sendagilea* in Unified Basque ("doctor"), *erejént* instead of *maisua* ("teacher"), *fotó* instead of *argazkia* ("photo"), *godalét* instead of *edalontzia* ("glass"), *llapí* instead of *untxia* ("rabbit"), *motó* instead of *motorra* ("motorbike"), and *otó* instead of *automobila* ("car"). A few old loanwords, however, have been adapted to Zuberoan Basque rules, for example *apostólü* ("apostle"), *gramatíka* ("grammar"), *katolíko* ("Catholic"), and *solído* ("solid"), as well as some words ending in *-zio* such as *ofizío* ("profession"), *prezío* ("price"), and *sakrifizío* ("sacrifice").

Similarly, foreign words ending in *-on* and *-ion* are emphasized on the last syllable, such as *arazú* or *arrazoi* in Unified Basque ("reason"), and *kamiú* or *kamioi* ("truck"). And, likewise, some suffixes take over the emphasis: *-ñí* and *-(xk)ót*, expressing smallness in size (*amañí* instead of *amona* in Unified Basque "grandmother," *alorxkót* instead of *alortxoa* "little field"); *-tár* and *-és* expressing origin (*mauletár* "an inhabitant of Maule," *frantsés* "French"); the allative case *-alát* (*mendilát* instead of *mendira* "to the mountain"); the quantifiers *-ná*/*-rá* (*biá* instead of *bira* "turn" or "spin around," *hiuná* instead of *hiruna* "three each"), *-báit* (*nurbáit* instead of *norbait* "someone"), *-kál* (*aldikál* instead of *aldi bakoitzeko* "of or pertaining to each side"), *-khói* (*gaznakhói* instead of *gaztazale* "cheese lover"), *-kór* (*ahalkór* instead of *lotsatia* "shy"), *-liár* (*egoiliár* instead of *egoilea* "inhabitant") and *-ús* (*amurús* "amorous," *seriús* "serious").

Morphology

Noun Morphology

There is a marked tendency to use words without an article. In fact, this can also be heard in other Eastern dialects, but it is particularly noticeable in Zuberoan Basque. This can be seen in the following examples:

gue aitá záhar da or (in Unified Basque)
gure aita zahar da
"our father is old."

Joháñe labuái da or
Johañe nekazari da
"Johañe is a farmer."

semía hun düzü or
semea on da
"he is a good son."

The indefinite is also used when a group is referred to:

ógi badít or
ogi badut
"I have bread."

bortín béhi ikhúsi dít or
mendian behi ikusi dut
"I have seen a cow on the mountain."

Similarly, the indefinite or the partitive can be used in questions:

náhi düzía ardú? / náhi düzía arduík? or
nahi duzu ardo/ardorik?
"do you want (some) wine?"

ógi badéa? / ogík badéa? or
ogi/ogirik bada?
"is there (any) bread?"

Proper and common nouns are distinguished between in the ablative and allative cases. In the ablative case, proper nouns have the suffix *-rik* added to them, and *-tik* is added to common nouns:

Máuleik jin da or
Maulerik etorri da
"he/she has come from Maule"

and

mendítik jin da or
menditik etorri da
"he/she has come from the mountain."

In the allative case, similarly, *-ra* or *-rat* is added to proper nouns and, *-ála* or *-alát* to common nouns. Thus, nowadays, people in Zuberoa say "*Máulea jun da*" or in Unified Basque "*Maulera joan da*," meaning "he/she has gone to Maule" and "*bortilát jun da*" or "*bortualat* (or *mendira*) *joan da*," meaning "he/she has gone to the mountain."

It should also be pointed out that while articles are included in the declension of common nouns, phonological factors mean that they often do not appear in the spoken language. In the above mentioned word *bortü* ("mountain"), for example, the transformation *-ü* + *a* → *-ia* has taken place, as in many eastern areas: *bortü* + *alát* → *bortialát*. After that, the usual Zuberoan assimilation of the article has taken place: *bortialát* → *bortilát*. The same thing happens with this example: *baratze* ("vegetable garden") + *alát* → *batzialát* → *batzilát* ("to the vegetable garden").

Words ending in *-on* and *-ion* from French and Spanish take on the nasal, accentuated *-ú*, for example in the cases of *arrathú* for *arratoi* ("rat"), *arrazú* for *arrazoi* ("reason"), *bunbú* for *bonboi* ("bonbon"), *buttú* for *botoi* ("button"), *fanfarrú* for *fanfarroi* ("show-off"), *lehú* for *lehoi* ("lion"), *melú* for *meloi* ("melon"), *sasú* for *sasoi* ("season"), and *kamiú* for *kamioi* ("truck").

The suffixes *-ót* and *-xkót*, expressing smallness in size, are frequently used in Zuberoan Basque, as is the feminine suffix *-sa* (in fact, the latter is common throughout the Basque Country, for example *konde/kondesa* "count/countess") and the prefix *arra-*, and all of these originate through contact with the people of Béarn. Here are a few examples:

- *-ót/-xkót*: *alorxkót* for *alortxoa* ("little field"), *apáidüxkót* for *jatordutxoa* or *mokadua* ("snack"), *herrixkót* for *herritxoa* ("hamlet" or "little village"), *parraxtót* for *mordoxka bat* or *pilatxo bat* ("bunch"), and *plaxót* for *plazatxoa* ("little [town] square"). However, this rule is no longer productive.
- *-sa*: *alhargüntsa* for *andre alarguna* ("widow"), *bulanjérsa* for *andre ogi-saltzailea* (from the French *boulanger* or *okina* in Unified Basque) ("[female] baker"), *kozinérsa* for *andre sukaldaria* ("[female] cook or chef"), *laburarísa* for *andre nekazaria* ("[female] farmer"), and *ostalérsa* for *andre ostalaria* ("[female] innkeeper").
- *arra-*: *arraberrítü* for *eraberritu* ("to renew" or "to renovate"), *arrabíldü* ("to collect"), *arrégin* ("to redo"), *arraérran* for *berriz esan* ("to tell again"), *arrahártü* ("to retake"), *arrahási* ("to start again"), *arrajún* and *arrajín* for *berriz joan/etorri* ("to go/come again"), *arralóthu* ("to rejoin" or "to re-attach"), and *arraphíztu* ("to relight" or "to switch on again"). Special words have also been created using this prefix: *arramáiatz* for *ekaina* ("June"), and *arraséme/arralhába* for *biloba* ("nephew/niece"). This prefix has also spread to Lower Navarre.

A further suffix seems to have been created in Zuberoa itself: *-ñí*, to express smallness in size. Here are a few examples: *-ñí*: *aitañí* and *amañí* for *aitona/amona* ("grandfather/grandmother"), *amiñí* for *apurtxoa* ("a smidgeon"), *apáidüñí* for *jatordutxoa* or *mokadua* ("snack"), *ebiñí* for *euri xehea* ("light rain"), *gutiñí* for *gutxitxo* ("a little"), and *ttipiñí* for *txikitxoa* ("tiny").

Verb Morphology

As well as the verb *ari izan* ("to be [doing something]"), *erantsu* (> *iáuntsi*) is also used in Zuberoan Basque, as in the following sentences:

labuantzán iáuntsi dit eretrétala artíno	or, in Unified Basque,
nekazaritzan aritu naiz jubilazioa arte "I was a farmer until I retired"	
iáuntsi diát bázter xahátzen	or
aritu nauk bazter garbitzen "I have been cleaning up"	
zórtzi úrthez gazná egíten iáuntsi dit	or
zortzi urtez gazta egiten aritu naiz "I made cheese for eight years"	

Furthermore, **eradun* is the root of absolutive-dative-ergative auxiliary verbs, as it is throughout the eastern Basque Country, but this has undergone a particular phonetic transformation in Zuberoa: **eradun* → **erau* → **erai* → *erei* → *ei*. Because of this, the verb form has a different appearance in Zuberoan Basque compared to other dialects: *deit* instead of *dit*, *deitáde* instead of *didate*, *déizüt* instead of *dizut*, *deiót* instead of *diot*, *déikü* instead of *digu*, and *deiégü* instead of *diegu*.

The plural infix *-(t)z-* is used in absolutive-dative-ergative and absolutive-dative auxiliary verbs to form the plural rather than *-zki-*, as in Central Basque. These are the absolutive-dative forms: *záitzat* (and *záizt*), *záitzak*, *záitzo*, *záizkü*, *záitzü*, *zaitzíe*, *záitze*. In absolutive-dative-ergative, on the other hand, forms such as *deizt* instead of *dizkit* in Unified Basque, *déizkü* instead of *dizkigu*, *deitzót* instead of *dizkiot*, *déitzüt* instead of *dizkizut*, and *deitzégü* instead of *dizkiegu* are used.

These pluralizing forms are strongly present in young people's speech and are also used beyond the absolutive-dative and absolutive-dative-ergative categories. Here are two examples of this:

> *fenomeno berik dütützak eta ene hipotesien arabera analisatü tiatzat* or
> *fenomeno berriak dituk eta ene hipotesien arabera analizatu ditiat*
> "these are new phenomena and I have analyzed them according to my hypotheses"

The past of the absolutive-dative category auxiliary verbs are not formed using *zit-*, as in the central Basque Country. As in Western Basque, they are formed using the present + *n*: *zéitan* instead of *zitzaidan* in Unified Basque, *zeián* instead of *zitzaian*, *zeión* instead of *zitzaion*, *zéikün* instead of *zitzaigun*, *zéizün* instead of *zitzaizun*, *zeizíen* instead of *zitzaizuen*, and *ze(i)én* instead of *zitzaien*.

Some people believe that the absence of *zit-* is something new, but that is not the case. For instance, Athanase Belaipere wrote in his Christian teaching materials in 1696: "*adin hortan zer heltü zaion?*" ("What happened to him at that age?") and "*bi aingürü xuriz estalirik agertü zaitzen*" ("two angels swathed in white appeared to them").[8] Thus, *zaion* = *zitzaion* and *zaitzen* = *zitzaizkien*.

Moreover, *-rik* is added to participles in Zuberoan. The new forms *-ta* and *-a*, used in some other areas, are unknown. Thus, *entzünik nízün* is the correct form in Zuberoan instead of *entzuna nuen* in Unified Basque ("I had heard about it"), *estonatüik züzün* instead of *harritua zen* ("he/she was amazed"), *otóa hartüik* instead of *automobila hartuta* ("by car," literally "having taken the car"), *úntsa beztitüik* instead of *ondo jantzita* ("well dressed"), and *konektatüik nük* instead of *konektatuta nauk* ("I am connected" in the familiar *hika* form).

Meanwhile, *baiko* is used in time clauses, but this is not used by young people: for example, in *etxéa báiko, lanái lóthü nündüzün* for *etxera heldu bezain laster, lanari lotu nintzen* (or *nintzaion*) "as soon as I arrived home, I got stuck into work."

Undeveloped Rules

In some words ending in *-e* and *-i*, the transformation → *-ü* has been affected: *bederatzü* for *bederatzi* ("nine"), *botxü* for *botxe* or *harkaitza* in Unified Basque ("rock" or "crag"), *hemeretzü* (> *himeretzü*) for *hemeretzi* ("nineteen"), *üllü* and *illi* for *euli* ("fly"), *üzkü* for *uzki* ("anus" or "butt"), and so on. What happens here is that when *-e* + *a*, *-i* + *a* and *-ü* + *a* come together, all three become *-ia*, and in the same way that the word *eskia* comes from *eskü* ("hand"), some people believe that the word *botxia* comes from *botxü* ("rock" or "crag") and that *üzkia* comes from *üzkü* ("anus" or "butt").

The transformation *tz* → *tx* takes places in some words: *atxeidü* for *altzairu* "steel," *hanitx* for *anitz* or *asko* in Unified Basque ("a lot [of]," "many," or "much"), *khütxe* for *gurutze* ("cross"), *zerbütxü* for *zerbitzu* ("service"), and so on.

The transformation *r* → *ll* has led to *bella* instead of *bera* or *bigun* in Unified Basque ("soft" or "tender"), *holli* instead of *hori* ("yellow"), and *hüllan* instead of *hurran* or *hurbil* ("near" or "close"). At the start of these words, furthermore, the transformation has been *l-* → *ll-* in the following words: *llabür* for *labur* ("short" or "brief") (this also exists outside Zuberoa) and *llapî* for *lapina* or *untxia* ("rabbit").

The occlusive is silent at the start of these words: *khorpitz* for *gorputz* ("body"), *khütxe* for *gurutze* ("cross"), *phakatü* for *pagatu* or *ordaindu* in Unified Basque ("to pay"), and *pharkatü* for *barkatu* ("to forgive").

Vocabulary

In addition to phonology, vocabulary is also special in Zuberoa, and here as well both the conservative and innovative nature of the Zuberoan Basque dialect is evident.

The following are loanwords from foreign languages: *baranthalla* instead of *otsaila* in Unified Basque ("February"), *bedezi* instead of *medikua* ("doctor"), *boronte* instead of *kopeta* or *bekokia* ("forehead"), *godalet* instead of *edalontzia* ("glass"), *khantü* instead of *ondo* or *aldamen* ("side"), *kota* instead of *gona* ("skirt"), *pera* instead of *madaria* ("pear"), *prefosta* instead of *jakina* or *noski* ("of course" or "naturally"), *seteme* instead of *iraila* ("September"), *sordei* instead of *gaiztoago* ("wickeder" or "worse"), and *uñhu* instead of *tipula* ("onion"). Most of these words are derived from Gascon.

Words that have disappeared from other parts of the Basque Country but that are still used in Zuberoa include: *baratxe* instead of *astiro* or *poliki* ("slowly" or "gently") (also used on the Lapurdi coast), *botxe* (> *botxü*) instead of *harkaitza* ("rock" or "crag"), *eden* instead of *hartu* or *kabitu* ("to hold"), *ediren* instead of *aurkitu* ("to find"), *eli* instead of *multzoa* ("bunch"), *erho* instead of *hilarazi* ("to kill"), *herots* instead of *hotsa* or *zarata* ("noise"), *naba* instead of *ibarra* ("valley"), *oski* instead of *oinetakoa* ("shoe"), and *zi* instead of *ezkurra* ("acorn"). It is commonly believed that the word *neskenegün* for "Saturday" (*larunbata* in Unified Basque) was particular to Zuberoa and to Erronkari, but Julio Caro Baroja states that this word was once also used in the Bortziriak area of Navarre.[9]

Zuberoans have also created their own words. Here are some of the best known examples:

A *aholkü* for *gomendioa* ("recommendation"), *ahüña* for *antxumea* ("kid" as in young goat), *aiñharba* for *armiarma* ("spider"), *aitañi/amañi* for *aitona/amona* ("grandfather/grandmother"), *altxatüra* for *orantza* or *legamia* ("yeast" or "leaven"), *amañ* for *armiarma sarea* ("spider web"), *amiñi* for *apurra* ("crumb" or "bit"), *aran* for *oihartzun* ("echo"), *arramaiatz* for *ekaina* ("June"), and *athe* for *meta* ("stack" or "haystack").

B *bedatse* for *udaberria* ("Spring"), *belhagile* for *sorgina* ("witch"), and *besainko* for *ukondoa* ("elbow").

D *düründa* (in Pettarra) and *ühülgü* (in Basabürü) for *trumoia* or *ostotsa* ("thunder").

E *egari* for *erabili* ("to use"), *ekhi* for *eguzkia* ("sun"), *ekhürü/ükhürü* for *geldi* or *lasai* ("still" or "calm"), *elhestatü/elherran* for *mintzatu* ("to speak"), *eñherik* for *nekatuta* ("tired"), and *eretz* for *aurrez aurre* or *aldea* ("face to face" or "area") as well as *etzin* for *eretzean* ("on the edge" or "at the side").

G *galtho* for *galdera* ("question").

H *haboro* for *gehiago* ("more"), *hatsarre* for *hasiera* ("beginning"), *heltübada* for *beharbada* ("maybe"), and *hurak* for *haiek* (the plural demonstrative "these" or the pronoun "they").

I *iñhazi* for *tximista* ("lightning"), *iresi* for *orraztu* ("to comb"), and *izei* for *abetoa* ("fir tree").

J *jesan* for *mailegutan hartu* ("to borrow").

K *khaldü* for *zartakoa* ("strike" or "slap").

L *latsün* for *karea* or *gisua* ("lime" as in the substance).

M *manex/manexina* meaning "an inhabitant of Lapurdi or Lower Navarre," and *marddo* for *bigun* or *beratz* ("soft" or "tender").

N *neskatsuna* for *neska gaztea* or *neskatoa* ("young girl" or "little girl").

O *ohiltü* for *bota* or *egotzi* ("to throw"), and *olha* for *borda* ("shepherd's refuge or hut").

P *phikoxte* for *zilborra* ("navel"), and *pikarrai* for *biluzik* ("naked").

S *süskhandera* for *sugandila* ("lizard").

T *thai (gabe)* for *etenik (gabe)* "endless" (literally, "without stopping").

U *ügatz* ("bearded vulture"), *ühaitz* for *ibaia* ("river"), *ülhaintx* for *mirua* ("kite" as in the bird), and *ürhentü* for *bukatu* ("to finish").

Z *zühain* for *zuhaitza* ("tree").

Many of the words in this list have spread to Erronkari and Zaraitzu in Navarre and Lower Navarre. It appears as if they originated in Zuberoa, spreading first to neighboring areas, and from there throughout the Basque Country.

Variants

The letter *e-* begins some words in Zuberoan Basque, and, in some cases at least, this is an old usage: *ebili* and *ibili* ("to walk"), *heraki* instead of *irakin* ("to boil" or "to ferment") (both of these variants also exist outside Zuberoa), *egürüki* and *ügürüki* for *iguriki* or *itxaron* in Unified Basque ("to wait"), *elkhi* for *ilki* or *irten* in Unified Basque ("to go out" or "to leave"), *erri* for *irri (barre)* ("to laugh"). Likewise, *-e* also appears at the end of some words: *orraze* for *orrazi* ("comb") (this also exists outside Zuberoa), *âhâtze* for *ahantzi* ("to forget"), and *hautse* for *hautsi* ("to break").

The following words were created by assimilation: *bohor* for *behor* ("mare"), *-gerren* instead of *-garren* (a suffix attached to cardinal numbers to make them ordinals), and *mithil* for *mutil* ("boy").

These further variants also exist in Zuberoan: *algar* and *alkhar* for *elkar* ("each other" or "one another"), *ardu* for *ardo* ("wine"), *bardin* for *berdin* ("same"), *bihamen* for *biharamun* ("hangover"), *ebi* for *euri* ("rain"), *ejer* for *eder* ("beautiful"), *ertzo* for *ero* ("crazy"), *gahün* for *hagun* or *aparra* in Unified Basque ("foam"), *hamazortzi* for *hemezortzi* ("eighteen"), *hariña* (> *haña*) for *hondarra* ("sand" or "rubble"), *heben* for *hemen* ("here"), *herrokan* for *lerroan* ("in a row" or "in an orderly fashion"), *herxe* for *heste* ("intestine"), *inkhatz* for *ikatz* ("coal" or "charcoal"), *khanbera* for *ganbara* ("chamber" or "loft"), *khirixti* for *kristau* ("Christian"), *lein* (> *leñ*) for *leun* ("smooth" or "soft"), *sakola* for *sakela* ("pocket"), *-tarzün* instead of *-tasun* (a suffix indicating a quality or a feature), *txeste/txestatü* for *dastatu* ("to taste" or "to try"), *ükhen* for *ukan* or *eduki* ("to have"), *ürsain* (> *ürsañ*) for *usin* ("sneeze"), and *zelü* for *zeru* ("sky").

Zuberoan Basque has many differentiating characteristics: indeed, it is clearly different from all the other Basque dialects. Its character is most distinguishable in it phonetics: the accent is strong, its *ü* vowel, the frequent use of aspirations, and so on. Many of these distinguishing features come from Gascon and, of course, the influence of Gascon is also very apparent in the vocabulary.

3
Western Basque

This dialect is spoken in Bizkaia, most of the Deba Valley in Gipuzkoa, and the towns of Aramaio and Legutio in Araba. Araba also used to belong to this area, together apparently with the Basque-speaking parts of Burgos and La Rioja. At any rate, the linguistic remains found there and place names look like Western Basque.[1] Taking this whole area into account, and seeing how many innovations from Western Basque have spread out to the Goierri area in Gipuzkoa, the Burunda, Ameskoa, and Lana Valleys in Navarre, it looks as if Vitoria-Gasteiz may have been located at the geographical center of this dialect. It was, at least, the largest urban center in which Western Basque was spoken and would therefore have served as a basis from which to extend the dialect.

In the area in which Basque is still spoken today, there are two highly differentiated sub-dialects: Western and Eastern, as I have termed them. With regards to these sub-dialects' boundaries, an eighteenth-century description by Agustin Kardaberatz was precise and accurate. In his short book *Cristiñau dotrinea* (Christian doctrine), he wrote:

> I have been able to see clearly that while the same type of Basque is spoken throughout Bizkaia, some words vary from town to town. I have heard, seen and learned some words that change from Orozko [Orozco] and Zeberio [Ceberio] to Plentzia [Plencia] and from Plentzia and the Matxitxako area to Mungia and to here. They are different mostly in the way they are pronounced. The way of speaking changes from Durango and Markina to here.[2]

Kardaberatz mentions Matxitxako in the north and Otxandio in the south, and, in fact, the line between these two places divides the two sub-dialects. Between those two main areas there are "intermediary areas" that serve as connectors: Busturialdea, which lies between the Uribe Kosta coastal area and Mungialdea in the west and the Lea-Artibai area in the east (including, among others, the towns of Ondarroa, Lekeitio, Markina, and Ispaster), and Zornotza (Amorebieta), which is located between the Arratia Valley (including, among others, Igorre, Lemoa, Dima, and Zeanuri) and the Durangaldea area (including, among others, Durango, Abadiño, Elorrio, and Berriz). Last-

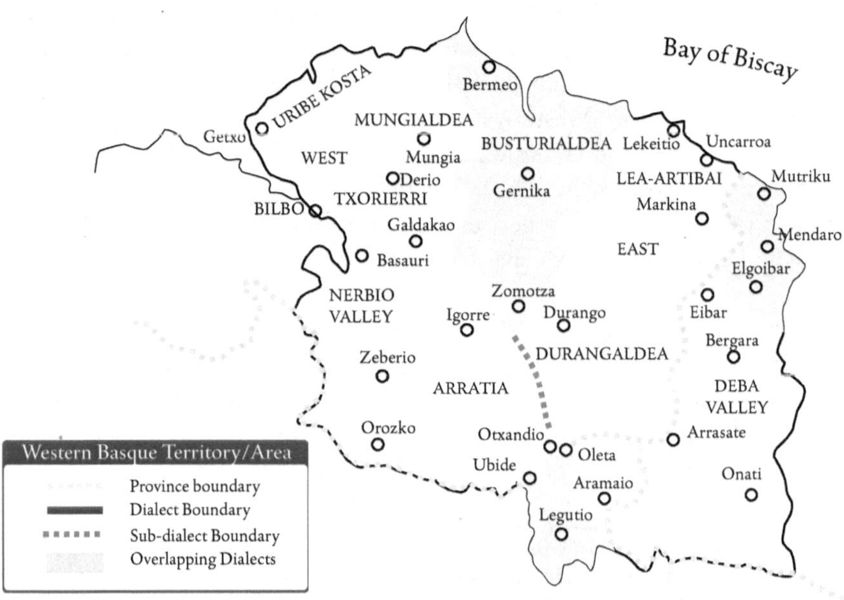
Bay of Biscay
URIBE KOSTA
Bermeo
Getxo
MUNGIALDEA
BUSTURIALDEA
Lekeitio
Uncarroa
WEST
Mungia
Derio
Gernika
LEA-ARTIBAI
Mutriku
BILBO
TXORIERRI
Markina
Galdakao
Mendaro
Basauri
EAST
Elgoibar
NERBIO
VALLEY
Zomotza
Igorre
Durango
Eibar
Bergara
DURANGALDEA
Zeberio
ARRATIA
DEBA
VALLEY
Orozko
Otxandio
Oleta
Arrasate
Ubide
Aramaio
Onati
Legutio
Western Basque Territory/Area
Province boundary
Dialect Boundary
Sub-dialect Boundary
Overlapping Dialects

ly, in the southern part of the area in which the dialects are still used today, Otxandio (Ochandiano) and Ubide (Ubidea) in Bizkaia, and Legutio and the Oleta district of Aramaio in Araba look both west and east at the same time. Thanks to these intermediate areas, there is an almost imperceptible, step-by-step route from one sub-dialect to the other.

There are also highly differentiated areas in this wide territory. This can be seen, above all, in the Deba Valley. Being administratively part of Gipuzkoa has brought it closer to the type of Basque spoken in Gipuzkoa, and this closeness can clearly be seen in the northern part of the area. At present, the Basque spoken in three towns in this area – Elgoibar, Mendaro, and Mutriku – cannot be clearly classified as being either Western or Central Basque because Basque speakers here use intermediate ways of speaking. The influence of Central Basque has also been considerable in Antzuola and Bergara, and nowadays Itziar and Deba are also in the Central Basque area.

Some parts of the coastal areas are also highly differentiated, and not only in Bizkaia. Because of their ways of life, they have particular ways of speaking. There are also differences in single towns between the fishing community and the farming community.[3] The differences can be found in intonation and, above all, in vocabulary, but separating forces can be seen in other aspects as well. In the streets of Ondarroa, for instance, the letter *-g* goes at the start of absolutive-dative auxiliary verbs: *gasta* instead of *zait* in Unified Basque, *gako* instead of *zaio*, *gasku* instead of *zaigu*, *gatzu* instead of *zaizu*, *gatzue* instead of *zaizue*, and *gakoe* instead of *zaie*. In the farming areas of the same town, however, the letter *j-* is pronounced, giving *jata*, *jako*, *jaku*, and so on to express the same thing. As in Ondarroa, so the ways of speaking in other coastal towns in Bizkaia such as Lekeitio, Elantxobe, and Bermeo also have their own marked character.

Some Notes on the Historical Evolution of Western Basque[4]

It is not surprising that sub-dialects and special areas should exist in such a wide area, but these differences have mostly arisen and their use has spread since the nineteenth century in particular. For instance, two different sixteenth-century publications – one, a list of songs and proverbs collected by the historian Esteban Garibai and the other, titled *Refranes y sentencias* (Refrains and maxims), a collection of proverbs – demonstrate a remarkable similarity in the kind of Basque cited.[5] Yet we should bear in mind that Garibai was from Arrasate and most of the proverbs in *Refranes y Sentencias* seem to be from the Bilbao area; in other words, they are from opposite ends of the Western Basque area. It is a similar case if one compares seventeenth- and eighteenth-century manuscripts; the differences between them are not that great or numerous.

A new era for Western Basque started in the nineteenth century. It was then that Basque in Bizkaia became separate from the rest of Basque and, at the same time, the differences between the two sub-dialects increased. In 1800, Joan Antonio Mogel, the former priest of Markina (Bizkaia), wrote *Erakasteak* (Teachings) in Gipuzkoan Basque, which displeased the Bizkaian church authorities. Mogel himself admitted this later on (1964: 63):

> It was barely even news in Bizkaia, the fact that a work in Basque and in the Gipuzkoan dialect had been published . . . and that the author was a priest of the said Seigniory, when all of a sudden there was great commotion among the Bizkaian clergymen, bitterly complaining that the Gipuzkoans had been given preference. What use can we make, they said, of a work written in a strange dialect and impenetrable for us? The author could give powerful reasons for its origins, or for the assumed preference, if he were to publish them.[6]

Mogel wanted as many Basque speakers as possible to read and understand his book and for that reason wrote it in Gipuzkoan Basque. However, some members of the church in Bizkaia saw things in a different way. They were interested in the inhabitants of Bizkaia itself and not in all Basque speakers or in the whole of the Basque Country. After the uproar, a working group was formed to promote Bizkaian Basque, and it was there that initial efforts were made to create a unified Bizkaian Basque, with the Franciscan friar Pedro Antonio Añibarro taking a leading role. From then on, Mogel himself wrote mostly in Bizkaian Basque, although he always preferred Gipuzkoan Basque from the Beterri area – comprising an area from Donostia to Tolosa and including towns such as Hernani, Andoain, and Villabona – which he believed to be the best type of Basque to appeal to all speakers. Because of this, he did not take part in work to create a unified Bizkaian Basque and wrote in the manner of his town, Markina.

This initiative led to the breakup of Western Basque. Mogel took his model from the eastern area, in other words, Lea-Artibai and Durangaldea, while the western area was the model for unified Bizkaian Basque. Meanwhile, in the Deba Valley of Gipuzkoa, where Bizkaian Basque had traditionally been spoken, people increasingly began to use Gipuzkoan Basque instead.

With regard to this effort to create a unified Bizkaian Basque, it should be pointed out that, as well as distancing Bizkaians from other Basque speakers, it also noticeably hindered the progress of Bizkaian Basque. Believing that the similarities Bizkaian Basque shared with all the other dialects had been "contaminated" by the Gipuzkoan way of speaking, the working group chose to replace these elements with irrelevant, strange, and recently invented things.

A grammar of Bizkaian Basque published in 1848 by Joan Mateo Zabala served as the pioneer of this policy.[7] He clearly explained in the foreword to the book that when there were two options within Bizkaian Basque, he would always choose the "most regular" and not the "most used" or the "most widely used" option. As a result, although most Bizkaians used the auxiliary verbs *ditugu* and *dituzu*, and *ginean* and *zinean,* he chose *doguz* and *dozuz*, and *gintzan* and *zintzan*, thereby reinforcing their use. Clearly, Zabala believed that *doguz, dozuz, gintzan*, and *zintzan* were of Bizkaian origin whereas *ditugu, dituzu, ginean*, and *zinean* had been borrowed from the Gipuzkoans. Zabala was, however, wrong because what he took to be Gipuzkoan was, in fact, common to the whole of the Basque Country and to all the Basque dialects. In contrast, the option he took to be "autochthonous" and "genuine" had in fact been invented by some speakers in several towns in Bizkaia. The following passage by Zabala is highly significant: "I will say nothing of the *ebazan, ebeezan, nebazan* of Lekeitio, the first two also present in Orozko; nor of the *nendun, nenduzan, eudeezan* throughout the whole center of Bizkaia, which undoubtedly are part of a form more in accordance with the rest of the conjugation than the *zituan, zituen, nituan* that have been adopted by our writers."[8] Therefore Zabala believed that Bizkaian writers had taken *zituan, zituen*, and *nituan* from Gipuzkoans and that pure Bizkaian was to be found in a single Bizkaian town (Lekeitio: *nebazan*) and in two Bizkaian towns (Lekeitio, once more, and Orozko: *ebazan* and *ebeezan*). He believed all this to be authentic Bizkaian, along with *nendun, nenduzan*, and *eudeezan* from central Bizkaia.

This was not actually the case. In fact, *nebazan, ebazan*, and *ebeezan* were very recent innovations that derived from the very strong use of the pluralizing letter *-z* in the western part of Bizkaia: *neban* (or *nuen* in Unified Basque) → *nebazan, eban* (or *zuen*) → *ebazan, ebeen* (or *zuten*) → *ebeezan. Nendun*, from central Bizkaia, was also a new form, invented along the lines of the plural auxiliary verbs *gendun* (or *genuen* in Unified Basque), *zendun* (or *zenuen*), and *zenduen* (or *zenuten*) and, by adding the pluralizing *-z, nendun* or *nenuzan* was then formed.

Nevertheless, Zabala's opinion gained adherents in Bizkaia through the nineteenth century and came to completely dominate in the twentieth century. Furthermore, when the idea of standardizing or unifying Basque was first mooted in the late nineteenth century, it was flatly rejected by the influential figure of Sabino Arana, the founder of the first Basque nationalist political party: the Euzko Alderdi Jeltzalea-Partido Nacionalista Vasco (EAJ-PNV, Basque Nationalist Party), in 1895. He wanted each region to maintain its own character, and, because of that, its own distinct dialect,[9] and he also denied the suitability of Gipuzkoan Basque as a standard reference point, which was put forward by many people. In Arana's opinion, Bizkaian Basque was the oldest, the most authentic, the most correct, and the richest dialect. Because of Arana's influence, opposition to a single unified Basque language grew, as, in

Bizkaia, did enthusiasm for its own dialect. An example of this is that when Euskaltzaindia was founded in 1918 and the debate about unified Basque began once more, his followers and members of the EAJ-PNV were against it.

However, another tendency also gained force and spread among Arana's followers: linguistic cleanliness, an objective with political overtones. Namely, because the Basque Country was different it had to be independent. They believed that the race was the most differentiating factor in the Basque Country, along with the Basque language, and, while language was different in itself, they made efforts to make it more so. Moreover, for this separateness to be visible, they modified Basque orthography and made use of graphemes that did not exist in the languages neighboring Basque; in particular, *l*, *r*, *d*, and *t* were written with accents over them. But these changes were not limited to the surface; they also revamped the internal language. Loanwords from foreign languages were banished, and new words were created to take their place. For instance, instead of the word *eliza* ("church"), which was used throughout the Basque Country, *txadona* (< *etxe deuna* "holy house") was invented, and all the words in the dictionary were "cleaned" and "corrected." Most of the support for Arana's EAJ-PNV party was, at this time, in Bizkaia and that is also where most of the effort to revolutionize the language was made.

Furthermore, at the end of the nineteenth century people understood that cleansing process in different ways. People who believed that Basque was completely corrupted and destroyed thought that the way the original Basques spoke was the key to resuscitating the language. Obviously, as there were no intermediaries to know how people had spoken in ancient times, the solution was to make it up. The Bizkaian, Resurreccion Maria Azkue, who was to go on to be the head of Euskaltzaindia, started from this premise. For example, in his grammar *Euskal Izkindea* (1891), he explained that Basques in ancient times had apparently used the verb *izan* ("to be" and the auxiliary for transitive verbs) in this way:

Ni nai	I am
I ai	You are (singular)
A dai	He/she/it is
Gu gaiz	We are
Zu zaiz	You are (plural)
Arek daiz	They are

In Azkue's opinion, the verb forms *naiz* and *aiz* were corrupt because they made superfluous use of the pluralizing *-z*. On the other hand, the very same *-z* was missing from the places where it should have been, and *gara, zara,* and *dira* were being used instead. Finally, the root of the verb, *-ai-*, had been corrupted in some verb forms and come up as *-a-*. Azkue's proposal solved all of these problems and took Basques straight back to the pure, pristine language of their ancestors. As the years went by, Azkue himself abandoned the route he had taken in his youth, but there were still people who continued trying to recover the so-called authenticity of Basque.

Chained to this vicious circle, a completely new language was invented in Bizkaia that was also given a new name: *euzkera barria* (New Basque). It was extremely difficult to understand for people who were not from Bizkaia and unknown and unfamiliar to many Bizkaians themselves. A few of the words coined then have found their way into Unified Basque and into common usage – for example *antzokia* (theater), *ikurriña* (flag), and *akeita* (coffee) – but this form was mostly used by a few elite groups (teachers, priests, and so on).

Similarly, throughout the twentieth century many inappropriate steps were taken in Bizkaia. For example, when the new standardized Unified Basque was being formed in the 1960s, people who were against it resurrected and encouraged the use of the most bizarre distinctive things in Bizkaian Basque. Some Bizkaians who were in favor of Unified Basque also damaged it considerably. Despising and denouncing the Basque that was spoken at the time, they combined sixteenth- and seventeenth-century Lapurdian Basque with things they had made up themselves and presented the mixture as a model for the new Unified Basque. That was unquestionably a mistake because it took Basque speakers too far away from the language they spoke. Recently, things have started to come back to a more sensible position, but there is still much work to be done and, above all, to be undone.

The Nature of Western Basque

Leaving the excesses of the nineteenth and twentieth centuries aside, Western Basque is a distinct dialect and the most distinctive of all the Basque dialects. As is usually the case, this distinctiveness is mostly due to the dialect being located on one edge of the Basque Country. That being so, and as noted in the case of Zuberoan Basque as well, it is both conservative and innovative at the same time. The nature of Western Basque is most noticeable in its morphology (especially with regard to verb forms) and its vocabulary. I will now explain its most significant characteristics.

Phonology

Vowels

One characteristic stands out: when the singular article is added to words ending in *-a*, that *-a* becomes an *-e* and, in some ways of speaking, an *-i*. For example, in the Deba Valley, *gauza* ("thing") + *au* → *gauziau*, *gauza* + *ori* → *gauziori* and *gauza* + *a* → *gauzia*. The transformation extends beyond the Western

Basque area; it also takes place in some parts of the Urolaldea area (around Azkoitia and Azpeitia) and throughout the Goierri area of Gipuzkoa, as well as in Burunda, Navarre. It would therefore seem to be an innovation that originated in Vitoria-Gasteiz long ago because, as noted, this would have been the main urban nucleus at the center of this general area.

This is a useful rule and is applied to most new words. The following words have been heard in the Deba Valley: *astronautia* instead of *astronauta* in Unified Basque ("astronaut"), *autistia* instead of *autista* ("autistic"), *biagria* instead of *viagra*, *kapsulia* instead of *kapsula* ("capsule"), *kokainia* instead of *kokaina* ("cocaine"), *koka-kolia* instead of *koka-kola* ("Coca Cola"), *sidia* instead of *sida* (AIDS, from the Spanish acronym), and *tangia* instead of *tanga* ("thong" as in the underwear).

This rule applies to the whole singular declension, except for cases expressing place; in other words *non* (inessive, "where"), *nondik* (ablative, "from"), *nongo* ("local-genitive, "of" or "from"), *nora* (allative, "where to"), *noraino* (modified allative, "as far as" or "until"), *noruko* (modified allative, "for" or "destined for"), and *norantz(a)/norutz* (modified allative, "toward"). Thus, people say both *tabernea* ("bar"), *taberneak*, *taberneari*, *tabernearen*, *tabernearentzat/tabernearendako*, *taberneagaz/tabernearekin*, and *taberneagatik* as well as the Unified Basque *tabernan*, *tabernatik*, *tabernako*, *tabernara*, *tabernaraino*, *tabernarako*, and *tabernarantz(a)/tabernarutz*. In the plural, similarly, the standard general forms are used: *tabernak*, *tabernei*, *tabernen*, *tabernetatik*, and so on.

As a result of the above mentioned transformation, the transformation *-e* → *-a* is common in word endings. The result is that, in the singular absolutive case, words ending in *-e* and *-a* become the same: *andre + a* → *andrea* ("lady"), *larrosa + a* → *larrosea* ("rose"). Because the word *larrosea* comes from *larrosa* it is believed that *andrea* derives from **andra* and that many other words that end in an *-e* are taken to end in an *-a*. This confusion has long existed in Western Basque: *andre* in Unified Basque → *andra*, *basurde* → *basurda* ("wild boar"), *bele* → *bela* ("crow"), the Latin *corte* → *korta* ("stable") instead of *ukuilua* in Unified Basque, *hobe* → *hoba* ("better"), *-kume* → *-kuma* (a suffix meaning a young animal, as in *txarrikuma* instead of *zerrikume* in Unified Basque for "piglet"), *labe* → *laba* ("oven"), *landare* → *landara* ("plant"), and *lore* → *lora* ("flower"), as well as the loanwords *padule* instead of *zingira* in Unified Basque → *padura* ("swamp"), *suge* → *suga/suba* ("snake"), and *untze* instead of *iltze* → *untza* ("nail").

This has gained strength in Bizkaia more than anywhere else in the Basque Country and also happens with new foreign loanwords in many cases. Eneko Barrutia, for example, finds these examples in the Bizkaian coastal towns of Mundaka and Bermeo:[10] *arenque* (Spanish for "herring") instead of *sardinzarra* in Unified Basque → *arenka*, *víveres* (Spanish for "provisions") instead of *jatekoak* → *bibera*, *viaje* (Spanish for "journey") instead of *bidaia* → *bieja*, *yate* (Spanish for "yacht") → *dxata*, *eje* (Spanish for "axle") instead of *ardatza* → *eja*, *guante* (Spanish for "glove") instead of *eskularrua* → *guanta*, *corriente* (Spanish for "current" or "draft") instead of *ur lasterra* → *korrenta*, *palangre* (Spanish for "fishing line with many hooks") instead of *tretza* → *palangra*, and *percebe* (Spanish for "barnacle") instead of *lanperna* → *pertzeba*.

In most of Bizkaia, the diphthong *-au-* tends to become *-eu-*. The following examples are from Fika in Mungialdea:[11] *ahuntz* in Unified Basque → *euntz* ("goat"), *ahuspez* → *euspes* ("face down"), *aurre* → *eurre* ("front"), *aurten* → *eurten* ("this year"), *auzo* → *euso* ("neighborhood"), *gaua* → *geube* ("night"), *gaur* → *geur* ("today"), *gauza* → *geuse* ("thing"), *hauspo* → *euspo* ("bellows"), *hautsa* → *eutze* ("dust"), *hautsi* → *eusi* ("to break"), *jaurti* or *bota* in Unified Basque → *yeurti* ("to throw"), *jausi* or *erori* in Unified Basque → *yeusi* ("to fall"), and *nagusi* → *neusi* ("boss" or "chief"). This is a rule for participles with *-au* or *-atu*: *dedikeu* instead of *dedikatu* in Unified Basque ("to dedicate"), *deklareu* instead of *deklaratu* ("to declare" or "to testify"), *separeu* instead of *separatu* ("to separate"), and so on.

This transformation has long been applied to the verb *eduki* ("to have") and, in this case, has gone one step further: *-au-* → *-eu-* → *-e-*. Furthermore, this is not recent and the auxiliary verbs *dekot*, *dekok/dekon*, *deko*, *dekogu*, *dekozu*, *dekozue*, and *dekie* and so on are now used throughout almost the whole of Bizkaia instead of the Unified Basque forms *daukat*, *daukak/daukan*, *dauka*, *daukagu*, *daukazue*, and *daukate* to say "I have," "you have," and so forth (with a singular object).

Consonants

Four of the sibilants have become two in Western Basque; *z* (approximating *s* in the English word "so") and *s* (approximating a sound halfway between *so* and *sh* in the word "show") have both become *s*, and *tz* (close to *ts* in English) and *ts* (halfway between *ts* and *ch* in the words "its" and "itch") have both become *tz*. This leads to the pronunciations *asi* for both *hasi* ("to begin") and *hazi* ("to grow" or "to raise"); *esi* for *hesi* ("fence" or "hurdle") and *hezi* ("to educate," "to tame," or "to raise"); *esker* for *esker* ("thanks") and *ezker* ("left"); *sartu* for *sartu* ("to enter") and *zahartu* ("to age" or "to grow old"); *su* for *su* ("fire") and *zu* ("you"); *sur* for *sudur* ("nose") and *zuhur* ("prudent" or "thrifty"); *ametz* for *ametz* ("Pyrenean oak") and *amets* ("dream"); *atzo* for *atzo* ("yesterday") and *atso* ("old woman"); *etzi* for *etzi* ("the day after tomorrow") and *etsi* ("despair" or "to give up"); and *otz* for *hotz* ("cold") and *hots* ("noise" or as a conjunction "that is to say"); with the sibilants becoming identical in each case. However, although this is usually considered to be a peculiarity of Western Basque, it is not exclusively so. The same thing occurs in most of northern Gipuzkoa, for instance in Irun and Hondarribia.[12]

There is, however, one distinctive sibilant used in Western Basque: after the semi-vowel *j*, *z* → *x* (with *x* approximating *sh* in "show") and *tz* → *tx* (with *tx* approximating *ch* in "chair"). As a result of palatalization, the *j* often disappears. Here are some examples of this:

- *j* + *z* → *(j)x*: *aizkora* → *axkora/askora* ("ax"), *eleiza* or *eliza* in Unified Basque → *elexa/elixa* ("church"), *goiz* → *gox* ("morning" or "early"), *haize* → *axe* ("wind"), *kereiza* or *gerezia* → *kereixa* (> *keixa*) ("cherry"), *leizar* or *lizar* → *lexar* ("ash tree"), *noiz* → *nox/nos* ("when"). This is also applied to the verb *izan* ("to be"): *naiz* → *nax* → *nas*, *haiz* → *ax* → *as*.
- *j* + *tz* → *(j)tx*: *aitzur* → *atxur* ("hoe"), *ekaitz* → *ekatx* ("storm"), *ereitzi* or *iritzi* in Unified Basque → *eretxi* ("opinion"), *gaitz* → *gatx* ("harm" or "ailment"), *hareitz* or *haritz* → *aretx* ("oak tree"), *haitz* → *atx* ("rock"), *hurreitz* or *hurritz* → *urretx* ("hazelnut tree"), *-koitz* → *-kotx* (*bakotx* or *bakoitz* in Unified Basque "each/each one").

However, we should remember, as previously noted in the introduction, that this rule is already obsolete.

Another transformation has recently appeared in Bizkaia that resembles the previous change: the vowel *i* also creates the shift *z* → *x*. The following are examples of this: *bizar* → *bixer* ("beard"), *bizi* → *bixi* ("life"), *gizen* → *gixen* ("fat"), *gizon* → *gixon* ("man"), *itzartu* → *ixartu* ("to wake up"), *izan/izen* → *ixen* ("to be"), *izar* → *ixer* ("star"), *izara* or *maindirea* in Unified Basque → *ixera* ("bedsheet"), *izerdi* → *ixerdi* ("to sweat"), *izotz* → *ixotz* ("ice"), and so forth. This is a rule in second person singular verbs: for example, *dakizu* → *dakixu*, *dakizue* → *dakixue*, *egizu* → *eixu*, and *egizue* → *eixue*.

This is a productive rule and applies to new words as well. The following words from Nabarniz (Busturialdea) reflect this characteristic:[13] *juizio* or *epaiketa* in Unified Basque → *juixidxo* ("trial"), *malizia* or *maltzurkeria* → *malixidxe* ("scheming"), *medizina* or *sendagaia* → *medixiñie* ("medicine"), *miliziano* → *milixianu* ("militiaman"), *ofiziala* → *ofixiala* ("official"), *paliza* or *jipoia* → *palixie* ("beating"), *polizia* → *polixie* ("police"), *postizo* or *ordezkoa* → *postixue* ("substitute" or "replacement"), *rizadu* or *kizkurra* → *rixaue* ("curly"), and *zerbizio* or *zerbitzua* → *serbixidxo* ("service").

Having examined innovations, let us now look at the conservative side of Western Basque; in a few isolated words, after the letters *l*, *n*, and *r*, the sibilant fricative (*tz*) is not pronounced, being replaced by the fricative (*z*): for example, *hil ziran* rather than *hiltziren* ("they died"), *egon zan* rather than *egontzen* ("he/she/it was"), and *zer zan* rather than *zertzen* ("what was it").

Morphology

As I mentioned above, this section includes most of the distinctive features of Western Basque, and I have divided it into two parts: noun morphology and verb morphology.

Noun Morphology

One demonstration of the conservative nature of this dialect is the survival of the article of proximity, which has been lost in so many other areas. The following example is from Mallabia:

> *amen berton esin bada, kánpuen erosi bikou etxioi* or in Unified Basque
> *hemen berton ezin bada, kanpoan erosi beharko dugu etxeori*
> "If it cannot be done right here, we will have to buy the house elsewhere"

In this example, the words used are *berton* rather than *bertan* ("right here") and *etxeori* rather than *etxea* ("house").

I will now examine innovations in Western Basque and the distinct options used in the dialect.

- The comitative or associative suffix *-gaz* is used in most of the Western Basque area: *lagunagaz* (> *lagunaz*) "with a friend." Furthermore, *-kaz* is also used in the plural in a wide area of Bizkaia (*lagunakaz* "with friends"), but *-kin* is used in the Deba Valley of Gipuzkoa and in eastern Bizkaia.
- The adlative suffix of approximation is distinctive, and also varies in the two sub-dialects. In the west it is *-rantz/-rantza* (*etzerantz/etzerantza* "toward home") and in the east *-rutz* (*etxerutz*).

When verbal nouns of movement express a direction or an objective, the usually inessive *zertan* case is used in most of Western Basque instead of the more generally used allative *zertara* case. The following example is from Iurreta (Durangaldea):[14]

> *etxera ikesten juen da* or
> *etxera ikasten joan da*
> "She/he has gone home to study"

Here, then, the form used is *ikasten*, not *ikastera* as it would be in Unified Basque.

The old ablative suffix *-rik* is used in expressions such as *bazterrik bazter* ("every corner"), *etxerik etxe* ("house to house"), *herririk herri* ("town to town"), *kalerik kale* ("street to street"), *mendirik mendi* ("mountain to mountain"), and *tabernarik taberna* ("bar to bar"). However, the more generally used instrumental suffix *-z* is also in use: *ahoz aho* ("mouth to mouth"), *aurrez aurre* ("face to face"), *bidez bide* ("on the road"), and *kaminoz kamino* ("along the way").

The demonstrative pronouns are the same in appearance in both singular and plural: *honek* instead of the *honek/hauek* distinction in Unified Basque, *horrek* instead of *horrek/horiek*, and *harek* instead of *hark/haiek*. In some areas, they are distinguished with a spoken accent: *honék* for *honek* and *hónek* for *hauek*, for example. Elsewhere, meanwhile, *-i-* appears in the plural: *hon(e)ik* for *hauek*, and *horr(e)itan* for *horietan*.

The emphatic pronouns of the *neu* group are used: *neu* ("me myself"), *heu* ("you yourself" in the familiar *hika* form), *geu* ("we ourselves"), *zeu* ("you yourself" in the more general *zuka* form), *zeuek* ("you yourselves"), as well as *neuk*, *neure*, *geuk*, *geuri*, and so on. However, forms such as *neroni* and *nihaur*, used in other areas, are unknown here.

The whole "*edo* + interrogative pronoun" series is used in Bizkaia: for example, in the case of *edonor* ("anyone/anybody"), as well as *edonori*, *edonoren*, *edonogaz/edonorekin*, *edonorengana*, *edonorengandik*, *edonorentzat*, *edonon*, *edonondik*, *edonongo*, *edonora*, *edonos*, *edozertan*, *edozertara*, *edozelan*, *edozelako*, and so on. It would appear that these all came from the generally used *edozein* ("anyone/anybody" or "any") model. At the same time, the pronoun *edozer* ("any/anything") is more widely used, and it is also used in Central Basque.

The whole "interrogative pronoun + *edo* + interrogative pronoun" series is used in Bizkaia: *nonor*, *nonok*, *nonori*, *nonoren*, *nonogaz*, *nonongana*, *nonongandik*, *nonontzat*, *nonon*, *nonondik*, *nonongo*, *nonora*, and so on. At present, there is also one such word that is also used beyond Western Basque: *zer edo zer* (> *zeozer*) "something." Similarly, the following forms have spread beyond Bizkaia and are also used in the Deba Valley and in Urolaldea: *noiz edo noiz* (> *noizonoiz*) "sometime," *non edo non* (> *nunonun*) "somewhere," and *nora edo nora* (> *nonora/nuanua*) "someone."

The Spanish ending *-(c)ión* becomes *-(z)ino*: for example, in *demonino* ("devil"), *erlijino* ("religion"), *espekulazino* ("speculation"), *espropiazino* ("expropriation"), *filtrazino* ("filtration"), *globalizazino* ("globalization"), *inseminazino* ("insemination"), *klonazino* ("cloning"), *obsesino* ("obsession"), *prekauzino* ("precaution"), *reunino* ("meeting"), and *sofistikazino* ("sophistication"). As can be seen, then, this is productive and is also applied to new words.

The ending *-n* is added to the adverbs of manner *zelan* instead of *nola* ("how" or "how come") in Unified Basque, *ezelan* instead of *inola* ("somehow" or "anyhow"), *edozelan* instead of *edonola* or *nolanahi* ("anyhow" or "anyway"), *zeozelan* instead of *nola edo hala* ("somehow or other"), *zelanbait* instead of *nolabait* ("somehow"), *zelango* and *zelako* instead of *nolako* ("what kind of"), *zelangure* instead of *nolanahi* ("anyway"), *honan* and *honantxe* instead of *honela(xe)* ("like this" or "in this way"), *holan* and *holantxe* instead of *horrela(xe)* ("like that" or "in that way"), *halan* and *halantxe* instead of *hala(xe)* ("like that" or "in that way")," and *bestelan* and *bestela* ("otherwise" or "or else").

Verb Morphology

The root of **edun* (*-o-*) and, in the third person, *-au-* appear in the present: *dot* ("I have"), *dok/don* ("you have" in the singular familiar *hika* form), *dau* ("he/she/it has"), *dogu* ("we have"), *dozu* ("you have" in the singular general *zuka* form), *dozue* ("you have" plural), and *daue* (> *dabe*) ("they have"). In the past tense, by contrast, *-eu-* appears in some verb forms: *neuan* (> *neban*) instead of *nuen* in Unified Basque ("I had"), *euan* (> *eban*) instead of *zuen* ("he/she/it had"), and *euen* (> *eben*) instead of *zuten* ("they had"). This also happens with conditional forms: *baneu/neuke* ("if I had/I would have"), *baheu/heuke* ("if you had/you would have" in *hika*), *baleu/leuke* ("if he/she/it had / he/she/it would have"), *geunke* ("we would have"), *zeunke* ("you would have" in *zuka*), *zeunkie* ("you would have" plural), and *balebe/leuke* ("if they had/they would have").

The verb *eutsi* is the root of absolutive-dative-ergative verbs. Due to contractions that have formed down the centuries, the shift *-eu-* → *-o-* has occurred in most places: *dostezu* from *deustazu* (*didazu* in Unified Basque), *dotset* from *deutsat* (*diot*), *dotso* from *deutso* (*dio*), *dosku* from *deusku* (*digu*), *doskuzu* from *deuskuzu* (*diguzu*), *doskue* from *deuskue* (*digute*), *dotsuet* from *deutsuet* (*dizuet*), and so on.

In imperatives, the potential and subjunctive root **ezan*, which was once used throughout the Basque Country, has been replaced by *egin*: for example, *ikusi leiket* instead of *ikus dezaket* in Unified Basque ("I can see it"), *ikusi egizu* (> *ikusizu*) instead of *ikus ezazu* ("see it"), and *ikusi daigun* instead of *ikus dezagun* ("let us see it").

The *ari izan* ("to be busy at" or "to be . . . -ing") form is not used in Western Basque and is replaced by *egon* and *ibili*: for example, *karate ikasten dago* or *karate ikasten dabil* is said, and not *karate ikasten ari da* as in Unified Basque ("he/she is learning karate"). In the eastern part of the area where Western Basque is spoken – mostly in the north of the Deba Valley – the synthetic verb *jardun* also survives to express the same thing: *karate ikasten dihardu*.

There has been a particular phonetic transformation in absolutive-dative verb forms; *y-/dx-/j-* starts to appear as you travel eastward rather than the more generally used *z-*. These are the most widely used verb forms: *yat* instead of *zait* in Unified Basque ("she/he/it is . . . to me"), *yak/yan* instead of *zaik/zain*, *yako* instead of *zaio*, *yaku* instead of *zaigu*, *yatzu* instead of *zaizu*, *yatzue* instead of *zaizue*, and *yake* instead of *zaie*. In the northwestern area, however, *d-* has recently gained strength: *dat, dako, daku, datzu, datzue, dake*.

The same transformation takes place in absolutive-dative-ergative *hika* verbs when the absolutive is *hura/haiek* (she/he/it/they): *yotsat/yotsanat* instead of *zioat/zionat* in Unified Basque, for example. This also happens in *hika* synthetic verbs: *yakik/yakin* instead of *zakik/zakin* in Unified Basque, and *yatozak/yatozan* instead of *zatozak/zatozan*.

Hika verb forms based on **edun* are special and *y-/dx-/j-* appears at the beginning of these words as well: *yoat/yonat* instead of *diat/dinat* in Unified Basque ("I have"), *yok/yon* instead of *dik/din*, *yoagu/yonagu* instead of *diagu/dinagu*, and *yoek/yone* instead of *ditek/diten*.

Furthermore, when any of these verb forms combine with the particle *ez*, there is a particular outcome: *etxako* for *ez zaio*, *etxotsat* for *ez zioat*, *etxakik* for *ez zakik*, and *etxok* for *ez dik*.

There is another phonetic transformation in verb forms based on **io*: specifically, an *-n-* is inserted. Thus, the following shifts take place in most of the Western Basque area: *dinot* instead of *diot* in Unified Basque, *dinok/dinon* instead of *diok/dion*, *dino* instead of *dio*, *dinogu* instead of *diogu*, *dinozu* instead of *diozu*, *dinozue* instead of *diozue*, *dinoe* instead of *diote*, *dinotsut* instead of *diotsut*, *dinostezu* instead of *diostazu*, *dinotso* instead of *diotso*, and so on. These verb forms are used very often. In the third person past tense, ø is the special characteristic of verbs in the absolutive rather than the more generalized *z-*: *eban* instead of *zuen* in Unified Basque (she/he/it had"), *osten* instead of *zidun*, *egoan* instead of *zegoen* ("he/she/it was" or "there was"), *euken* instead of *zeukan/zeukaten* ("he/she/it had"/"they had"), *etorren* instead of *zetorren* ("he/she/it was coming"), *etozen* instead of *zetozen* ("they were coming"), *ekien* instead of *zekien/zekiten* ("she/he/it knew"/"they knew"), and so on. There are also exceptions; in *izan* verb forms (*zan*, *ziren*), in **edun* verb forms with plural objects (*zituen*) and, in some areas at least, in **edin* and *egin* verb forms as well: *zeiken* instead of *zitekeen*, *zeixen* instead of *zegien/zegiten* (*zezan/zezaten* in Unified Basque). Similarly, *z-* is taken on by *jardun* and *iruditu* verb forms (*zirudien; ziharduen*).

Thus, when the form is ø-, as in most verbs, and it combines with the particle *ez*, this is pronounced as a fricative, and not as an affricate as in most of the Basque Country: *ezekien* (generally *etzekien* "she/he/it did not know"), *ezeban* (generally *etzuen* "she/he/it did not have"), and *ezan* (generally *etzen* "she/he/it was not").

In plural verbs, *-z* is almost always used: *dagoz* instead of *daude* in Unified Basque ("they are"), *dekoz* instead of *dauzka* ("he/she/it has" with plural object), *dabiz* instead of *dabiltza* ("they are walking"), *leikez* instead of *daitezke*, *dotsaguz* instead of *dizkiogu*, *jakoz* instead of *zaizkio*, and so forth. This does not happen with all **edun* verb forms, but there, too, *-z* is often used throughout Bizkaia: for example, *dodaz* instead of *ditut* in Unified Basque ("I have" with plural object), *dauz* instead of *ditu* (he/she/it has" with plural object), and *nebazan/nenduzen* instead of *nituen* ("I had" with plural object). Verb forms with two pluralizing elements are also often used by speakers of a certain age: *dituz*, *ditudaz*, *nituzen*, *gaituz*, *zaitudaz*, and the like.

The Spanish participle *-ado* becomes *-au* and *-ido* becomes *-idu*. Examples of this include *aluzinau* ("staggered"), *aparkau* ("parked"), *depilau* ("depilated"), *estresau* ("stressed"), *flipau* ("amazed"), *inplikau* ("implicated"), *reziklau* ("recycled"), and *sofistikau* ("sophisticated"); and *dibertidu* ("interesting"), *entretenidu* ("entertaining"), *inbertidu* ("reversed"), *kabidu* ("fitting"), *kubridu* ("covered"), and *mantenidu* ("preserved"). As can be seen from the examples, this rule is very much alive.

Verbal nouns are easily formed. On the one hand, *-ten* is used more extensively than in Central Basque. This is used when participles are formed using *-a*, *-e*, *-o*, *-gi*, *-ki*, and *-{l, n, r}i*: for example, *bota* ("to throw") → *botaten* ("throwing"), *bete* ("to fill") → *beteten* ("filling"), *jo* ("to hit") → *joten* ("hitting"), *jagi* or *jaiki* in Unified Basque ("to get up") → *jagiten* ("getting up"), *euki* or *eduki* in Unified Basque ("to have") → *eukiten* ("having"), *ibili* ("to walk") → *ibilten* ("walking"), *ipini* ("to put") → *ipinten* ("putting"), and *ekarri* ("to bring") → *ekarten* ("bringing"). However, when endings are formed using *-a* and *-e*, in some areas, *-etan* is then taken on: for example, *botetan* and *betetan*.

In Western Basque, *-etan* is often used when the participle ends in *-au*: *kantau* → *kantetan* ("singing"). In northwestern and coastal Bizkaia, the older form *-ten* is still in use: *kantaten*.

When participles end in *-tu*, *-atu*, *-itu*, and *-idu*, on the other hand, *-tuten* is used throughout Western Basque: *apurtu* ("to break") → *apurtuten* ("breaking"), *konturatu* ("to realize") → *konturatuten* ("realizing"), *garbitu* ("to clean") → *garbituten* ("cleaning"), *entendidu* ("to understand") → *entendiduten* ("understanding").

Finally, *urten* or *irten* in Unified Basque ("to go out" or "leave") and *igon* or *igo* ("to go up," "ascend," or "climb") are transitive; thus, one says, for example, *urten dot* ("I went out") and *igon dot* ("I went up") in Western Basque (rather than the intransitive forms *irten naiz* and *igo naiz* in Unified Basque).

Morphology and Syntax

The word *ala* is often used at the end of "*bai/ez*" ("yes/no") type question clauses, the second part being silenced: *ez zatoz, ala?* ("are you coming or not?").

The word *arren*, used to express a contrast of ideas, and which was once used throughout the Basque Country, survives in Western Basque. It has recently become widely used once more thanks to its inclusion in Unified Basque. The following example is from Aramaio, Araba:[15]

> *emenguek isen es arren, euskeldun sentitten dittuk or hemengoak izan ez arren, euskaldun sentitzen dituk*
> "even though they are not from here, they feel Basque"

As well as *arren*, the suffix *-tearren* also originates from Western Basque. It is used to express causes and objectives. The following examples are from

Zeberio, Bizkaia:[16]

lartxu edatearren moskortu'ok ori or
gehiegi edatearren mozkortu duk hori
"because he wanted to drink a lot, he got drunk"

diruek itearren, txarto yanda bixi de or
diruak egitearren, gaizki janda bizi da
"because he wants to make a lot of money, he doesn't eat very well"

In some clauses, the suffix *-(e)na* is used in subordinate clauses. This is used when the meaning is completely clear but is not the focus of the sentence. The following example is from Elgoibar, Gipuzkoa:[17]

badakixe gurekin ezin leikena ezer eiñ or
badakite gurekin ezin daiteekena ezer egin
"they know they cannot do anything with us"

In clauses expressing time, *-keran* is used in Bizkaia. The following example is from Iurreta, in the Durangaldea area of Bizkaia:[18]

etxetik urtekeran ankie okertu'ot or
etxetik irteterakoan hanka okertu dut
"I twisted my leg on leaving my house"

Demonstratives are placed before the noun in most of the Western Basque area. The following examples are from Aramaio, Araba:[19]

fixetan nas orreikin gisonokiñ or
fidatzen naiz gizon horiekin
"I trust that man"

setan dabis, bañe, orreik umiok? or
zer ari dira, baina, haur horiek?
"what on earth are those children doing?"

The tendency to place the quantifier *bi* ("two") after the noun has been generally kept in Western Basque (in Unified Basque, this rule only applies to the number *bat* or "one"): *gorringo biko arrautzia* ("an egg with two yokes"), *kontu bi kontau* ("to tell two stories"), and *kalimotxo bi edan* ("to drink two kalimotxos" – a drink made up of red wine and cola) are examples of how this is generally used.

When synthetic verbs are the focus of a sentence, the structure 'participle + conjugated verb' is used in most of Western Basque. The following example is from Urduliz, in the Uribe Kosta area of Bizkaia:[20]

txikitxu ixen arren, iñurrik eron doro bera baño astunau dan karge or
txikitxoa izan arren, inurriak eraman darama bera
baino astunagoa den zama
"even though it is very small, an ant carries a load heavier than itself"

euri seiñ aterri, yon gos or
euri nahiz ateri, joan goaz
"whether rain or shine, let's go"

kostaten dana kostaten dala, ekarri dakargu te kittu! or
kostatzen dena kostatzen dela, ekarri dakargu eta kito!
"whatever it takes, let's bring it and that's that!"

orasiño itten bere yakin dakitzu faltzo orrek or
otoitz egiten ere jakin daki faltso horrek
"that fake also knows full well how to pray"

euki dekola, eser emon estek emoten daust amorrurik andiena or
eduki daukala, ezer eman ez egiteak ematen dit amorrurik handiena
"given that she/he has something, it makes me very angry that she/he doesn't give anything"

Undeveloped Rules

Some words start with *-u* rather than with the more usual *-i*: *ugaraxo* or *igela* in Unified Basque ("frog"), *ule* or *ile* ("hair"), *untza* or *iltze* ("nail"), *huri* or *hiri* ("city"), *urten* or *irten* ("to go out" or "leave"), *urun* or *irin* ("flour"), and *uzan* (> *uzen*) or *izain* ("leech"). In most of Bizkaia, the word *uger* or *igeri* in Unified Basque ("swimming") is used, and in a few areas around Bilbao, the word *uzen* or *izen* ("name") is also used.

In many parts of the Basque Country, there is an *e* → *a* before vibrant sounds, and there are also some differentiating variants to this in Western Basque: *bardin* (which is also used in Zuberoa and in some areas of Lower Navarre) instead of *berdin* in Unified Basque ("same"), *barri* instead of *berri* ("new"), and *txarri* instead of *txerri* ("pig"). In western Bizkaia, *garri* instead of *gerri* ("waist") and *garriko* instead of *gerriko* ("belt" or "sash") is also used.

The transformation *-ain* → *-an* takes place in the following words: *ezpan* instead of *ezpain* in Unified Basque ("lip"), *laban* instead of *labain* ("slippery" or "slip"), *uzan* (> *uzen*) instead of *izain* ("leech"), and *zan* instead of *zain* ("waiting" or "wait"). In most of Western Basque, *erran/erren* instead of *errain* ("daughter-in-law") is also used, as is *gan* instead of *gain* ("top" or "apart from") in Bizkaia.

The transformation *-uin* → *-un* takes place in the words *bigun* instead of *biguin* and *mun* instead of *muin*. At the same time, the words *asun* (not *asuin*, *ausun*, or *osin* "nettle") and *lurrun* (not *lurrin* or *urrin* "scent") are used.

It is common to confuse occlusive consonants (*p*, *t*, *k*, *b*, *d*, *g*) with one another throughout the Basque Country, and in Western Basque these particular changes take place: *ahizta* instead of *ahizpa* in Unified Basque ("sister"), *bagerik* (> *barik*) instead of *gabe* ("without") and *bako* instead of *gabeko*, *kereixa* (> *keixa*) instead of *gerezia* ("cherry"), *ki(n)pula* instead of *tipula* ("onion"), and *lebatz* instead of *legatz* ("hake"). There are variants to this when the occlusive consonant is at the start of a word, or even when it is not, throughout the Basque Country, but the following is particular to Western Basque: *bere* (> *be*) instead of *ere* ("also").

Furthermore, the *p* and *t* are kept in the following loanwords from Spanish: *altara* instead of *aldare* in Unified Basque ("altar"), *denpora* instead of *denbora* ("time"), and *jente* instead of *jende* ("people").

In most areas, the transformation *l* → *r* is used in the following words: *arkondara* instead of *alkandora* in Unified Basque ("shirt"), *armozu* (from the Spanish *almuerzo*) instead of *gosaria* ("breakfast"), *aurki* instead of *aulki* ("chair"), and *orio* instead of *olio* ("oil"). However, in the word *solo* ("field"), instead of *soro* (or *alorra*, but more generally, *soro*), the *l* has been maintained.

The previous *-r-* has been preserved as *-d-* in the following four words: *bedar* instead of *belar* in Unified Basque ("grass"), *edur* instead of *elur* ("snow"), *idar* (>ider) instead of *ilar* ("pea"), and *zidar* (>zider) instead of *zilar* ("silver").

An *n-* is used at the start of the word *nasai* instead of *lasai* in Unified Basque ("calm") (this also happens outside Western Basque) and in *narru* instead of *larru* ("skin" or "leather").

There are variants with *-n-* in Western Basque: for example, *inuntz* instead of *ihintz* in Unified Basque ("dew"), *ipuin* ("story," which is *ipui* in Central Basque), *mamin* instead of *mami* ("essence"), *mihin* instead of *mihi* ("tongue"), *premina* instead of premia ("necessity"), *suhin* instead of *suhi* ("son-in-law"), and *zentzun* instead of *zentzu* ("sense" or "meaning"). In western Bizkaia, *sein* instead of *sehi* ("child") is used.

As in the Northern Basque Country, the transformation **-ani* → *-ain* takes place in the following words: *arrain* ("fish"), *usain* ("smell"), and *zain* ("waiting"). It should be remembered that the *-ai* transformation has taken place in most of Gipuzkoa and Navarre.

The suffix *-to* is used in a few adverbs: *ederto* instead of *ederki* in Unified Basque ("well," "fine," or "beautifully"), *polito* instead of *egoki* or *ongi* ("appropriate" or "well"), *txarto* instead of *gaizki* ("wrong" or "badly"), and so on. There are also two words that are used beyond Western Basque as well: *ondo* as opposed to *ongi* ("well") and *hobeto* in contrast to *hobeki* ("better").

The *-gi* ending is used in a few participles: *ebagi* (> *ebai*) instead of *ebaki* in Unified Basque ("to cut"), *erabagi* (> *erabai*) instead of *erabaki* ("to decide"), *eralgi* instead of *eralki* ("to sieve"), *esegi/eskegi* (> *esei/eskei*) instead of *eseki* or *zintzilikatu* ("to hang (up)"), *iregi* (> *irei*) instead of *ireki* ("to open"), *jagi* (> *jai*) instead of *jaiki* ("to get up"), and *jaurtigi* (> *jaurti*) instead of *bota* ("to throw").

Vocabulary

Being situated at one edge of the Basque Country and on the boundary with Spanish, Western Basque has many words that have disappeared from other dialects, as well as many loanwords taken from Spanish, and also many words formed in the area itself. Here are some examples of this.

The following words were borrowed from Spanish long ago and their use is deeply rooted in Western Basque: *abade* instead of *apaiz* in Unified Basque ("priest"), *adore* instead of *kemena* ("energy" or "vigor"), *amatatu* instead of *itzali* ("to put out" or "to turn off"), *armozu* instead of *gosaria* ("breakfast"), *atondu* instead of *gertatu* ("to happen"), *azoka* instead of *merkatua* ("market"), *berba* instead of *hitza* ("word") and *berbeta* instead of *hizkuntza/hizkera* ("language"), *bezero* instead of *klientea* ("client" or "customer"), *enparauak* and *gainerakoak* ("the rest"), *ganora* instead of *fundamentua* ("substance"), *garau* and *alea/pikorra* ("grain"), *gura* and *nahi* ("wish" or "will"), *izara* instead of *maindirea* ("bedsheet"), *karu* instead of *garestia* ("expensive"), *kirikino/kirikolatz* instead of *sagarroia* or *trikua* ("hedgehog"), *korta* instead of *ukuilua* ("stable"), *kuma* instead of *sehaska* ("cradle"), *lau* instead of *ordokia* ("plain"), *olgau* instead of *jolas egin* ("to play"), *ortu* instead of *baratzea* ("vegetable garden") and *ortuari* instead of *barazkia* ("vegetable"), *oste* instead of *atzealdea/ondoren* ("after"), *padura* instead of *zingira* ("swamp"), *pernil* instead of *urdaiazpikoa* ("ham"), *piku* instead of *mokoa* ("beak" or "bill"), *praka/fraka* instead of *galtza* ("pants" or "trousers"), *puxika* instead of *maskuria* ("bladder"), *saniatu* instead of *sendatu* ("to cure" or "to heal"), and so on. *Ogigaztai* ("weasel"), instead of *erbinudea*, is a translation of the Spanish *paniquesa*.

The following words have been lost or almost lost in the other Basque dialects and only survive in Western Basque: *argal* instead of *mehea/ahula* in Unified Basque ("weak"), *bider* instead of *aldiz* ("time"), *eroan* instead of *eraman* ("to carry" or "to take"), *ha* instead of the demonstrative *hura* ("that" [one]), *ipini/imini* instead of *jarri* ("to put"), *jaurti* and *bota* ("to throw"), *oratu* instead of *heldu/atxiki* ("to join" or "to connect"), and *orri* instead of *hostoa* ("leaf" or "petal").

The following words seem to have been created within the dialect. As I noted above, there are many of them, and they are frequently used. For example, the days of the week: *martitzen* instead of *asteartea* in Unified Basque ("Tuesday"), *eguazten* instead of *asteazkena* ("Wednesday"), *eguen* instead of *osteguna* ("Thursday"), *bariku* instead of *ostirala* ("Friday"), *zapatu* instead of *larunbata* ("Saturday"), and *domeka* instead of *igandea* ("Sunday"). In a few parts of western Bizkaia, *ilen* instead of *astelehena* ("Monday") is also used.

A few month names are also particular, though they are very seldom used nowadays: *zezeil* instead of *otsaila* in Unified Basque ("February"), *marti* instead of *martxoa* ("March"), *bagil* instead of *ekaina* ("June"), *garagarril* instead of *uztaila* ("July"), and *zemendi* instead of *azaroa* ("November"). On the other hand, the Bizkaia word *irail* ("September") has regained strength on being included in Unified Basque.

The pronouns *nortzuk* ("who" or "who all"), *zertzuk* ("what" or "what ones"), and *zeintzuk* ("which ones") are used in the plural, and *nor* ("who"), *zer* ("what"), and *zein* ("which") are used in the singular.

Another special features of this dialect is the use of *zein* to express equality (more generally, *nahiz* "as ... as"), *baino* to express contrast (more generally, *baizik* "but" or "but rather"), *lako* to make comparisons (more generally, *bezalako* "like" or "such as"), and *legez* to express manner (more generally, *bezala* "like" or "as").

Many other special words in Western Basque are used throughout the area, although often this does not extend to the Deba Valley in Gipuzkoa. Meanwhile, in some other cases, words have gone beyond Western Basque and are used in Urolaldea and the Goierri in Gipuzkoa, and Burunda in Navarre. The following are the most important examples of this:

A *abarketa* for *espartina* ("espadrille"), *adur* for *lerdea* ("drool" or "spittle"), *ahalegindu* for *saiatu* ("to try"), *aitita/amama* for *aitona/amona* ("grandfather/grandmother"), which is also used in Oztibarre in Lower Navarre, *albo* and *aldamen* ("side"), *amaitu* for *bukatu* ("to finish"), *aratoste* for *inauteria* ("carnival"), although in disuse in many areas, *ardi* for *arkakuso* ("flea"), *arerio* for *etsaia* ("enemy"), in disuse in many areas, *arineketan* for *lasterka* ("running" or "race"), *arrankari* for *amuarraina* ("trout"), *artaziak* for *guraizeak* ("scissors"), *astiro* for *poliki* ("slowly"), *astun* for *pisua* ("weight"), and *atzamar* for *hatza* ("finger").

B *behar* for *lan* ("work") and *behargin* for *langilea* ("worker"), *berakatz* for *baratxuria* ("garlic"), *birrindu* for *apurtu* or *zehatu* ("to crush" or "to pulverize"), and *bits* as well as *apar* ("foam") in a few areas.

E *ei* for *omen* ("it is said that"), *eragin* – and, mostly to the south of Bilbao, *a(ra)zo* – for *arazi* ("to make [somebody else do something]"), *erpe* for *atzaparra* ("claw" or "paw"), and *esegi/eskegi* for *zintzilikatu* ("to hang [up]").

G *Gabon zahar* for *Urtezahar* ("New Year's Eve"), *gaitz* (> *gatx*) for *zail* ("difficult"), *garun* for *burmuina* ("brain"), *garo* and *inontz* for *ihintza* ("dew"), *gatzatu* for *mami* or *gaztanbera* ("curds"), *geriza* for *itzala* ("shade") and *gerizpe* for *itzalpea* ("shady place").

H *hazbizar* for *ermamia* ("fingertip"), and *hur/hurran* for *hurbil* ("close" or "nearby").

I *inausi* and *kimatu* ("to prune" or "to trim"), *indaba* for *babarruna* ("bean"), *inor* for *beste* ("other" or "else"), *ira* for *iratzea* ("fern"), *i(re) targi* for *ilargia* ("moon"), *isiotu* and *piztu* ("to light" or "to turn on"), *itaundu* for *galdetu* ("to ask"); in disuse in most areas, *itzal* (> *itzel*) for *berebizikoa* ("special"); and *izeko* for *izeba* ("aunt"), although in many places the Spanish word *tía* is used.

J *jaramon* for *kasua* or *arreta* ("attention" or "heed"), and *jausi* for *erori* ("to fall").

K *(kata)mixar* for *katagorria* or *urtxintxa* ("squirrel"), in disuse in many areas.

L *lain* as well as *beste* and *adina* ("as much as" or "as many as"), *lantzean (behin)* and *noizean (behin)* ("occasionally" or "from time to time"), *lapiko* for *eltzea* ("pot" or "stewpot"), and *itsulapiko eltzeitsua* ("piggy bank"), *lar/larregi* for *gehiegi* ("too much" or "too many"), *legar* for *gatzagia* ("rennet"), *lei* and *izotz* ("ice"), and *lorrin* for *lardatsa* ("dirty").

N *neba*, meaning a female's brother.

O *odoloste* and *buzkantz* for *odolkia* ("blood sausage"), *okaran* ("plum"), *osatu* for *sendatu* ("to cure" or "to heal"), *ostean/ostantzean* and *bestela* ("otherwise" or "or else"), *ostera* for *aldiz* ("on the other hand"), and *otzara* for *saskia* ("basket").

P *pizta* for *makarra* ("bleariness of eyes").

S *sama* ("neck") and *lepo* – which means "neck" in Unified Basque – used instead of *bizkarra* ("back"), *sarri* for *maiz* ("often"), and *sats* for *ongarria* ("manure" or "fertilizer").

T *txarto* for *gaizki* ("badly" or "wrong").

U *udagoen* for *udazkena* ("Fall"), *ugar* (< *uhar*) for *herdoil* ("rust"), *ugaraxo* for *igela* ("frog"), *ugazaba* and *jabe* ("boss"), and *urten* for *atera* or *jalgi* ("to take out").

Z *zarata* and *hots* ("sound" or "noise"), *zela(n)* for *nola* ("how") and *zelako* for *nolako* ("what (kind) of"), and *zil* for *zilborra* ("navel").

Variants

Those words created by assimilation include: *ete* instead of *ote* in Unified Basque (the interrogative particle implying "perhaps?" "maybe?" or "by any chance?"), *gitxi* instead of *gutxi* ("little" or "few"), *guntzurrun* instead of *giltzurdin* ("kidney"), *guzur* instead of *gezur* ("lie"), and *lehelengo* and *lehenengo* instead of *lehenbizi* ("first," "firstly," or "before"). The following has appeared due to dissimilation: *urrin* instead of *urrun* (or *urruti*) "far" or "faraway."

The pronoun *eurak* is used instead of *berak* "they" (together with *eurei*, *eurena*, *eurekin/eurekaz*, *eurengana*, and so on), as are similar pronouns.

There are more particular variants in Western Basque, including the following: *ardao* instead of *ardo* ("wine"), *aterri* instead of *ateri* ("to clear up"), *baltz* instead of *beltz* ("black"), *emon* instead of *eman* ("to give"), *eperdi* instead of *ipurdi* ("bottom"), *esku(bi)tur* instead of *eskumutur* ("wrist"), *etzun/itxun* instead of *etzan* ("to lie down"), *gaztai* instead of *gazta* ("cheese"), *gorpu* instead of *gorputz hila* ("corpse") and *gorputz bizia* ("[live] body"), *hamazortzi* instead of *hemezortzi* ("eighteen"), *hamen* (and *hemen*) ("here"), *hazur* instead of *hezur* ("bone"), *iruntsi* instead of *irentsi* ("to swallow" or "to devour"), *itxi* instead of *utzi* ("to leave" or "to abandon"), *mailuki* instead of *marrubi* ("strawberry"), *mustur* instead of *mutur* ("end" or "snout"), *nahi* and *nahiz* ("although" or "though" and "as well as," expressing both contrast and similarity), *postura* instead of *apostu* ("bet" or "wager"), *txixa* instead of *pixa* ("pee"), and *zal* instead of *zail* ("difficult").

Western Basque is the most particular of all the dialects. At present it is spoken in Bizkaia and the Deba Valley in Gipuzkoa, but it used to be spoken in Araba as well. Some innovations from Araba spread to the Goierri and Urol-aldea areas in Gipuzkoa as well as to three valleys in Navarre close to Araba: Burunda, Ameskoa, and Lana. It also seems that many areas in what are now La Rioja and Burgos used to form part of this Western dialect area. As far as the dialect's characteristics are concerned, its morphology is the most separate from all the other dialects.

4
Navarrese Basque

Navarre is the largest of all the Basque regions and is territorially nearly as large as the other six regions put together. The Basque-speaking area was once very extensive as well, but much of it was lost between the eighteenth and nineteenth centuries. Dialects have survived in the north of the region, specifically in the northwest, while the dialects of the Zaraitzu and Erronkari Valleys have been lost and those of Ultzama and the Aezkoa Valley are also in danger of disappearing.

With regard to the structure of Navarrese Basque, leaving the Zaraitzu and Erronkari Valleys aside, there are not many differentiating factors compared with other dialect areas. However, Navarrese Basque it not especially homogeneous, and four sub-dialects can be distinguished within it.

Clearly, the unity of the dialect came from Iruñea. It was the only developed urban center for northern Navarre, and became the meeting place for inhabitants of this area. Furthermore, Iruñea used to enjoy an even wider influence, extending to practically the entire Basque Country. It was the seat of power of the Navarrese monarchy, a diocese from the sixth century onward, and an infrastructural center; specifically, the main route from Astorga to Bordeaux went through Iruñea. The Road to Santiago de Compostela also went through Iruñea, and, thanks to the merchants and craftsmen who were based there, it was an important economic center up to the fourteenth century.

Iruñea's importance is also to be seen in language, and it seems that many innovations originated there. To be more precise, it seems that Iruñea and Vitoria-Gasteiz were the birthplaces of today's Basque dialects, which emerged in the early Middle Ages. We will examine some of the innovations that may have originated in Iruñea in the second part of the book.

However, Iruñea's influence has always been greater in southern Navarre. All the valleys in northern Navarre were always closer to market towns in the Northern Basque Country than to Iruñea: towns such as Donibane Lohizune, Ezpeleta, Baigorri, Donibane Garazi, Maule, and Atharratze. In recent centuries, however, this connection to the Northern Basque Country has been considerably weakened, and the northern Navarrese areas have increasingly

The Territory of Basque Dialects in Navarre

Province boundary

looked toward Iruñea. This is partly explained by the growing economic weakness of the Northern Basque Country, but also by the strengthening of the border between France and Spain during this time.

Of course, the boundaries have never been completely closed, but circumstances have changed considerably ever since Castile conquered Navarre in the early sixteenth century, and Lower Navarre became a separate entity. At the same time, in the sixteenth century, Phillip II of Spain removed several areas from the Baiona diocese and included them in the Iruñea diocese, which he controlled as king of Castile: the Bortziriak, Malerreka, Bertizarana, Baztan, Urdazubi, Zugarramurdi, and Luzaide. Furthermore, in 1659, the Treaty of the Pyrenees was signed between the kingdoms of France and Spain. That was the first step toward specifying the border, a process that concluded with the Treaty of Baiona in 1856–66.[1]

These changes also left their mark on the language; the linguistic influence of the Northern Basque Country on northern Navarre declined and these areas increasingly adopted Navarrese. However, the historical connection to the north has not been entirely lost in Baztan, Urdazubi, Zugarramurdi, and, above all, Luzaide.

Northwestern Navarre was, likewise, more distant (geographically as well as culturally) from Iruñea. It also had traditionally better access to other market places and towns. For example, the proximity to Gipuzkoa is apparent in the Basque of the Araitz-Betelu, Larraun, Basaburua and Imotz Valleys. This is also true for Sakana and for most of the Navarrese towns bordering the Goierri area of Gipuzkoa: the Burunda Valley, Etxarri Aranatz, and Ergoiena, for example.

Below in my discussion of Central Basque we will see the influence of the road that runs from Iruñea to Tolosa and Donostia. Araitz-Betelu, Larraun, Basaburua, and Imotz are all located along that road, which has almost certainly facilitated an increasingly close relationship with Gipuzkoa.[2] Sakana, by contrast, has moved away from that axis and maintained its more specifically Navarrese linguistic character.

Meanwhile, the Baztan-Bidasoa area is close to Irun in Gipuzkoa, and the Irun-Elizondo railroad was built to make that connection stronger and easier. Construction began in 1911, and the railroad reached Elizondo (Navarre) in 1916, linking Irun and Elizondo until 1956. It comes as no surprise, therefore, that there are still signs of this in the language spoken in this area, particularly in the Bortziriak, but also in Malerreka, Bertizarana, and Baztan.

As regards unifying factors in Navarrese Basque, thus far I have only mentioned the influence of Iruñea, and, in fact, there is no evidence to suggest that there has ever been any other similar unifying factor. Neither written literature nor oral tradition has been especially influential in this regard. Nor have there been any other important towns or cultural centers in Navarre to fulfill such a task. At the same time, the loss of Basque in Iruñea and in the surrounding areas has left its mark on Basque itself, splitting the language up, so that while it still survives, it does not enjoy anything like its previous homogeneous nature. Today, Basque is at its healthiest in western Navarre, where its proximity to Gipuzkoa has converted that region into its model and protector in Navarre as a whole.

Navarrese Dialects and Sub-Dialects

Bonaparte was the first to study the language of Navarre and distinguished seven dialects on his journey: all of them, except for Bizkaian Basque. Bonaparte did not study Bizkaian Basque and left it out of this categorization. He noted Zuberoan Basque in Erronkari; Eastern Lower Navarrese Basque in Zaraitzu; Western Lower Navarrese Basque in Aezkoa and Luzaide; Lapurdian Basque in Baztan, Urdazubi, and Zugarramurdi; and Gizpuzkoa Basque in Etxarri Aranatz, Ergoiena, and Burunda. He classified all other ways of speaking in Navarre as Navarrese Basque, which he divided into two dialects: Northern and Southern Navarrese Basque.

I already mentioned the changes that occurred in northern Navarre, and Koldo Mitxelena long ago pointed out that Bonaparte's classification had not been correct.[3] Instead, Mitxelena classifies the Baztan Valley as an area of Navarrese Basque, while the Basque spoken in Aezkoa, Zaraitzu, and Erronkari was a separate dialect in itself. Subsequently, Iñaki Camino added Basque from the Aezkoa Valley to Navarrese Basque.[4] In contrast, I have combined the Zaraitzu and Erronkari Valleys into a single, separate dialect: Eastern Navarrese Basque. Moreover, I have classified the language spoken in the Aezkoa and Baztan Valleys as "intermediate ways of speaking," which also applies to Urdazubi and Zugarramurdi, although these latter two towns had until now been classified as within the area of Lapurdian Basque.

The influence of the Northern Basque Country is still very deep in Urdazubi and Zugarramurdi, but new innovations from that area have not reached those two towns. For example, the vowel ü, which comes from French, and the uvular [*R*] (pronouncing *r* → *g*) are not used there; however, the Spanish influenced pronunciations [*x*] and /ø/ are standard there, as are words taken from Spanish, such as *garaje* ("garage") and *gozada* ("a pleasure" or "an absolute delight"), which have become commonly used throughout the Southern Basque Country. Vocabulary and expressions, too, come from the Southern Basque Country and from Spanish; the word for "unemployment," for instance, is *paro* (from Spanish) rather than *xomadxa*, which is the word used in the Northern Basque Country and taken from French. Furthermore, this tendency toward change is even more apparent among young people, who generally live and study in Navarre and the Southern Basque Country.[5]

Let us now examine northwestern Navarre, and specifically the Araitz-Betelu, Larraun, Basaburua, and Imotz valleys. I believe that Bonaparte classified the Basque of this area incorrectly. Firstly, he did not know the Basque of this area directly himself or study it in detail. The instructions he gave his assistant, Bruno Etxenike, in order to classify the Basque spoken there are very significant; in short, he was to examine the following three characteristics:[6] whether the forms *gara*, *zara*, and *zarete* or *gera*, *zera*, and *zerate* were used to express "we are," "you are" (singular), and "you are" (plural); whether the forms *dut* or *det* were used to express "I have"; and whether the prefix *bait-* or the suffix *-(e)n* were used in structures, such as *zeren ona baita/zeren ona den* to express "because it is good."

In my opinion, at least, a way of speaking cannot be known and then classified based on only three characteristics, and, leaving Bonaparte's criteria aside, there is another factor that must be taken into account: the model for the inhabitants of this area has long been Gipuzkoan Basque and, nowadays, above all, Unified Basque, which is largely derived from Gipuzkoan Basque. Clearly, then, Navarrese characteristics have lost strength at the expense of the increasing influence of Gipuzkoan since Bonaparte's time. The old Navarrese character has been maintained in Beintza-Labaien, Basaburu Txikia (Basaburúa Menor), and, to some extent, in Goizueta and Saldias. In the Imotz Valley, however, the town of Muskitz (Músquiz) is an exception in that we still classify it today as lying within the area of Navarrese Basque.

In mentioning Basaburu Txikia, it is worth some additional discussion because of the special situation there. There are eight towns in the area. In Arano and Areso, the Basque spoken is similar to Gipuzkoan Basque; the former looks toward Hernani while the latter is connected to Tolosa, both significant towns in Gipuzkoa. The proximity to Gipuzkoa can also be heard in Leitza, Ezkurra, and Eratsun, but the old Navarrese Basque roots are stronger there. Beintza-Labaien, on the other hand, is near the more significant urban center of Doneztebe, and that is its reference point. Saldias is located between Leitza and Doneztebe, and the influences of both places can be heard in its speech. Finally, Goizueta is geographically and linguistically closer to the Bortziriak and, until very recently, was very isolated. Because of that, it has maintained its Navarrese linguistic character more than other areas around it.[7]

There are reasons behind the diverse situation in Basaburu Txikia. To start with, the decision to administer these eight towns together was made relatively late, dating back to only 1757, and while administrative unity has been achieved, this has certainly not been the case in terms of linguistic unity. It should also be added that the people of the area do not feel that they belong to a unified entity. Furthermore, the main market place for people of this area is Doneztebe, which the people from northern Basaburua have always maintained strong links with.

When examining southwestern Navarre, there is another debate about the Etxarri Aranatz, Ergoiena, and Burunda areas. Bonaparte classified them as speaking Gipuzkoan Basque, but, in fact, he only used a single criterion to take this decision: the presence of the root *-e-*, from **edun*, in the auxiliary verbs. This is the case in Etxarri Aranatz, where *det, dek/den, dezu, dezubie*, and *debie* are used. In Ergoiena and Burunda, on the other hand, this root is only to be found in the verb forms for *zuk* and *zuek* ("you" in singular and plural respectively); thus, they say *dezu* and *dezie* in Ergoiena, and *dezu* and *dezai* in Burunda. Along with these, however, the Western Basque forms *dot, dok/don*, and *dau* instead of *du* (in Unified Basque) are used in that area. However, Bonaparte classified the area as speaking Navarrese Basque because the Eastern root *-u-* is used from Arbizu onward (*dut, duk/dun, dugu, duzu, duzubie, dubie*).

Once again, I believe that using a single criterion is too weak a basis for this argument; but, in addition, his researchers in the area were partly to blame for the mistake. Bonaparte commissioned the translation of Christian teachings into the language used in Etxarri Aranatz and Urdiain, but they were instead translated into the "official" Basque that is spoken in the Beterri area of Gipuzkoa. Obviously, the translators had not understood what Bonaparte wanted: he wanted the local speech, just as it was, in order to study it, and instead they gave him the most elegant Basque there was. I have therefore included Ergoiena and Etxarri Aranatz in the Navarrese Basque-speaking area and Burunda as a location of an intermediary way of speaking.[8]

We still have to examine the differences that Bonaparte saw between the two sub-dialects in Navarrese Basque. In fact, Bonaparte himself admitted in his book *Le verbe basque* (The Basque verb, 1869) that the basis for separating them was weak and that the two could be considered to be a single dialect;[9] indeed, Azkue proposed this in his later argument,[10] and I agree with him. Of course, there are noticeable differences in the Navarrese Basque spoken from one part of Navarre to another. Basque spoken in Etxalar is by no means the same as that spoken in Mezkiritz (Mezquíriz), and there are also differences between that of Arbizu and that of Eugi, but there are no breaks or gaps between the various different areas. The changes are gradual and without any sudden jumps.

Furthermore, the differences between one area and another are neither so numerous nor so significant, and it would thus be more appropriate to use the term sub-dialect instead of dialect. There are, then, four such sub-dialects of Navarrese Basque:

1. Northwestern. Spoken in the Bortziriak, Malerreka, Bertizarana, and a few nearby areas: in Oronoz-Mugairi, in Baztan, and in Beintza-Labaien, in Basaburu Txikia, and in Goizueta and Saldias.
2. Southwestern. Spoken in Sakana.
3. Central. Spoken in Ultzama, Lantz, Atetz, Anue, and Odieta.
4. Eastern. Still used in Erroibar and Esteribar.

The Western sub-dialects are the most distinct. On the one hand, many Navarrese innovations have not reached those areas, and, on the other, the influence of Gipuzkoan Basque is very noticeable among them. The proximity of the Northern Basque Country is also evident in the Northwestern group.[11]

There are two distinctive features in the Eastern sub-dialects. They have not taken on many of the innovations that have emerged in Central Basque and they have developed a few of their own special characteristics. Three of these are worth mention here:[12]

1. The letter *i* is omitted between some vowels: *anaia* → *anae* ("brother"), *baietz* → *baetz* ("of course!"), *behia* → *bea* ("cow"), *maiatz* → *maetz* ("May"), and so on.
2. The suffix *-n* disappears from some verbs in the past tense: *nuen* → *nue*, *zen* → *ze*, *zegoen* → *zego*, *zekon* or *zion* in Unified Basque → *zeko*, and so on.
3. The letter *g-* appears in some demonstrative pronouns: *gau* instead of *hau* in Unified Basque, *gori* instead of *hori*, *gura* instead of *hura*, and so on. It is not clear whether this is an innovation or an archaic form. I am inclined to think the latter, but cannot be sure.

There are two very noticeable lexicographical features in the Eastern sub-dialects: *jarduki* is used instead of *hitz egin* ("to talk") and *orre* instead of *ipurua* ("juniper tree"). Finally, among variants, the most important are *eile* (> *elle*) instead of *ile* or *artilea* ("wool"), *ereki* instead of *erein* ("to sow" or "to scatter"), and *yago* instead of *gehiago* ("more").

I would repeat, however, that these do not constitute a significant amount of distinguishing features, and, furthermore, they are not common to all areas. There is, then, no reason to classify this as a dialect in itself, and the term "Eastern sub-dialect" is more appropriate.

The structure of Navarrese Basque can be summed up by saying that it is based around the central part of the region, Iruñea, and the surrounding area.[13] Some innovations from the central area have not reached western Navarre, but those from Gipuzkoa have and continue to do so. However, the

Bera
Zugarramurdi
Urdazubi
BORTZIRIAK
BAZTAN
Goizueta
Oronoz Mugairi
Elizondo
THE NORTHWEST
MALERREKA
BERTIZARANA
Doneztebe
Beintza-Labaien
Saldias
CENTRAL AREA
THE SOUTHWEST
ULTZAMA
Lantz
Muskitz
ESTERIBAR
ERROIBAR
Orbaizeta
ATETZ
ANUE
Etxarri
Aranatz
ODIETA
AEZKOA
Bakaiku
Uharte-Araki
THE EAST
SAKANA
BURUNDA
Urdiain
Navarrese Basque Territory/Area
Dialect Boundary
Sub-Dialect boundary
Overlapping Dialects

sub-dialects in the center and in the east are very similar. There is a small difference, for example, between the Anue Valley in central Navarre and the Esteribar Valley in the east. As a result, I do not believe that Bonaparte was right to distinguish two dialects there.

As well as the four sub-dialects, there are also three areas with very distinctive characteristics: the Aezkoa Valley, the Baztan-Urdazubi-Zugarramurdi area, and Burunda. In these areas, the dialect spoken is mostly Navarrese Basque, but, because they are all located in border areas of Navarre, they also share close links with areas beyond these borders; Baztan Basque shares links with Navarrese-Lapurdian Basque, above all in Urdazubi and in Zugarramurdi. Aezkoa is connected to Eastern Navarrese Basque, and more precisely with Zaraitzu and Erronkari Basque. Burunda Basque, meanwhile, is related to Central and Western Basque.

Baztan, on the Boundary

As I noted above, the northern valleys of Navarre used to be mostly influenced by the Northern Basque Country and, nowadays, look mostly toward Navarre and the Southern Basque Country in general. To explain this further, I will take Baztan as an example. I will also use the example of Baztan Basque to explain how I categorize a particular local way of speaking as part of one dialect or another. As I have already explained, the key to my decisions on this matter is where newly introduced innovations come from.

Where to place Baztan Basque is a source of debate. After having his doubts, Bonaparte finally classified it as Lapurdian Basque,[14] but did not explain his reasons for doing so, and the question has not been properly cleared up since then. Mitxelena, as mentioned above, categorized it as Navarrese Basque;[15] but more recently, Pedro Irizar included it in Lapurdian Basque once more.[16] In recent years, there have been many studies on Baztan Basque, and thanks to these we now have a firmer basis for classifying it.[17]

Innovations from the Northern Basque Country used to reach Baztan, as we can see by these examples: before nasal consonants (*m*, *n*, *ñ*), *o* → *u*. In Baztan, this can be heard in demonstrative pronouns such as *honek* → *unek*, *honetan* → *unten*, and *honi* → *uni*. There are further examples of this, such as *ongi* → *ungi* ("good" or "well") and *ontzi* → *untzi* ("boat" or "container"), most significantly, but there are no more examples of this transformation. Furthermore, this rule is no longer productive.

As in Navarrese-Lapurdian Basque, *x*- appears at the start of words rather than *tx*-: *xapela* ("beret"), *xerri* ("pig"), *xerto* ("graft" or "vaccination") and *xertatu* ("to graft" or "to vaccinate"), *xistorra* (a kind of sausage), *xoko* ("corner" or "joint"), *xori* ("bird"), and so on. This had also been applied to loanwords from Spanish: *xaflan* (Spanish *chaflán*) rather than *kantoia* ("corner") in Unified Basque, *xapin* (Spanish *chapín*), meaning a kind of clog, and so forth. This tendency is no longer productive, and, recently, *tx-* has become common at the start of many words taken from Spanish: for example, *txantxullo* ("racket" or "fiddle"), *txapuza* ("a botched job"), *txikle* ("chewing gum"), *txorrada* ("something stupid"), *txuleta* ("chop [of meat]"), *txupa* ("jacket"), and *txupada* ("lick," "suck," or "puff").

In foreign loanwords, the transformation *-on* → *-oin* takes place. This can be seen in many old Baztan words: for example, *arratoñe* ("mouse"), *arrazoñe* ("reason"), *botoñe* ("button"), *kantoñe* ("canton"), *matoñe* ("bully"), *pozoñe* ("posion"), and *sasoñe* ("season" or "time"). In recent loanwords, however, *-on* is used, as it is in Navarrese Basque: *balkona* ("balcony"), *balona* ("ball"), *bidona* ("can" or "drum"), *kamisona* ("gown" or "nightdress"), *limona* ("lemon"), *melona* ("melon"), *melokotona* ("peach"), *xabona* ("soap"), *zinturona* ("belt"), and so on.

As in the Northern Basque Country, the variant *-rat* is used in the allative case, but this appears in very few words and is no longer a productive rule. It is mostly used in adverbs of place like *unet* ("[to] here"), *orrat* ("[to] there" as in somewhere close), and *arat* ("[to] there as in somewhere far), and also in the following words: *noat* rather than *nora* in Unified Basque ("where to?"), *aitzinet* rather than *aitzina* or *aurrera* ("forward"), and *gibelat* rather than *gibelera* or *atzera* ("backward"). In the most northerly towns in the Baztan Valley, it can also be heard in some other words, but it is mostly used by elderly people.

As in the Northern Basque Country, elderly speakers from Baztan occasionally use the structure *-ri buruz* to express direction: *mendiari buruz gan naiz* ("I went toward the mountain"). This is not usual among younger people, who use this structure with a different notion meaning "about (something)," as in Unified Basque.

Pronouns such as *nior* rather than *inor* in Unified Basque ("anyone," "someone," or "no one") are sometimes heard in the northern Baztan: as well as *niork*, *nion*, *nioiz*, and so on. But they are not common and, furthermore, are only used by elderly speakers.

Elderly speakers from Baztan use simple participles in relative clauses: for example, *zuk utzi tokien dago* ("it's where you left it").[18] However, it would be very unusual to hear a young speaker use this form.

As in the Northern Basque Country, *-ain* is the word ending for *arrain* ("fish"), *usain* (> *usein*) ("smell"), and *zain* ("keeper" or "waiting") as well as *artzain* ("shepherd"), not *-a* as it is in Navarrese and Gipuzkoan Basque.

Now let me turn to innovations from Navarrese Basque that have reached Baztan.

As in most of Navarre, the accent is marked and is placed on the penultimate syllable: *launbéta* for *larunbata* in Unified Basque ("Saturday").

Apheresis and syncope, on the other hand, are very typical with unaccented syllables. The following are examples of initial syllables being lost as a result of apheresis: for example, *ekarri* → *kárri* ("to bring"), *eman* → *mán* ("to give"), *emazteki* → *maztéki* ("woman"), *etorri* → *tórri* ("to come"), *ezagutu* → *zázu-tu* ("to know"), *ikusi* → *kúsi* ("to see"), *ikuzi* → *kúzi* ("to wash"), *ipurdi* → *púrdi* ("bottom"), *itsusi* → *tsúsi* ("ugly"), *iturri* → *túrri* ("spring"), and *izaten* → *záten* ("being"). As a result of syncope, vowels disappear from the middle of the following words: *atera* → *átra* ("to take out"), *batere* → *bátre* ("at all"), *harrapatu* → *arpátu* ("to catch"), *haserretu* → *asértu* ("to get mad"), and so on.

It is customary in the future tense for the transformation *-tuko* → *-tiko* to take place: *akituko* rather than *bukatuko* in Unified Basque → *akitiko* ("[will] finish"), *hartuko* → *artiko* ("(will) take"), *konprendituko* → *konprenditiko* ("[will] understand), *pasatuko* → *pastiko* ("(will) happen"), *salatuko* → *salatiko* ("[will] denounce"), and so on.

In second person singular *hika* verb forms, the use of *y-* is common in Baztan, particularly in the southern Basaburua area: *haiz* → *yaiz*, *hintzen* → *yitzen*, *huen* → *yuen*, *habil* → *yabil*, *haut* → *yaut*, and so on.

The pluralizing *-it-* has reached Baztan in the absolutive-dative-ergative, although it is not typical. It is mostly used when the indirect object is third person singular: for example, *ditiot* (> *tiot*) instead of *dizkiot* in Unified Basque, and *nition* instead of *nizkion*.

A *g-* is placed at the start of words beginning with *oa-* in the words *goaie* instead of *hoa* in Unified Basque ("you are going" in the *hika* form), *goartu* instead of *ohartu* ("to realize" or "to notice"), *goatze* instead of *ohatze* or *ohea* ("bed"), and *guai* instead of *orain* ("now").

The following innovations did not originate specifically in Navarrese Basque but, more generally, in the Basque spoken in the Southern Basque Country.

As in extensive areas of Navarre and the whole of the Southern Basque Country, the transformation *a* → *e* takes places after the vowels *i* and *u*. This rule is very much in use and highly productive, as the following examples demonstrate: *animatu* → *animetu* ("to encourage" or "to cheer up"), *juntatu* → *yuntetu* ("to join" or "to unite"), *aitarendako* → *aiteindeko* ("for father"), *gizonarengatik* → *gizoneingetik* ("from the man"), *gizonarengana* → *gizoneingena* ("to the man"), *lagungarri* → *lagungerri* ("helpful"), *ehizelari* or *ehiztari* in Unified Basque → *izileri* ("hunter"), *harrika* → *arrike* ("throwing stones"), *hirugarrena* → *irugerna* ("the third [one]"), *herri bat* → *erri bet* ("a people" or "a village"), *heldu da* → *eldu de* ("he/she/it has arrived"), *heldu gara* → *eldu gera* ("we have arrived"), *baldin badu* → *balin bedu* ("if he/she/it has (it)"), and so on.

As in the whole of the Southern Basque Country, the pronunciation [*x*] is used in many loanwords from Spanish: for example, *fijo* ("fixed" or "definitely"), *majo* ("nice"), *jeneral* ("general"), *makillaje* ("make-up"), and *peaje* ("toll").

As in most of Bizkaia, western Gipuzkoa, and Navarre, the vowel *i* often leads to the palatized sounds *ñ*, *ll*, and *tt* in Oronoz-Mugairi, Arraioz, and the southern Baztan area of Basaburua: *ilargi* → *illergi* ("moon"), *zinen* → *ziñen* ("you were"), *nituen* → *nittun* ("I had" with a plural object), and so on.

As in some other areas of the Southern Basque Country, it is very common for young people in Baztan to use the absolutive-ergative instead of absolutive-dative-ergative verb forms, so they will say *kusi datzut* instead of *ikusi zaitut* ("I have seen you").

With regard to vocabulary, the old connection to the Northern Basque Country is still apparent in that many words from there are still used today in Baztan: for example, *abantxu* instead of *ia* ("nearly" or "almost") in Unified Basque , *agorril* instead of *abuztua* ("August"), *aiher* instead of *gorrotoa* ("hate" or "spite"), *aizturrak* instead of *guraizeak* ("scissors"), *alatu* instead of *bazkatu* ("to feed" or "to graze"), *alimaleko* instead of *sekulakoa* ("great" or "excellent"), *alta* instead of *ordea* ("however" or "but"), *andana* instead of *mordoa* ("bundle" or "bunch"), *azantz* instead of *hotsa* ("sound" or "noise"), *Besta Berri* instead of *Korpus Eguna* ("Feast of Corpus Christi"), *bihi* instead of *alea* ("grain"), *buruil* instead of *iraila* ("September"), *ereiaro* instead of *ekaina* ("June") as well as *garagarril* ("July") and *garagarzaro* ("June"), *eskuzarta* instead of *txaloa* ("applause"), *etxilar/ilar biribil* instead of *ilarra* ("pea"), *fitsik* instead of *ezer* ("nothing"), *guri* instead of *bigun* ("soft" or "smooth"), *iskilin* (a kind of needle or pin), *kalapita* instead of *iskanbila* ("disturbance" or "disorder"), *kofoin* instead of *erlauntza* ("beehive"), *orga* instead of *gurdia* ("cart" or "wagon"), *ortzadar* ("rainbow") rather than the Navarrese Basque *jainkoaren gerrikoa/jainkoaren paxa* (literally "God's belt" or "God's sash"), *papo* instead of *paparra* ("chest"), *piro* instead of *ahatea* ("duck"), *pittika* instead of *antxumea* ("kid," as in young goat), *suntsitu* instead of *desegin* ("to undo" or "to come apart"), *ukaldi* instead of *zartakoa* ("slap"), and *xingar* instead of *urdaia* ("pork"). Some loanwords have also been imported from French: *afera* instead of *auzia* ("controversy" or "dispute"), *deliberatu* instead of *erabaki* ("to decide"), *fier* instead of *sendoa* ("strong," "firm," or "robust"), *fite* instead of *laster* ("fast"), *kapable* instead of *gai* ("capable" or "able"), *kausitu* instead of *aurkitu* ("to find"), *pozoin* ("poison"), *propie* instead of *polita* ("pretty" or "nice"), and *xeka* instead of *bila* ("in search of").

But, at the same time, there are also words that link Baztan with Navarre and the rest of the Southern Basque Country: for example, *asots* for *hotsa* ("sound" or "noise"), *atrije* for *usina* ("sneeze"), *banabar* (but *ilar* in northern Baztan) for *indaba* ("bean"), *barride* for *auzoa* ("neighborhood"), *beratz* for *biguna* ("soft" or "smooth"), *bota* for *erori* ("to fall"), *dermio* for *eremua* ("area" or "domain"), *eskatu* ("to ask for") instead of *galdegin* in the Northern Basque Country, *goatze* for *ohea* ("bed"), *ilbeltz* for *urtarrila* ("January"), *ja* for *ezer* ("nothing"), *maindire* ("bedsheet") instead of *mihise* in the Northern Basque Country, *mingain* for *mihia* ("tongue"), *nekazari* ("farmer") instead of *laborari* in the Northern Basque Country, *orantz* for *legamia* ("yeast"), *ortots* for *trumoia* ("thunder"), *sor* for *gor* ("deaf"), and *ugalde* for *ibaia* ("river"). Nowadays, furthermore, models from the Southern Basque Country and, of course, loanwords from Spanish are also more and more frequent among younger speakers.

With regard to variants, there are several that link the area to the Northern Basque Country: for example, *barda* instead of *bart* in Unified Basque ("last night"), *eskuara* instead of *euskara* ("the Basque language," which in fact is a variant common to many parts of the Basque Country), *etsi* instead of *itxi* ("to close"), *gan* instead of *joan/eraman* ("to go/to take"), *gasna* instead of *gazta* ("cheese"), *jinko* as well as *jainko* ("God"), and *saindu* instead of *santu* ("saint"). Yet along with this, there are also words that are typically Navarrese Basque: for example, *atzendu* and *ahantzi* instead of *ahaztu* ("to forget"), *aunitz/aunditz* instead of *anitz* ("a lot," "much," or "many"), *bulkatu* instead of *bultzatu* ("to push" or "to promote"), *eke* instead of *ke* ("smoke"), and *negal* instead of *igel* ("frog").

In short, Baztan Basque is a good example of continual linguistic change, and these changes are very clearly distancing the area from the Northern Basque Country and bringing it closer to Navarre and the Southern Basque Country. This can sometimes be seen as a difference between generations and, on other occasions, between different places. The Navarrese and Southern Basque influence is very apparent in Almandoz, Aniz, Berroeta, and Ziga in the Basaburua area. This is also true in Arraioz and Oronoz-Mugairi where, in addition, influence from Irun can also be heard. On the other hand, older Baztan Basque has been better maintained in the northeastern area, in Arizkun, Azpilkueta, Amaiur (Maya), and Erratzu.

Characteristics of Navarrese Basque

Rules

Accent is the most significant differentiating factor in Navarrese Basque.[19] It is strong, and, in the Central and Eastern sub-dialects, the emphasis is on the penultimate syllable, as it is in Zuberoan Basque. These following examples are from Amaiur, in the Baztan area: *larunbata* → *launbéta* ("Saturday"), *lagunarekin* → *launéikin* ("with the friend"), and *lagunarendako* → *launeindéko* ("for the friend"). The Spanish word *fábrica* ("factory"), for example, becomes *fabríke*.

The Northwestern sub-dialect accent is also strong, but the emphasis is on a different place, namely on the second syllable in each word, as in many areas of Bizkaia and Gipuzkoa. In Bera, in the Bortziriak area, for instance, *larunbata* → *larúnta*, and this model also applies to several old loanwords from Spanish: *chocolate* → *txokólte*, *escopeta* → *eskópeta* ("shotgun"), *fábrica* → *fabríka*, and *música* → *musíka*. In Sakana, in what has been classified here as the Southwestern sub-dialect, the accent is not as strong and is closer to the accents of Western and Central Basque.

There is another clear feature of Navarrese Basque as regards accent. As noted, there is a strong emphasis on accentuated vowels, and non-accentuated vowels are much weaker, so much so that they are sometimes lost. The initial vowel sometimes disappears, and already mentioned variants such as *ekarri* → *kárri* ("to bring"), from Baztan Basque, can be heard. In other examples, meanwhile, vowels within words are lost and changes such as *haserretu* → *asértu* ("to get mad") take place. Of course, Sakana is different in this respect; vowels are not lost when there are other strongly accentuated vowels.

Erronkari Basque is often mentioned in connection to syncope, the loss of vowels within words, and, in fact, unusual consonant groups, for Basque, were formed there when non-accented vowels disappeared: *-gr-* (*gara* → *gra*), *-tr-* (*egitera* → *egitra*, *harturen* → *artren*, *harturik* → artruk), *-zr-* (*bazkaltzera* → *bazkalzra*, *ziren* → *zren*), and so on. However, on the other side of Navarre, in Arantza in the Bortziriak area, similar consonant groups can be heard nowadays as well: *guztanbera* → *gaztánbra*, *abilena* or *trebeena* → *abílna*, *politena* → *polítna*, *dituzte* → *zte*, *zaitez* → *stti*, and so on.

Furthermore, the following transformations are rules:[20]

- In the genitive, *-neko* → *-nko* (*gaineko* → *gáinko* "top" or "surface"), *-netako* → *ntko* (*oinetakoak* → *óintkuk* "shoes"), *-reko* → *-rko* (*bazterreko* → *baztérko* "of the edge"), *-etako* → *-etko* (*honetako* → *unétko* "of this").
- In the plural inessive, *-ketan* → *-ktan*: *hanketan* → *ánktan* ("on the legs").
- In verbal nouns, -teko → -tko eta -tzeko → -tzko: *jatekoa* → *yátkua* ("edible"), *jotzeko* → *yótzko* ("playable").
- In clauses expressing cause, *-elakoz* → *-elkoz*: *dutelakoz* or *dutelako* in Unified Basque → *dutélkoz* ("because they have").

The Northwestern sub-dialect is also different in that *p/b* → *u* at the end of syllables. In Arantza, for example, *akabatu* → *akáutu* ("to finish"), *arrapatu* → *arráutu* ("to catch"), *eskapatu* → *eskáutu* ("to escape"), *hilabete* → *illáute* ("month"), *irabazi* → *iráuzi* ("to win"), and *kalabaza* → *kaláuza* ("pumpkin").

Spanish words ending in *-(i)ón* are left as such in most of Navarre; *ba-*

jona ("slump"), *frontona* ("pelota court"), *kolokona* ("high"), *marrona* ("pain" or "mess"), *melokotona* ("peach"), *mogollona* ("tons of"), *abiona* ("plane"), *kamiona* ("truck") are all loanwords taken from Spanish, and, as can be seen in these examples, this rule is productive.

It is characteristic of Navarrese Basque to have *-s* at the end of words in *zertaz/nola* ("how?") instead of *-z*; *oines* ("on foot"), *eskus* ("by hand"), *burus* ("by memory" or "by heart"), *etorri delakos*, and *etorri eskeros* are used throughout much of the dialect area. This does not affect the Northwestern sub-dialect or Baztan but, on the other hand, most of the Imotz, Basaburua, and Larraun areas are affected.

In second person singular verbs, *y-* is used in most of Navarre: *haiz* → *yaiz* ("you are" in the *hika* form). This is an old innovation that also reached as far as Zaraitzu and Erronkari. This can also be heard in northeastern Gipuzkoa, from Lezo to Irun.

Plural verb forms in absolutive-dative-ergative are formed using *-it-* in part of Navarre: for example, *ditio* instead of *dizkio* in Unified Basque, *ditizu* instead of *dizkizu*, and *ditit* instead of *dizkit*. In the spoken language, *ditio* → *tio/ttio*, *ditit* → *tit/ttit*, but the pluralizing *-it-* clearly appears in the past tense: *nition/nittion* instead of *nizkion*, and *nitizun/nittizun* instead of *nizkizun*. This innovation does not seem to be very old; it has spread throughout most of central and western Navarre. This excludes Burunda, Ergoiena, and Etxarri Aranatz, and is very weak in Baztan. On the other hand, it is present in Imotz, Basaburua, northern Basaburu Txikia, and eastern Larraun. It can also be heard in the northeastern Gipuzkoa, although it has recently started to disappear. It has best survived in Hondarribia (Gipzukoa).

The root of absolutive-dative past tense verb forms in many areas of the dialect is *-ki-*: *zakidan* instead of *zitzaidan* in Unified Basque, *zakion* instead of *zitzaion*, *zakigun* instead of *zitzaigun*, and so on. This is not the case in the Northwestern dialect or in Baztan. In most of Sakana, however, this is very strong and has also been extended to the present tense: *dakit* instead of *zait*, *dakik/dakin* instead of *zaik/zain*, *dakiyo* instead of *zaio*, *dakigu* instead of *zaigu*, *dakizu* instead of *zaizu*, *dakizubie* instead of *zaizue*, and *dakiyobie* instead of *zaie*. In that area, then, it is the rule to say *ahaztu dakit* instead of *ahaztu zait* ("I have forgotten"), and *gustetzen dakizu?* instead of *gustatzen zaizu?* ("do you like it?").

In the central and eastern areas, there is a *u* → *i* tendency. This takes place in the following two situations: when the suffix *-ko* is added to form the future tense *-tuko* → *-tiko* and *-tu behar* → *-tiar*. Examples of the first transformation are *ailegatuko* → *allaatiko*, *pasatuko* → *pasatiko*, and so on. The second transformation has reached as far as Aezkoa, and the following examples are from that area: *goratu behar* → *goratiar*, *zikindu behar* → *zikindiar*, *frakasatu behar* → *frakasatiar*.[21]

Undeveloped Rules, Vocabulary, and Variants

Among undeveloped rules, *g-* before *oa-* must be mentioned. This happens with four words: *goa/goaye* instead of *(hi) hoa* in Unified Basque ("you are going" in the *hika* form), *guai* instead of *orain* ("now," which can also be heard outside Navarre), *goartu* instead of *ohartu* ("to realize" or "to notice"), and *goatze* instead of *ohatzea* or *ohea* ("bed").

As Navarrese Basque is very divided, there are very few words that are used throughout the area in which it is spoken, the following being among the most widely used: *arroitu* and *asots* instead of *hotsa* or *zarata* in Unified Basque ("sound" or "noise"), *at(r)ija* instead of *usina* ("sneeze"), *banabar* and *alubia* instead of *indaba* ("bean"), *barride* instead of *auzunea* ("neighborhood"), *beratz* instead of *biguna* ("soft" or "smooth"), *dermio* instead of *eremua* ("area" or "domain"), *estrabila* instead of *ukuilua* ("stable"), *galtzin* instead of *karea* ("lime"), *goatze* instead of *ohea* ("bed"), *jainkoaren gerriko/jainkoaren paxa* instead of *ostadarra* ("rainbow"), *listu* instead of *tua* ("spit"), *nekazari* for ("farmer" or more generally "someone who works the land"), *orantz* instead of *legamia* ("yeast"), *ostots/ortots* instead of *trumoia* ("thunder"), *sor* instead of *gor* ("deaf"), and *ugalde* instead of *ibaia* ("river").

The following can be heard in limited areas: *amina* instead of *amona* in Unified Basque ("grandmother"), *bota* instead of *erori* ("to fall"), *hagitz* and *(t)xoil* instead of *oso* or *arrunt* ("common" or "ordinary"), *ja* instead of *ezer* ("nothing"), *kalma* instead of *hodeia* ("cloud"), and *udondo* instead of *udazkena* ("Fall").

The names of some months are distinctive: *garagarzaro* instead of *ekaina* in Unified Basque ("June"), *garil* instead of *uztaila* ("July"), *urri* instead of *irail* ("September"), and *lastail* instead of *urria* ("October"). In some areas, *izotzil* instead of *urtarrila* ("January") is also used.

There are very few variants that are used throughout the dialect. These are the most widely used: *atzendu* instead of *ahaztu* ("to forget," which is also used in some parts of Gipuzkoa), *aunitz/aunditz* instead of *anitz* or *asko* ("a lot," "much," or "many"), *bulkatu* instead of *bultzatu* ("to push" or "to promote"), and *negel/legen* instead of *igel* ("frog").

The following are also used in many areas of Navarre: *altzin* instead of *aitzina* or *aurrea* ("forward"), *altzur/ailtzur* instead of *aitzur* ("hoe"), *etzin* instead of *etzan* ("to lie down," also used in the Deba Valley), *eke* instead of *kea* ("smoke"), *ekendu* instead of *kendu* ("to remove"), and *esene* instead of *esnea* ("milk"). The following are mostly used in the central and eastern areas: *erte* instead of *arte* ("until") and *ertsi* instead of *itxi* ("to close").

It seems that Iruñea was especially important in the general development of contemporary Basque. Specifically, features that emerged there spread all over the Basque Country. As the centuries went by, however, the importance of Iruñea declined as other cities and urban areas grew to compete with it: for example, Vitoria-Gasteiz in the west, Maule and Atharratze in the east, and the Donostia-Hernani-Tolosa axis in the central Basque Country. As a result, Iruñea's influence within Navarre itself was also more limited, and the dialect has few differentiating factors.

5
Central Basque

The dialect from the center of the Basque Country has become especially important in the development of Basque, among other reasons because it mostly serves as the basis for Unified Basque. There are both sociolinguistic and purely linguistic explanations for this importance. Among the sociolinguistic factors, the fact is that Basque is strongest in Gipuzkoa, which is a province with several large towns and significant infrastructure. In terms of linguistic factors, three mains features were taken into consideration when drawing up Unified Basque: as Gipuzkoa is in the center of the Basque Country, the way of speaking there is what most Basque speakers most easily understand; there is quite a rich Gipuzkoan literary tradition; and its dialect was prestigious and highly esteemed from the eighteenth century onward. Let us now examine this dialect's development and structure in greater detail and depth.

The Beterri area has always been the heart of this dialect, specifically that part of the axis that connects Iruñea and the Gipuzkoan coast. This is an ancient route, along which many urban centers emerged and developed in importance: for example, Donostia, Hernani, Andoain, and Tolosa.

The influence of this axis has spread to its surrounding areas, and this includes its local way of speaking. In fact, old records attest to the prestige attached to this way of speaking. *El borracho burlado* (The ridiculed drunk, 1764), a comic opera published by Xabier Munibe, the Count of Peñaflorida, is an example of this. It seems that Munibe wanted to write it in Basque, but he could not do so in the Basque from Azkoitia, his hometown, because the local way of speaking was not sufficiently prestigious. Nor did he feel he could write it in Beterri Basque because he was afraid that the actors would not be able to use it appropriately. This is what Munibe wrote about the matter: specifically, his doubts and the solution he came up with for the problem:[1]

> My first idea was that the whole opera should be in Basque, but then I became aware of the difficulty of the dialect I would have to use to do so. If I used that of Azkoitia it would not have been very welcome in the rest of the [Basque] Country, right up to the border with France, because of the concerns they have with Basque or the dialect of the Goierri, and if I wished to use the dialect of Tolosa, Hernani, Donostia, etc. I would run

> the risk of making the actors look ridiculous, since it would be difficult for all of them to imitate it well. For this reason, then, I had to make do with reserving Basque for all the sung parts, meaning that all the acting parts were in Spanish.

Gipuzkoan Basque in the Deba Valley

This local way of speaking spread beyond the boundaries of Gipuzkoa and reached the neighboring regions. In the mid-eighteenth century, Agustin Kardaberatz wrote the following about the situation in Bizkaia:[2] "However, two things must be taken into account in this issue. Many people from Bizkaia also prefer to speak in our dialect rather than in their own, and many preachers in Bizkaia give their sermons in our dialect."

What Kardaberatz says is significant; the people of Bizkaia preferred the neighboring form of Basque to their own and, indeed, felt at home with it. He also mentions who extended the prestige of the neighboring local way of speaking: the Church. But, as we have seen when looking at Western Basque, this situation was not to last much longer because in the early nineteenth century Bizkaians began to revive their own dialect.

In the Deba Valley, however, the situation was very different. As the area is administratively part of Gipuzkoa and also part of the Diocese of Donostia, the influence of Gipuzkoan Basque there was much deeper. The Franciscan friar Uriarte, while preaching in the Leintz Valley (part of the Upper Deba Valley), wrote to Louis-Lucien Bonaparte in February 1859:[3] "Last Sunday, we commenced the mission that we will conclude on the seventeenth. We preach in the Gipuzkoan dialect of the Beterri, since they are accustomed to that dialect in the pulpit."

According to Uriarte, then, as well as the priests, churchgoers were also used to Gipuzkoan Basque. In May that same year, Uriarte wrote Bonaparte another letter in which he explained the situation in the whole of the Deba Valley:[4] "It is the case among all those populations that look with disdain at the Basque of Bizkaia and that are very devoted to the dialect of the Beterri: sermons and homilies are preached in that Beterri dialect and a lot of people study that dialect thereby mixing [their dialects]; yet they have still not been able to 'Gipuzkoanize' the common people."

Uriarte's testimony is worth bearing in mind. The prestige of Basque from the Beterri was already well known, but here he also tells us that the people of the Deba Valley looked down on their own local way of speaking. He states that, in addition to the people of the Church, other important people in society also gave up their own way of speaking and studied and used Basque from the Beterri. At the end of the day, speaking in one way or another was a sign of social status; and upper class people in the Deba Valley used Beterri Basque, while their lower class counterparts used Western Basque. In an 1863 letter, Bonaparte told Bruno Etxenike, from Navarre, that he had seen the same thing in Bergara:

> When I say that the dialect spoken in Bergara is Bizkaian Basque, and not Gipuzkoan Basque, I know that many important people in Bergara who try to be pure Gipuzkoans are not happy about this denomination. I admit that priests and educated people speak in Gipuzkoan Basque in their daily life, and, furthermore, they speak in the clear Gipuzkoan Basque from the Beterri. But this does not change my opinion. The question is not whether the people of Bergara like people from Bizkaia and their dialect or not, the thing is that ordinary people and farmers speak using the Eastern Bizkaian dialect.[5]

Turning, now, to a more contemporary reference, this time from the mid-twentieth century, Seber Altube wrote the following about his home town of Arrasate (in the Upper Deba Valley), which resembles what we have already seen described above:

> It is well-known that, at the point at which the two territories of Bizkaia and Gipuzkoa come together, there is a vast area that is linguistically Bizkaian, but which administratively forms part of the province named Gipuzkoa. . . . Well, all these thousands of inhabitants, whose own language is pure and solely Bizkaian, prefer to read in Gipuzkoan; they understand it perfectly and most even speak it in an acceptable way. What explains this phenomenon? Simply, that the Diocese of Vitoria-Gasteiz almost always sent priests from Gipuzkoa to the parishes of these towns, but in all this, did so regardless of linguistic areas. . . . Every sermon and all the other religious acts in the churches of Gipuzkoans who spoke Bizkaian were carried out, then, with few exceptions, in the Gipuzkoan dialect, and this was enough for the inhabitants of these areas, as has been remarked, to understand it without any difficulty, to speak it reasonably well, and, most interesting of all, to prefer it in missals, in the Christian Doctrine, and in all kinds of readings.[6]

A noticeable change had then taken place during the twentieth century. Language was no longer, apparently, a characteristic of social status, and lower as well as upper class people now tended to favor the use of Beterri Basque.

The last testimony I will quote here is very recent, and comes from the Fransican friar, Luis Villasante (born in Gernika, Bizkaia), who for many years lived in the Arantzazu Monastery near Oñati in Gipuzkoa, also in the Debagoiena or Upper Deba Valley. Reading these words, we likewise see admiration for Beterri Basque and shame about the local Basque, together with the influence of the Church in spreading the use of Beterri Basque. Yet as well as the Church, Villasante also mentions another key factor encouraging Beterri Basque use: *bertsolaritza* (improvised oral poetry). He writes: "I believe there is another reason behind this complex about bad quality. The expression 'Good Basque, from around Tolosa, from Gipuzkoa' is often used. That is the type of

Basque that is always used in sermons, lectures, and books. And that is what people ask for, even here in Oñati. Basque from over there is taken to be smart and elegant and *bertsolaris* love it as well."[7]

I mentioned Basque from the Deba Valley in the section about Western Basque. The influence of Gipuzkoan Basque in Bergara and Antzuola in the Upper Deba Valley is particularly deep, and is even deeper in Elgoibar, Mendaro, and Mutriku, in the Lower Deba Valley. Nowadays, it would be very difficult to decide if the Basque from the latter three towns is Western or Central Basque. Old Western roots and new Central innovations are combined in the way of speaking there. In the town of Deba itself, furthermore, the influence of Gipuzkoan Basque is even greater.[8]

Gipuzkoan Basque in Northeastern Gipuzkoa

Thus far, I have concentrated on the influence of Gipuzkoan Basque toward the west, but its shadow has also been cast to the east. I will first examine the area between Errenteria and Irun.

The Basque spoken in this area has not always been classified as the same dialect. In 1745, Manuel Larramendi categorized the area as speaking Gipuzkoan[9] although, especially in terms of accent, the proximity of Oiartzun, Hondarribia, and Irun to Lapurdi was very noticeable. In the nineteenth century, Bonaparte classified these same three towns as speaking Navarrese Basque and, furthermore, added Lezo along with them.[10] More recently, and following Mitxelena, Pedro Yrizar included Errenteria in the same group.[11]

However, Bonaparte was correct and astute on this occasion. He was sixty-four years old when he wrote the report *Observations sur le basque de Fontarabie, d'Irun, etc.* (Observations on the Basque of Hondarribia, Irun, etc.) and had been studying Basque for around thirty years. This is what he wrote about the area's Basque:

> The local way of speaking in Irun and Hondarribia, and above all in Lezo, has been severly damaged by Gipuzkoan Basque. The verb forms *dut, duk, dun, duzu, dugu,* and *duzute,* rather than *det, dek, den, dezu, degu,* and *dezute,* the Gipuzkoan forms, are some of the few things to be kept, as well as some highly significant individual words as well: *deus* (not *ezer*), *eldu naiz* or *naz* (not *(ba)nator*), *eldu nitzan* (not *(ba)nentorren*), *iratze* (not *iñastor/garo*). This, for the moment, is the Navarrese Basque that the area has preserved, although this will not be for long.[12]

It is very clear from this passage that Bonaparte himself was also aware of changes taking place in the language, and in the same work he mentions another change in the local way of speaking in Oiartzun. A century earlier, Larramendi heard the future tense forms *jain* (< *janen*) "I will eat," *joain* (< *joanen*) "I will go," *emain* (< *emanen*) "I will give," and *egoin* (< *egonen*) "I will be" in

Oiartzun, whereas Bonaparte only heard the Western and Central Basque forms *jango*, *joango*, *emango*, and *egongo*.

Bearing all of this in mind, one may ask why, with so little reason to include this type of Basque in Navarrese Basque, and taking the direction of the changes taking place into account, Bonaparte included the way of speaking bewteen Lezo and Irun in this dialect. In chapter 3 on Navarrese Basque, I noted that Bonaparte took very few factors into account when he studied it. At the end of the day, his objective was to classify and to draw up a map of the dialects; he did not aim to give exact explanations about Basque as a whole and its dialects. The explanation he gives in his report *Observations sur le formulaire de prône* is very helpful in order to understand how he classified the Basque dialects. Specifically, he distinguished the following five dialects:[13]

1. Gipuzkoan: Uses the verb forms *det*, *dezu*, and so on.
2. Bizkaian: Uses the verb forms *dot*, *dozu*, and so on.
3. Navarrese-Lapurdian: Uses verb forms such as *dut* and *naiz*.
4. Lower Navarrese: Uses verb forms such as *niz* and does not use the personal pronoun *zu*.
5. Navarrese-Zuberoan: Does use the personal pronoun *zu*.

Consequently, he only took three characteristics into account: the root **edun* in present tense verb forms (*-e-*/*-o-*/*-u-*), the root *izan* in present tense verb forms (*-ai-*/*-i-*) and the use or not of the personal pronoun *zu*. Bonaparte's words in an 1884 letter to the Gipuzkoan Jesuit Jose Ignazio Arana are also significant: "In Irun, Lezo, Oiartzun, and the surrounding areas, although the dialect currently used is highly influenced by Gipuzkoan, they say *dut* instead of *det* and, because of this, it must be classified as Northern Navarrese." It is clear, then, that the reason for still classifying the way of speaking Basque between Lezo and Irun as Navarrese Basque was the use of verb forms such as *dut* rather than *det*.

However, Bonaparte included other factors that differentiated the area from Gipuzkoan in his 1877 report:[14] the root *-a-* in *izan* verb forms (*gara*, not *gera*), *-e-* in the third person singular of *izan* (*zen*, not *zan*), the root *-a-* in past tense synthetic verbs (*zakien*, not *zekien*), and *-ki* in verb suffixes (*izaki*, *jakinki*). He also mentioned many different words and variants.

Without wishing to criticize Bonaparte for being mistaken, things are different in the early twenty-first century. Furthermore, several studies have been published about the Basque spoken in the area: specifically, that spoken in Pasaia (Pasajes), Lezo, Oiartzun, and Irun-Hondarribia.[15] Using these studies, together with material I have collected myself, my view is that the characteristics that Bonaparte mentions are not specifically Navarrese features; rather, they are more generally Eastern Basque characteristics. To put it another way, while they are Navarrese characteristics, they are also features of the Basque spoken in the Northern Basque Country; while there have been real Navarrese distinguishing features, they are very few and can be heard less and less frequently; and, since the eighteenth, and especially in the twentieth century, this area became more closely linked with Gipuzkoa as a whole, so, as one might imagine, this has also had a linguistic influence.

Similarly, in the same way I discussed Baztan in the previous chapter, in this chapter I will examine the forces at work in the Errenteria-Irun area as an example of the Basque spoken here. More specifically, I will look at Navarrese and Gipuzkoan influences as well as Eastern and Central Basque influences. Let us begin with influences from Navarrese:

- A *y-* is used in the second person singular throughout the area: *yaiz* instead of *haiz* in Unified Basque ("you are" in *hika*). However, this is being lost among younger people.
- From Oiartzun eastward, apheresis (*ikusi* "to see" → *kúxi*) and syncope (*abisatu* "to warn" → *abístu*) are common.
- The pluralizing *-it-* was used in absolutive-dative-ergative verb forms (*nittion* rather than *nizkion* in Unified Basque) but nowadays this is only common in Hondarribia, and it is also falling into disuse among younger people there.[16]
- The Navarrese tendency to put *g-* before the vowel group *oa-* is only to be found in Irun and Hondarriba in the verb form *gua* instead of *hoa* ("you are going" in *hitano*) and; furthermore, the variant *ua* is also used there.

Let us now turn to tendencies originating from Eastern Basque, in other words from Navarre and the Northern Basque Country:

- In Hondarribia and Irun, ascending diphthongs are common: *a.rran.tzá.lja* to pronounce *arrantzalea* ("fisherman"), *sé.mja* for *semea* ("son"), *al.go.dóis.kwa* for *kotoizkoa* ("[of] cotton"), and *bár.kwa* for *barkoa* ("boat," or *itsasontzia* in Unified Basque).
- A *-u-* is the root from **edun* throughout the whole area: *dut*.
- The root *-e-* is used in the third person singular of *izan* throughout the area: *den*, *dela*, and so on. However, *-a-* is also used in Errenteria.
- The verb suffix *-ki* is used in Irun and Hondarribia: *deus izáki ez, ta emán in bjartzén* to render *deus izan ez, eta eman egin behar zen* "we had nothing, but we had to give it our all."[17] This was once used in Oiartzun as well, but nowadays *izaki* is the only form of this frequently used there.

From Oiartzun eastward, the variant *-(e)larik* is sometimes used in clauses of time and manner: *gu ttikiyak giñalaik beti amairjin belarra izate genun* to render *gu txikiak ginelarik beti amabirjina belarra izaten genuen* "when we were young, we always used to use tutsan (a plant used to cure minor cuts and grazes)."[18] However, the Western and Central Basque form *-(e)la* is more typical, particularly among younger people.

From Oiartzun eastward, the suffix *bait-* is also used in relative clauses: *or nola da beste bat, arotzeya baitu* to render *hor nola da beste bat, aroztegia duena* "there's another one, the one that has a carpenter's shop."[19] This is falling into disuse among younger people.

In Irun and Hondarribia, the suffix *-(e)n* has been used with verbs expressing belief in subordinate clauses: *estut uste itxiak iñak diren* to render *ez dut uste etxeak eginak diren* "I don't think the houses are ready."[20] This, too, is falling into disuse among younger people.

There is also vocabulary that connects the area to Eastern Basque: *aieka* instead of *alderdia* in Unified Basque ("side"), *altxatu* instead of *gorde* ("to put away"), *arrastelu* instead of *eskuarea* ("rake"), *heldu da* instead of *dator* ("he/she/it is coming"), *hurbil* instead of *gertu* ("close" or "nearby"), *iratze* (not *irastor/garoa*, for "fern"), *kukuso* instead of *arkakusoa* ("flea"), *pizar* instead of *apurra* ("crumb"), *tenore* instead of *sasoia* ("season" or "time"), and so on. The following are also in use in Irun and Hondarribia: *andana* instead of *mordoa* ("bunch" or "bundle"), *atxiki* (> *itxeki*) instead of *heldu* ("to arrive"), *atzaman* instead of *harrapatu* ("to catch"), *aztal* instead of *berna* ("leg [from the knee to the ankle]"), *ebatsi* (> *ibatzi*) instead of *lapurtu* ("to steal"), *galdetu* instead of *eskatu* ("to ask [for])," *iduri du* instead of *dirudi* ("he/she/it appears/looks like"), and *txilko* instead of *zilborra* ("navel").

Lastly, the following variants in Irun and Hondarribia should be mentioned: *aipatu* (not *aitatu* "to mention"), *borroka* (not *burruka* "fight"), *elkar* (not *alkar* "each other" or "one another"), *iguzki* instead of *eguzki* ("sun"), and *kider* instead of *kirten* ("handle"). Throughout the area, *biño(n)/miño(n)* is used instead of *baina* ("but" or "although").

After examining the influences from Navarrese and Eastern Basque, let us now look at influences from other areas. First of all, influences from Gizpukoan which have reached the Errenteria-Irun area are:

- In verb forms in absolutive-ergative, *-au-* → *-a-* takes place throughout the area: *nauk* → *nak*, *nauzu* → *nazu*, *nauzute* instead of *nauzue* → *nazute*.
- The pronunciation [*x*] at the start of words now predominates throughout the area: *jan* (not *yan* "to eat").
- The root *-e-* in *izan* plural verb forms now also predominates in most of the area except for Oiartzun: *gera* ("we are"), *zera* ("you are" in singular), *zerate* ("you are" in plural), and so on.
- The *joan* verb forms *nijua* instead of *noa* in Unified Basque ("I am

going"), *dijua* instead of *doa* ("he/she/it is going"), *dijuazte* instead of *doaz* ("they are going"), *nijuan* instead of *nindoan* ("I was going"), *zijuan* instead of *zihoan* ("he/she/it was going"), and *zijuazten* instead of *zihoazen* ("they were going") are now used throughout the area.

Except for Hondarribia, the interrogative particle *al* has gained strength thoughout the area: for example, *ez al dakizu nun den?* "don't you know where he/she/it is?"

As in Gipuzkoan, there is a considerable *e* → *a* tendency before fast vibrant syllables. In Oiartzun, for instance, *baserritar* → *basarritar* ("farmer"), *eder* → *ear* ("beautiful"), *eguberriak* → *eguarriyak* ("Christmas season"), *eguerdi* → *eguardi* ("midday"), *izerdi* → *izardi* ("to sweat"), *izter* → *ixtar* ("thigh"), and *pitxer* → *pitxar* ("pitcher" or "jar").

There are also words from Gipuzkoan in use: *attona* and *amona* (not *aitatxi/amatxi* "grandfather/grandmother"), *eskumuinak* (> *eskumiñak*) instead of *goraintziak* ("regards" or "best wishes"), *esnatu* instead of *iratzarri* ("to wake up"), *isats* instead of *buztana* ("tail"), *korrika* instead of *lasterka* ("running"), *mami* instead of *gaztanbera* ("curds"), *mingain* instead of *mihia* ("tongue"), *neskame* (not *neskato* "maid"), *triku* instead of *sagarroia* ("hedgehog"), *txukun* instead of *aratza* ("clean"), and *zein* instead of *nor* ("who").

There are also Gipuzkoan variants: *apaiz* (not *apez* "priest"), *bixki* instead of *biki* ("twin"), *eskubi* (not *eskuin* "right"), *igo/iyo* (not *igan* "to go up"), *osin* instead of *asun* ("nettle"), *pake* instead of *bake* ("peace"), *parra/farra* instead of *barre* ("laugh"), *txingurri* instead of *inurri* ("ant"), and so on.

And, lastly, let us look at the many innovations from Gipuzkoa, Araba, and Bizkaia that have reached the Errenteria-Irun area. They are significant and can be used in order to classify the way of speaking used in the area:

As in Western and Central Basque, spoken emphasis changes many words' meanings. Koldo Mitxelena, for example, records *basúa* for *basoa* or *oihana* ("forest") and *básua* from the Spanish *vaso* instead of *edalontzia* ("glass"), *eltzía* instead of *eltzea* or *lapikoa* ("cooking pot"), and *éltzia* instead of *heltzea* ("arrival" or "seize"), *iltzía* instead of *iltzea* ("nail"), and *íltzia* instead of *hiltzea* ("death") in Errenteria.[21]

The consonant group *-st-* is used, not *-rtz-* as in Navarrese: *beste* ("other"), *bost* ("five"), *heste* ("intestine"), *ostegun* ("Thursday"), and so on.

Adverbs are undefined or partitive, but not in the singular absolutive case: *justu-justu heldu da* ("he/she/it just arrived," not *justu-justua*).

In distributive quantifiers, the suffix *-na* is used, not *-ra*: *seina* ("six each," not *seira*).

Foreign loanwords ending in *-on* become *–oi*, not *-ona* or *-oina*: *meloi* ("melon," not *melona/meloina*).

The future suffix *-go* is used, not *-en*: *egingo* ("will do," not *eginen*).

The suffix *-(e)nik* is common in subordinate clauses, *-(e)la* is not always necessarily used: *nik enekin itzik ere fan bartzuenik* instead of *nik ez nekien hitzik ere joan behar zuenik* "I didn't even hear that he had to go" in Unified Basque.[22]

The structure 'verb + *eta*' is also common in clauses expressing cause. This example is from Oiartzun: *beandu torri da, etxea jun bertzun ta* instead of *berandu etorri da, etxera joan behar zuen eta* "he/she was late because he/she had to go home."

The use of the reinforcing verb *egin* is a rule; *beandu, biño torri in da* instead of *berandu, baina etorri egin da* "he/she was late, but he/she made sure to come" is an example from Oiartzun.

Much of the vocabulary used in the area is from the Western and Central Basque dialects: *agindu* instead of *manatu* ("to order"), *alkandora* instead of *atorra* ("shirt"), *arotz* instead of *zurgin* ("carpenter"), *asko* instead of *anitz* ("a lot (of)"), *aukeratu* instead of *hautatu* ("to choose"), *aurre* and *atze* rather than *aitzin/gibel* ("front/behind"), *azkar* meaning *laster* ("soon") rather than meaning *indartsua* ("strong"), *barru* instead of *barne* ("inside"), and *baserritar* rather than *nekazari* or *laborari* ("farmer"), together with words such as *bertan* ("right there"), *bertatik* ("from right there"), *bertako* ("from there") and not *berean, beretik, bereko*, and so on, *bi* ("two") is always used rather than *bi* and/or *biga*, *bidali* rather than *igorri* ("to send"), *doministiko* instead of *atija* or *usin* ("sneeze"), *eskerrak!* rather than *beharrik!* ("thank God!"), *eskerrik asko* and not *mila esker/esker mila* ("thank you"), the demonstratives *honuntz* ("toward here" or "in this direction"), *horruntz* ("toward there" or "in that direction," in the sense of farther away), and *haruntz* ("toward there" or "in that direction," in the sense of farther away still) instead of *honata, honara*, and so on, *hirurogei* ("sixty") and *laurogei* ("eighty") rather than *hiruetan hogei* or *lauetan hogei*, *kale* instead of *karrika* ("street"), *kanpana* instead of *ezkila* ("bell"), *laster* and not *sarri* ("immediately"), *morroi* instead of *mutil* ("boy"), *ohe* instead of *goatze* ("bed"), *parra/farra* rather than *irri* ("snigger"), *saguzar* and not *gauenara* ("bat"), and *trumoi* instead of *ortots* ("thunder"). Some other words also coincide with the words used in Western and Central Basque: for example, *igurtzi* ("to rub") and *malko* ("tear" or "teardrop").

In variants, too, Western and Central Basque often coincide: *ahaztu* ("to forget," although in Hondarriba port *ahantzi* is also used), *belarri* rather than *beharri* or *begarri* ("ear"), *bildur* instead of *beldur* ("fear"), *bultzatu* and not *bulkatu* ("to push" or "to promote"), *esan* rather than *erran* ("to say"), *gutxi* rather than *guti* or *gutti* ("little" or "few"), *hamaika* instead of *hameka* ("eleven"), *ikuttu* and not *ukittu* ("to touch"), *itxi* rather than *hetsi* or *hertsi* ("to close"), *izu* instead of *izi* ("terror" or "panic"), *jantzi* ("to put on" or "to wear") and *erantzi* ("to take off") instead of *jauntzi/erauntzi*, *orain* rather than *orai* or *guai* ("now"), and so on.

In short, I have included the Basque of Oiartzun and, above all, Hondarribia and Irun as intermediary ways of speaking and, as well as being connected with Central and Navarrese Basque, they are also linked to the Navarrese-Lapurdian dialect. Lezo and Errenteria, on the other hand, have almost become part of the Central Basque dialect. That said, the Gaintxuirzketa district, which is part of Lezo and next to Hondarribia, still keeps Eastern characteristics as a result of its close relationship with Hondarribia and with Irun.

In Irun and Hondarribia, in fact, the influence of Central Basque has not been decisive, and they have more successfully preserved their old local way of speaking. There are several reasons for this. Irun has long been an important market center in its own right and has not always looked toward Donostia and Gipuzkoa in general. Furthermore, people from the neighboring towns in Navarre and Lapurdi use it as a meeting point, as well as a market place, medical, and leisure center, and many people from the Bortziriak and Malerreka in Navarre also moved to Irun to live and work there. Because of the influence of people who moved there from Navarre, Eastern characteristics have been better preserved.

I have mentioned the specific nature of Basque in Irun and Hondarribia, and this can also be seen in various linguistic features.

In Irun and Hondarribia, the dative case of the plural is formed using the suffix *-akeri* (*txoru oyekeri* instead of *zoro horiei* "[to] those crazy people"), the genitive plural is formed using the suffix *-aken* (*Portuarraken Asoziaziyua* instead of *Portuarren Asoziazioa* "Port Association"), and the *norentzat* (benefactive, "for [whom]") plural case is formed using the suffix *-akentzat* (*gizonakentzat* instead of *gizonentzat* "for the men"). This has also spread to the Bortziriak.

Between Lezo and Irun, absolutive-ergative verbs are used rather than absolutive-dative-ergative ones: *esan nau*, not *esan dit* ("[someone] told me"). This can also be found in southwestern Lapurdi and probably originated there. In fact, though, this has become more common in this area of Gipuzkoa, and absolutive-dative category verbs are also used instead of absolutive-ergative and absolutive-dative-ergative ones: *gustatu nau*, not *gustatu zait* ("I liked it") and *gustatu dio*, not *gustatu zaio* ("he/she liked it").

In Irun and Hondarribia, habit is expressed using the suffix *-ketu*: *ibiliketu da* instead of *ibili ohi da* ("he/she usually walks"), and *parte hartuketu dute* instead of *parte hartu ohi dute* ("they usually take part"). This has also spread to the Bortziriak and Malerreka.

To sum up, I would highlight two main consequences: firstly, when people in the Southern Basque Country hear the words *erran* ("to say") and *deus* ("nothing"), they think of Navarrese Basque, but those who understand the wider picture of the Basque language know that *erran* and *deus* are also used in the Northern Basque Country, as well as in Navarre. One should therefore conclude that these characteristics are more generally "Eastern" rather than specifically "Navarrese." Indeed, it is this kind of misunderstanding that led to this way of speaking being originally categorized as Navarrese Basque.

Secondly, it is clear that the Irun-Errenteria model has taken from both Eastern and from Central Basque, although things have changed over recent years, particularly since 1960. In the movements between the dialects, Central Basque has gained in strength, and the Eastern dialects have weakened.

From 1926 to 1935, for example, Gerhard Bähr published verb forms he had collected, including those of Errenteria. In this collection, we see the competition between the two roots: namely, *dut* and *det* appear simultaneously. Around half a century later, Pedro Irizar asked Koldo Mitxelena the reason for this, describing the situation thus:

> Bähr made a note of the *dut* and *det* forms as being used indiscriminately in Errenteria. I asked Professor Mitxelena his opinion on the use of these forms in his hometown. He replied: "For me the forms are *dut*, etc. As regards *det*, the difference is gender more than anything else. I have never heard a woman [say it] ever. When I was young, the children of both sexes began with *dut*, and later moved on to *det*, in a somewhat solemn way, influenced by adult males. I get the impression that the contracted forms are still said, even by men, *eitteut*, *-euk*, *-euzu*, etc.[23]

Mitxelena's answer is significant. On the one hand, it was gender that determined whether to use one root or the other; it seems that the Gipuzkoan root *-e-* only appeared in men's speech. On the other, it was also used in educated speech; the root *-u-* seems to have been predominant between friends.

Mitxelena saw that people used to choose between Central Basque and educated Eastern Basque characteristics depending on whether they were with friends or not. On seeing the way the nineteenth-century *bertsolari* Xenpelar used the language, he wrote: "Xenpelar was from Errenteria and from the Oiartzun side of Errenteria: in compositions he used *det*, *zan*, and *zebillen* instead of the *dut*, *zen*, and *zabillen* used among his friends."[24]

In the past, then, what one was doing – and even one's gender – determined the use of Central or Eastern Basque characteristics, but those nuances have long been lost. The language has become more homogeneous, and Central Basque characteristics have become more widely used at the same time. The following testimony confirms this.

In the mid-twentieth century, Mitxelena was the first observer to record that verb forms such as *dan* and *zan* were being more widely used and forms such as *den* and *zen* less so: "I had always thought . . . that the blend of High Navarrese and Gipuzkoan that could be observed in the speech of Errenteria was explained by a continual diffusion of Gipuzkoan forms onto the primitive

Navarrese base. This is undoubtedly true today: e.g., *den* and *zen* tend to be relaced by *dan* and *zan*."[25]

Koldo Artola later spoke about the plural forms in the absolutive-dative-ergative case. According to data from Irun, the Navarrese form *-it-* was losing ground and the Gipuzkoan form *-zki-* was gaining in strength:

> His mother and father used forms such as *nittion* and *zittion* and, when he was young, Basque was almost the only language used in Lapitze [a neighborhood of Irun] and, in general, in the whole of Irun, and his family was very typical in this respect. He says that these same forms are used in Pausua [also known as Behobia, a neighborhood of both Irun in Gipuzkpoa and Urruña in Lapurdi] nowadays. At present, however, forms such as *nizkion*, *zizkion*, and other such Gipuzkoan verb forms are used in many districts of Irun, and these forms were introduced by schools, television, and other media.[26]

Naturally, the changes that Mitxelena and Artola mentioned were not the only ones taking place in the area. For instance, the suffixes *-kotz*, *-(e)lakotz*, and *-tekotz* are heard less and less, and *-ko*, *-(e)lako*, and *-teko* now predominate among young people: *ekarri duelako* ("because he/she/it has brought [it]"), not *duelakotz*. The same is true for clauses of time and manner: the Eastern form *-(e)larik* is not unknown (*gu gaztiak giñelik hiltzen ama* "mom died when we were young"), but Western and Central Basque forms are now more usual *-(e)la* and *-(e)nean* (*gaztiak giñela/gaztiak giñenian* "when we were young").

This competition can also be seen in the vocabulary used. The following are pairs (and trios) of words used in Irun and Hondarribia:[27] *ahate/piro* (general/Lapurdian variants of "duck"), *antzeko/iduri* ("similar"), *behera/beheiti* ("down" or "downward"), *gora/goiti* ("up" or "upward"), *ezer/deus* ("nothing"), *gogoratu/oroitu* ("to remember"), *jela/horma* and *izotz* in general ("ice"), *kare/kisu* ("lime"), *lehor/idor* ("dry") and *xukatu* ("to dry"), *nahikoa/aski* ("enough"), *ondo/ongi* ("well" or "good"), *hobeto/ho[be]kiyo* ("better"), *oso/arront* ("very" or "completely") and *txoil* ("very" or "totally"), and *ukuilu/eia* ("stable").

In summary, young people's tendencies should be very much taken into account because they indicate future trends. In traditional Basque dialectology, however, this has not been taken into consideration very much, and more work has been done to collect and study the way older speakers use the language. To put it bluntly, there has been more "archeology" than "dialectology" in the Basque Country. Naturally, if a study's objective is to restart a process of transmission that has stalled and to develop and strengthen a language, then taking older speakers into account is indispensable; but if the objective is to classify certain ways of speaking as part of one dialect or another, then speakers from all age groups must be taken into account, including young people, obviously.

Gipuzkoan Basque in Western Navarre

Language development in western Navarre has been similar to that in the Errenteria-Irun area of Gipuzkoa, and the influence of Gipuzkoan Basque is obvious there as well. Here I will not explore the language characteristics one by one, as I did above, because they are similar to those of the Errenteria-Irun area. Instead, I will just cite the testimonies of Basque speakers and scholars of the speech in this area in order to gain some idea about the way Basque is spoken in the area.

The Navarrese writer Arturo Campión, for example, long ago realized that Gipuzkoan Basque had moved beyond the Errenteria-Irun area and into Navarre (especially to the Bortziriak, Araitz, and Burunda areas). He wrote about this, assisted by Pierre Broussain, stating that this dialect had a gift for creating a unified form of Basque: "Invasory traits can be distinguished in it; it is ousting Northern High Navarrese from the towns of Gipuzkoa in which it was spoken and interstitially infiltrating Navarre through the area of the Bortziriak and the Araitz and Burunda Valleys."[28]

Pedro Irizar, on the other hand, when studying the use of verb forms in Navarre, saw competition between Navarrese and Gipuzkoan verb forms in Azpirotz, a village in the Larraun area of Navarre, and recorded one of his collaborator's explanations: "This collaborator is not consistent in verbal inflections and thinks that there are perhaps two levels, one that has been used by the previous generation and another influenced quite strongly by Tolosa [Gipuzkoa], which currently and due to the ease of [access to] the media, has been able to influence these people for whom the best Basque is that of Tolosa."[29]

Errazkin is next to Azpirotz, and one collaborator from there admitted similarly that he had always admired the Basque of Tolosa in an interview with Mikel Olano: "I've always liked Basque from Tolosa! I've always envied it! What's more, who can speak the way they do? You have to come from there . . . You have to be from there to speak like that, originate from there!"[30]

Rodolfo Bozas Urrutia compiled a dictionary in the mid-1960s in Arano (Navarre), and observed the following about the local way of speaking there:

> The Basque of Arano, as everyone knows, is included in the Northern High Navarrese dialect. But it is quite different from the other villages in Basaburua, such as Leitza, Goizueta, etc., and suffers a Gipuzkoan influence. The relations between this village – and also between Goizueta – and Hernani and Donostia [in Gipuzkoa] are very close. In contrast, they are practically inexistent with the rest of Navarre, except in official matters, whether civil or religious.[31]

Koldo Artola reached the same conclusion in his study of Basque in Arano: "It seems that in many things the Basque spoken in Arano is connected to that of the Urumea Valley, Astigarraga, Hernani, Ereñotzu, etc."[32]

As well as these opinions, now we also have access to precise explanations of why these transformations are taking place thanks to the studies of Juan Joxe Zubiri and Mikel Olano on the form of Basque in, respectively, Arano and Goizueta, and Areso and Leitza.[33] Furthermore, Amaia Apalauza and Kontxi Arraztio have studied the names for agricultural implements in Araitz-Betelu.[34] And Apalauza also examines the most significant characteristics in the same area.[35] A cursory glance at the names given to those implements in this latter area reveals the extent to which the influence of Gipuzkoan Basque has spread: to Araitz-Betelu and most of western Larraun, to a lesser extent to western Basabura and eastern Larraun, and even less so to eastern Basaburua and Imotz. However, one person from Oskotz did not hide his enthusiasm for the Basque of Tolosa. When the researcher Orreaga Ibarra told him that she wanted to study his way of speaking, this was his astonished reply: "You should go to Tolosa and speak with somebody from there; they have a beautiful accent and everybody understands them."[36]

The influence of Gipuzkoan Basque can also be found in Bortziriak, Malerreka, and Sakana. Further inland too, Ibarra quotes something heard in Ultzama: "Basque from Tolosa is beautiful Basque: ours is rougher, we say *erran* and they say *esan*."[37]

A Few General Observations

I will now turn to a few of the factors behind the increasing influence of Beterri Basque in general. One clear and often mentioned influence is that of the Church. Likewise, *bertsolaritza* (improvised oral poetry) has also been mentioned, and it, too, has been important in this case. Literature, however, has not yet been mentioned although it has had a significant role in the process. Frantzisko Ignazio Lardizabal, for example, is often taken to be one of the best Gipuzkoan writers. Although he was from Zaldibia (in the Goierri area of Gipuzkoa), he wrote in Beterri and not Goierri Basque, as did another writer from the same town, Joan Ignazio Iztueta. Moreover, as noted, the writer Joan Antonio Mogel, born in Eibar (Gipuzkoa) but long resident in Markina (Bizkaia), also chose Beterri Basque to write his first book, in 1800, and might well have continued to do so had his decision not provoked such a commotion in Bizkaia at that time. Yet later Bizkaian writers still continued to use Beterri Basque, such as Txomin Agirre in the novel *Garoa* (The fern, 1912), published in the early twentieth century.

The development of Basque-language literature in the Southern Basque

Country started in the mid-eighteenth century. Basque as a written language was reignited at that time, and Gipuzkoan served as the bellows in fanning the flames of this reignition. Indeed, ever since then, Gipuzkoan has been the de facto driving force among the different forms of Basque and, because of this, a kind of model for the other dialects. And echoes of its leadership in this regard are to be found in the regions and dialects around it.

Linguistic norms are usually created when literature comes into existence. When writing starts to be used in a language, doubts and difficulties appear, and grammars and dictionaries are written to try to solve those problems. These are then used depending on how helpful they are, and they are influential to the extent to which they are used. In the Basque Country, Manuel Larramendi was for a long time the main reference in this sense. He published the first Basque grammar in 1729 and the first dictionary in 1745. They were very widely used throughout society and became highly successful. As well as Central Basque, this also helped to homogenize Basque itself.

Along with other unifying forces, the Beterri area (based around Tolosa, Andoain, Hernani, and Donostia) has often been mentioned. Its influence is obvious in the surrounding areas and also in the nearby areas of Navarre and has also reached the Urolaldea area of Gipuzkoa, particularly Zumaia, Errezil (Régil), and Beizama.

However, the structure of Gipuzkoa itself must be taken into account. It does not have a single urban center, like Maule and Atharratze in Zuberoa, or Iruñea in Navarre, Vitoria-Gasteiz in Araba, and Bilbao in Bizkaia. Its structure is based on multiple urban centers, often comprising a series of towns: Irun-Hondarribia, Lezo-Errenteria-Pasaia, Donostia itself, Hernani-Andoain, Tolosa, Beasain-Ordizia, Urretxu-Zumarraga-Legazpi, Azkoitia-Azpeitia, Arrasate, and Bergara-Eibar-Elgoibar have been the most significant centers, and they have in turn influenced the areas around them in structure and in ways of speaking. This structure also explains why there are so many different ways of speaking in Gipuzkoa and why there are so few features common to the whole dialect. Nowadays, however, there is a more established network that includes all of these centers and this has led to linguistic homogenization. This network has also helped to extend Unified Basque and make it widely accepted.

Central Area Sub-Dialects

Central Basque is not, then, a completely homogeneous dialect. However, the core of both this dialect and its main sub-dialect is Beterri Basque.[38]

I noted above that this is the dialect spoken in the Basaburua, Imotz, Larraun, and Araitz-Betelu Valleys in Navarre. Specifically, the Larraun towns

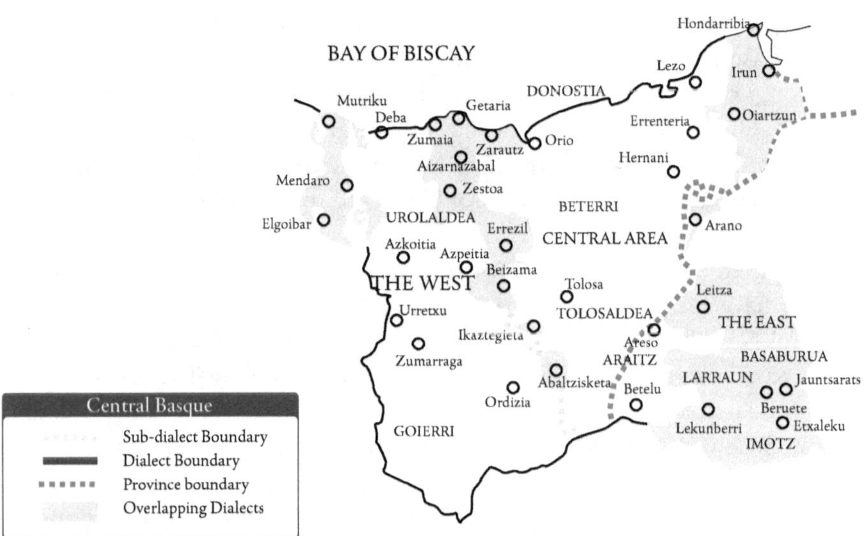

BAY OF BISCAY
Hondarribia
Lezo
Irun
DONOSTIA
Mutriku
Getaria
Deba
Oiartzun
Errenteria
Zumaia
Zarautz
Orio
Aizarnazabal
Hernani
Mendaro
Zestoa
BETERRI
Elgoibar
UROLALDEA
Errezil
Arano
CENTRAL AREA
Azkoitia
Azpeitia
Beizama
THE WEST
Tolosa
Leitza
Urretxu
TOLOSALDEA
THE EAST
Ikaztegieta
Areso
Zumarraga
ARAITZ
BASABURUA
Abaltzisketa
LARRAUN
Jauntsarats
Betelu
Ordizia
Beruete
Lekunberri
Etxaleku
GOIERRI
IMOTZ
Central Basque
Sub-dialect Boundary
Dialect Boundary
Province boundary
Overlapping Dialects

in the Araitz-Betelu and Azpirotz Valleys (Errazkin, Gorriti, Azpirotz, and Uitzi) have close ties with Tolosa and their local way of speaking is similar to that of Tolosa. To the east, the Beterri influence lessens, and, while the language there has been linked to Central Basque, that connection has long been lost and its Navarrese character is now more pronounced. It is an intermediate local way of speaking; in other words, it links Central and Navarrese Basque. I term this the Eastern sub-dialect of Central Basque and include three towns in northeastern Gipuzkoa in this way of speaking: Oiartzun, Hondarribia, and Irun.

There is a third local way of speaking, made up of the language spoken in two areas of Gipuzkoa: the Goierri and Urolaldea. The way of speaking is different in these two areas, but I have included them in the same sub-dialect: Western Central Basque.

Basque from the Goierri has a very marked character; it is highly homogeneous, although there are differences from west to east: between Segura, Zegama, and Legazpi on the one hand and Zaldibia and Legorreta on the other, for example.

The towns of Ordizia and, since the twentieth century, Beasain have been the principal meeting places in the Goierri. The area has its own very distinct personality. It has not looked exclusively to Beterri Basque, and has historically borrowed from the Basque of both Navarre and Araba. The road over the Lizarrusti Pass from the Goierri into Navarre is an ancient trade route, as are those over the Etxegarate Pass and through the San Adrian tunnel (formerly the Lizarrate Pass) into Araba. The latter two have been highly significant, especially since the thirteenth century, being the road between Araba and the Gipuzkoan coast. Because of its location, then, a distinctive way of speaking developed in the Goierri.[39] However, the Basque spoken in the Goierri is not completely distinct from other ways of speaking in Gipuzkoa. That of Abaltzisketa and Ikaztegieta, for example, links it to the Tolosa area, while that of Urretxu and Zumarraga links the Goierri and Urolaldea.[40]

Basque in Urolaldea is not as homogeneous nor is it so markedly different. Here, furthermore, influence from Beterri Basque has been deeper and nowadays, at least, the transition from one area to another is unnoticeable. At present there is an intermediate way of speaking in Zarautz, Getaria, Zumaia, Aizarnazabal, Zestoa, Errezil, and Beizama; or, to put it another way, Azkoitia and Azpeitia are the towns with the most differentiated local way of speaking in Urolaldea. Furthermore, this intermediate group now includes Itziar and Deba in the Debarrena area.[41]

These Western sub-dialects are marked by two main charcteristics. On the one hand, they display several features of Western Basque while on the other, some innovations from Central Basque have not taken root among them. In the Goierri, furthermore, its enduring and close relationship with Araba has also left a trace on the Basque spoken there. I will now consider some examples in order to illustrate this:

> When the article is added to words ending in *-a, -a + a → -ea (> -ia, -ie): patata + a → patatea/patatia/patatie* ("potato").
> The suffix *-rik* is used in expressions, such as *etxerik etxe* ("from house to house").

The *egin* root is used in the potential: *daiket* instead of *dezaket* in Unified Basque ("I can"), *daikezu* instead of *dezakezu* ("you can"), and so on. It is also used in absolutive-dative-ergative subjunctives and imperatives, but this is also used in a wider area; namely, in the whole of Gipuzkoa and in the Sakana area of Navarre, at least, there are verb forms such as *botaiozu* instead of *bota iezaiozu* ("throw it to him/her"), and *kendu deiola* instead of *ken diezaiola* ("let him/her take it away").

The *-au* suffix is used in participles and, furthermore, more commonly than in Western Basque. Unlike in Western Basque, in the Goierri it is used in old loanwords and in Basque verbs: for example, *aukerau* instead of *aukeratu* ("to choose"), *barkau* instead of *barkatu* ("to forgive"), *bukau* instead of *bukatu* ("to finish"), *eskau* instead of *eskatu* ("to ask for"), *gerau* instead of *geratu* ("to stop" or "to remain"), *ingurau* instead of *inguratu* ("to surround" or "to go around"), *jokau* instead of *jokatu* ("to play" or "to gamble"), and *nazkau* instead of *nazkatu* ("to loathe").

The transitive use of the verbs *irten* and *igo* are intransitive in Unified Basque: for example, *erten degu* instead of *irten gara* ("we have left") and *igo degu* instead of *igo gara* ("we have gone up"). In Urolaldea, the verb *jardun* is used and that, too, is transitive: *jardun degu* ("we have spoken").

-(e)na is used in subordinate clauses. This example is from Zaldibia:[42] *nik antzeman nion ilko zana* "I guessed that he would die."

The linking word is *ala* in interrogative clauses. This example is also from Zaldibia:[43] *gaztiñea ugarie izango zan, ala?* or *gaztaina ugaria izango zen, ezta?* (in Unified Basque) "there would have been a lot of chestnuts, right?"

The connection is also seen in vocabulary: *albo* instead of *aldamena* ("side"), *astun* instead of *pisua* ("weight"), *irten/erten* instead of *atera* ("to leave" or "to go out"), *izara* instead of *maindirea* ("bedsheet"), *lain* instead of *beste* or *adina* ("as much as" or "as many as"), *lapiko* instead of *eltzea* ("pot" or "stewpot") and *itsulapiko eltzeitsua* ("piggy-bank"), *praka* instead of *galtza* ("pants"), *sarri* instead of *maiz* ("often"), *zapatu* instead of *larunbata* ("Saturday"), and so on. These words are also used in the Goierri: *indaba* instead of *babarruna* ("bean"), and *pits* instead of *aparra* ("foam" or "froth").

Western variants are similarly used in some forms of speech: *alkondara* instead of *alkandora* ("shirt"), *ete* instead of *ote* (the interrogative particle, meaning "perhaps?" or "by any chance?"), *gaztai* instead of *gazta* ("cheese"), *keiza/keixa* instead of *gerezia* ("cherry"), *narru* instead of *larru* ("skin" or "leather"), *txixa* instead of *pixa* ("pee"), and so on.

Western Basque's influence is greater in Urolaldea than in the Goierri. Because it is a flatter area allowing easier communications and, above all, because of the industry in the Eibar-Elgoibar agglomoration, the relationship has been closer and more frequent. In the Goierri, however, the connection with Western Basque declined over time because of the disappearance of Basque in Araba. In 1921, Gerhard Bähr from Legazpi wrote the following to the linguist Hugo Schuchardt: "On a recent excursion to the coast, between Ondarroa and Zarautz, I had a number of opportunities to make observations. I was especially able to verify that Bizkaian and Gipuzkoan, which here in Legazpi and Oñati are very clearly separate from each other, are merging into one another."[44]

The connection can most clearly be seen in vocabulary. Agurtzane Azpeitia, for example, heard the following Western Basque words in Zestoa (Gipuzkoa): *abade* instead of *apaiza* ("priest"), *abarketa* instead of *espartina* ("espadrille"), *adur* instead of *lerdea* ("drool" or "spittle"), *aitita* and *amama* instead of *aitona/amona* ("grandfather/grandmother"), *izeko* instead of *izeba* ("aunt"), *katamuxar* instead of *katagorria* ("squirrel"), *kerizpe* instead of *itzala* ("shade"), *okela* instead of *haragia* ("meat"), *osterantzian* instead of *bestela* ("otherwise" or "or else"), *puxika* instead of *maskuria* ("bladder"), and *zarata* instead of *hotsa* ("sound" or "noise").[45]

As well as in vocabulary, the influence of Western Basque can also be seen in the following features of the language as used in Urolaldea:

Neuk is the emphatic personal pronoun ("I myself"); but *neronek* and so on are also used in eastern Urolaldea.

In clauses expressing cause and purpose, the suffix *-tearren* is used in some areas; *jendiak ez ikustiarren, gauez ibiltze[n] zan* ("he moved around at night so people couldn't see him") was recorded in Zestoa.

In the Azkoitia-Azpeitia area in particular, *-iu* is used in participles, and, unlike in Western Basque, this also appears in Basque verb forms: *garbiu* instead of *garbitu* in Unified Basque ("to clean"), *geldiu* instead of *gelditu* ("to stop" or "to remain"), *txikiu* instead of *txikitu* ("to chop up" or "to break"), and so on.

However, some of these Western characteristics have weakened and are used less among younger people, for instance the subordinate *-(e)na*, and placing the quantifier *bi* ("two") to the right of nouns. With regard to the latter, Azpeitia records these examples from an elderly speaker in Zestoa: *atta batenak eta ama birenak eo orrela zian* ("they had the same father and two different

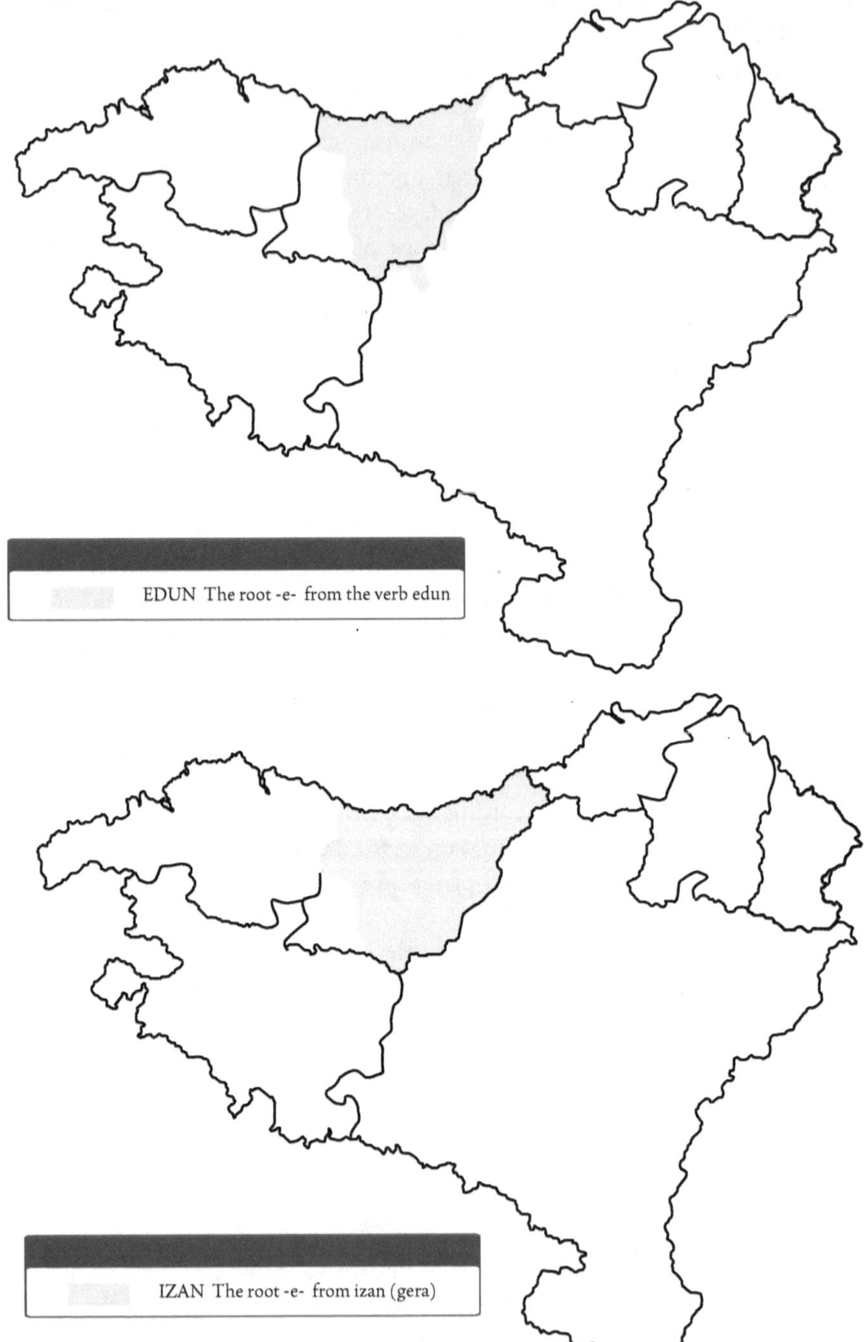
EDUN The root -e- from the verb edun
IZAN The root -e- from izan (gera)

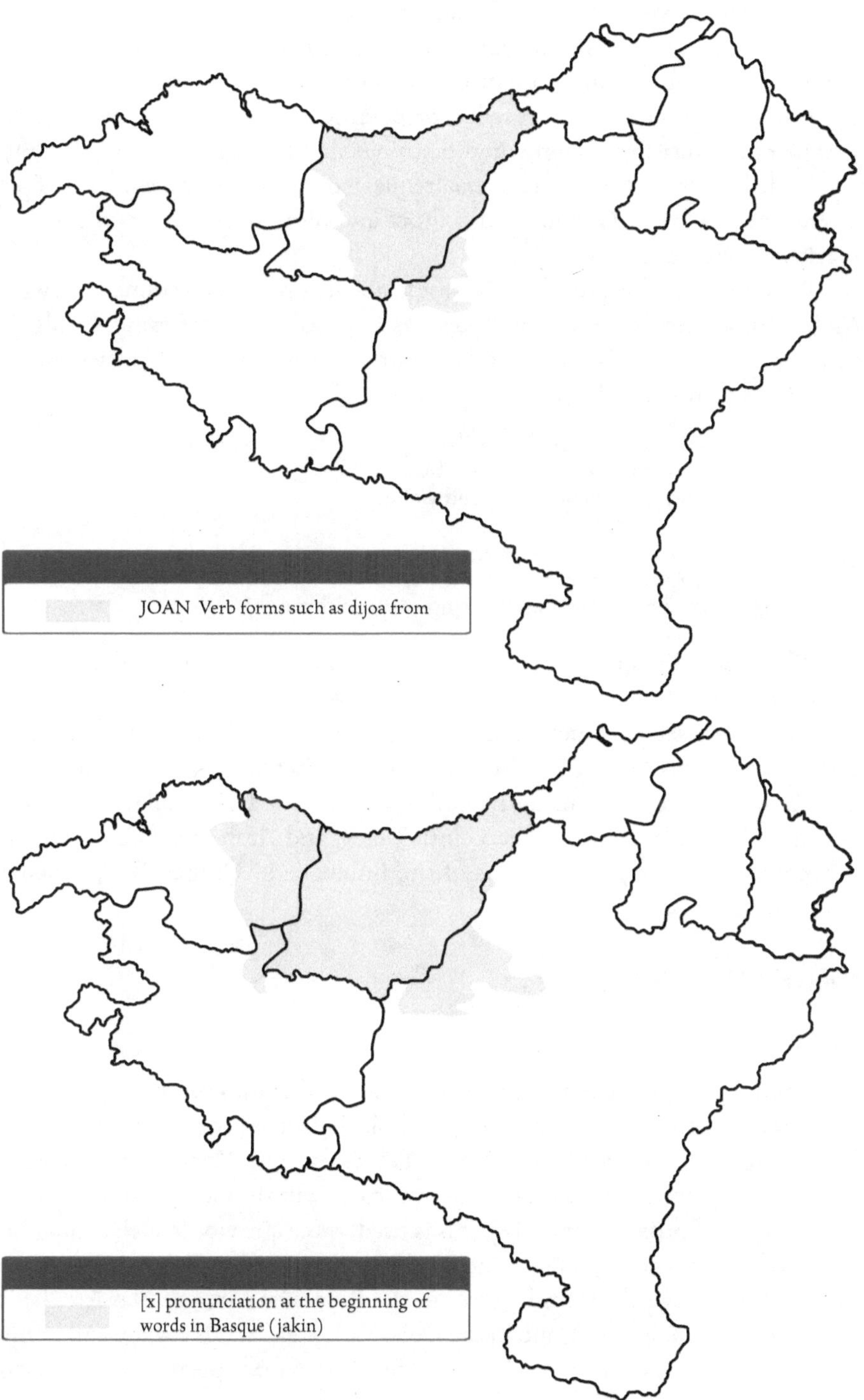
JOAN Verb forms such as dijoa from
[x] pronunciation at the beginning of words in Basque (jakin)

mothers, or something like that"), *eun bitik bat juten giñan eskola* ("we [only] went to school every other day"), and *puntu bietan lotu lokarriyak* ("tie the ropes in two places").[46] Among younger people, however, this way of speaking is not used anymore, and the quantifier *bi* goes to the left of nouns.

But not everything has receded or been lost, and some other Western Basque characteristics are growing in strength and extending in area; *-au* in participles (*okupau* "busy" and *eskau* "requested") is an example of this. This has reached as far as Zarautz, and is more and more noticeable as the age of speakers decreases.

Finally, as regards the Goierri, I noted above how the old connection with Araba is most clearly noticeable, and an example of this is not using the plural verb forms in absolutive-dative and absolutive-dative-ergative. The following examples are from Zaldibia:[47]

guri eamatentziun bokadillok instead of
guri eramaten zigun ogitartekoak
"they used to bring us sandwiches"

asi zaio umei ortzak atatzen instead of
hasi zaio umeari hortzak ateratzen
"the baby's teeth are starting to come through"

Thus, *zigun* (singular) is used rather than *zizkigun* (plural), and *zaio* rather than *zaizkio*.

This innovation, which seemingly first emerged in Araba (and almost certainly in Vitoria-Gasteiz), also exists in the Urretxu-Zumarraga area; as it does, and even more significantly, in the south of the Deba Valley, from Bergara and Antzuola to Oñati, the Leintz Valley, and Aramaio. This, however, is becoming less frequent because of the influence of Unified Basque being taught in schools.

Central Basque Features

Rules

As I mentioned previously, Central Basque has few differentiating features, and those it has are not common to the whole dialect area or, in other cases, go beyond the dialect's boundaries into the Navarrese and Western areas. In fact, there are only two features that are used throughout the Central Basque area:

Firstly, the pronunciation [*x*]: this is used in Basque words such as *jan* ("to eat"), *jakin* ("to know"), *jo* ("to hit"), and *josi* ("to sew"). Two nuances must be noted with regard to this feature: in the Basaburua area of Navarre, [*j*] is pronounced (*yan*; not *jan*), and in the Deba Valley, eastern Navarre, and in the whole of Sakana (Navarre), [*x*] is used. Amaia Apalauza specifies the towns in

Basabura in which [*j*] is pronounced:[48] Erbiti (Erviti), Gartzaron (Garzarón), Beruete, Arrarats (Arrarás), and Orokieta (Ororquieta); in other words, in the north and the east of Basaburua.

And secondly, in questions, the intonation is very marked, as is the use of the particle *al*: *etorriko al haiz?* "will you come?"

Now I will turn to features that only appear in certain areas. They are mostly used in Gipuzkoa or, to be more precise, in areas where Gipuzkoan Basque is spoken.

The *-e-* root from **edun* in the present: *det*, *dek/den*, *degu*, *dezu*, and *dezu(t) e*. In the Deba Valley, this is used in Deba, Mutriku, Mendaro, and the Altzola district of Elgoibar. In Navarre, it is used in Areso and Etxarri Aranatz. In Burunda and Ergoiena (both in Navarre), it is also used in plural verbs: *dezu* instead of *duzu* and *dezai* instead of *duzue*, for example, in Urdiain.

The use of the *-e-* root in izan plural verb forms: *gera* ("we are"), *zera* ("you are" in singular), and *zerate* ("you are" in plural). In the Deba Valley, it is used between Elgoibar and Deba. In Navarre, it is used in Arano and Areso. And on the Lapurdi coast, *ge* instead of *gara* and *ze* instead of *zara* are used.

Joan ("to go") verb forms such as *nijoa* ("I'm going"), *dijoa* ("he/she is going"), and *dijoaz* ("they are going") are used instead of *noa*, *doa*, and *doazte*. This is also the case in Deba and Mutriku and, although with special forms, in Elgoibar and Mendaro: *nixe* instead of *noa*, *dixe* instead of *doa*, and so on. In Navarre, the Araitz-Betelu and Burunda Valleys, Arano, Ergoiena, Etxarri Aranatz, and Arbizu form part of the area that uses these *joan* verb forms.

The following characteristcs are new and, because of that, are used in a smaller area. Furthermore, they are neither closed nor continual features. Thus, from a dialectological point of view, they are of little value.

The transformation *-au-* → *-a-* in absolutive-ergative auxiliary verbs. In Arano, Navarre, for example, *nauk/naun* → *nak/nan*, *nauzu* → *nazu*, *nauzue* → *nazue*, *haut* → *yat*.[49]

The transformation *-ai-* → *-a-* in absolutive-dative auxiliary verbs. This transformation is a rule in the Western sub-dialect (Goierri and Urolaldea). It also exists in the Eastern dialect in some areas of Araitz-Betelu, Larraun, and Basaburu Txikia. In Arano, for instance, it is used in most verb forms: *zait* → *zat*, *zaik/zain* → *zak/zan*, *zaigu* → *zau*, *zaizu* → *zazu*, *zaizue* → *zazue*.[50]

An innovation originating from the Beterri is adding *-tx-* to *hitano* verbs. This is seen mostly in the absolutive-ergative, absolutive-dative-ergative in the past tense, and in synthetic verbs. This has also spread to Urolaldea, and the following examples are from Zumaia:[51] *nau* → *natxiok/natxion*, *gaitu* → *gatxibek/gatxiben*, *ninduen* → *nitxuan/natxionan*, *gintuzten* → *gitxibian/gatxibenan*, *nion* → *nitxuan/nitxionan*, *nago* → *natxiok/natxion*, *noa* → *natxiak/natxian*, *nator* → *natxitorrek/natxitorren*, and *nabil* → *natxibillek/natxibillen*.

In the Beterri, the pluralizing *-zki-* is used in **edun hitano* verb forms rather than the generally used *-it-*: *ditut* → *dizkiat/dizkinat*, *ditu* → *dizkik/dizkin*, and so on. This has spread to most of Urolaldea and, recently, it has also reached the Goierri, with *zituat/zitunat* falling into disuse.

Finally, to complete the potential, the structure 'nominalized verb + *eduki/egon*' is used in the central Beterri area: *ekar dezaket* → *badakat ekartzia / badago ekartzia* ("I can bring it"). This has spread to most of Urolaldea and is also starting to be used in the Goierri. It is also used in Burunda, Navarre.

Undeveloped Rules

Among the undeveloped rules, the *e* → *a* tendency before fast vibrant sounds should be mentioned. This happens to some extent throughout the Basque Country, one example being *berdin* → *bardin* ("same") in Zuberoa and Bizkaia. However, this is stronger than anywhere else in Central Basque: *baserri* → *basarri* ("farm") and *baserritar* → *basarritar* ("farmer"), *eder* → *e(d)ar* ("beautiful"), *eguberri* → *eguarri* ("Christmas"), *eguerdi* → *eguardi* ("midday"), *izerdi* → *izardi* ("sweat"), *izter* → *iztar* ("thigh"), *musker* → *muskar* ("lizard"), *piper* → *pipar* ("pepper"), *pitxer* → *pitxar* ("pitcher"), *puzker* → *puzkar* ("fart"), and so on. This is used in a wider area with the words *baztar* instead of *bazter* ("corner" or "edge") and *hasarre* instead of *haserre* ("anger").

Throughout Gipuzkoa, the suffix *-raka* (> *-aka*) is used to express direction ("toward"), in the way that *-rantz/-rutz* and *-ri buruz* are used in other areas. However, this is not used with all words, and, although it is more frequent in some places than in others, it is more commonly used by younger people than it is by older speakers; *honeaka*, *horreaka*, and *hareaka* ("[toward] here, there [close], and there [far]"), *goraka* and *beheraka* ("upward" and "downward"), *aurreaka* and *atzeaka* ("forward" and "backward"), *ezkerreaka* and *eskubiaka* ("to the left" and "to the right"), *barruaka* and *kanpoaka* ("inward" and "outward"), and *etxeaka* and *kaleaka* ("[toward] home" and "out" or literally "[toward] the street") are the most common uses. It has reached as far as Oiartzun, from where this example comes from:

eldu za Uniaka? instead of
bazatoz Unibertsitaterantz?
"are you coming to the uni(versity)?"

Vocabulary

These words are particular to Central Basque. Some of them are not used throughout the dialect, while others have gone beyond it and reached the Deba Valley and Lower Navarre:

A *agor* instead of *iraila* ("September," although now extinct), *aitona* and *amona* ("grandfather" and "grandmother"), *apreta* instead of *espartina* ("espadrille"), and *aurren* instead of *lehenbiziko* ("first").
B *babarrun* instead of *indaba* ("bean"), *bailara* instead of *ibarra* ("valley"), *basur* instead of *ihintza* ("dew"), *behatz* instead of *hatz* ("finger"), *belaze* instead of *landa* ("field"), and *beta* instead of *astia* ("free time").
E *eskumuinak* (> *eskuminak*) instead of *goraintziak* ("regards"), and *esnatu* instead of *iratzarri* ("to wake up").
G *garagarril* instead of *ekaina* ("June," in extinction) and *garo* instead of *iratze* ("fern").
H *hots egin* instead of *deitu* ("to call").
I *iaio* instead of *trebea* ("skilled"), *ilbeltz* instead of *urtarrila* ("January"), *iritsi* instead of *heldu* ("to arrive"), *isats* instead of *buztana* ("tail"), and *iskanbila* instead of *zalaparta* ("upheaval" or "disorder").
J *jator* instead of *zintzoa* ("good" or "sincere"), *jela* instead of *izotza* ("ice"), and *jipoi* instead of *astindua* ("beat" or "hit").
K *katagorri* instead of *urtxintxa* ("squirrel") and *korrika* instead of *lasterka* ("running").
L *laiotz* instead of *ospela* ("shady side"), *lapurtu* instead of *ostu* ("to steal"), and *legamia* instead of *orantza* or *altxagarria* ("leavening").
M *mami* instead of *gatzatu* or *gaztanbera* ("curds"), *mikatz* instead of *mingotsa* ("bitter" or "tart"), and *mingain* instead of *mihia* ("tongue").
N *neskame* instead of *zerbitzaria* ("maid").
P *peto* instead of *benetakoa* ("real" or "true").
S *sona* instead of *ospea* ("fame").
T *triku* instead of *sagarroia* ("hedgehog"), *txistu* instead of *tu* ("spit"), and *txukun* instead of *apaina* or *egokia* ("charming" or "suitable").
U *ukuilu* instead of *korta* ("stable").
Z *zilbor* (> *txilbor*) "navel."

It is also worth noting that the pronoun *nor* ("who") has been almost completely lost, and *zein* has taken its place: *Zein etorri da?* "Who has come?"

It is likewise worth noting that two words, long since lost in other areas, have been maintained in Central Basque: *bukatu* instead of *amaitu* ("to finish") and *eseri* instead of *jarri* ("to sit"). The Central Basque word *arkakuso* ("flea") is clearly an old term. The first part of it has been kept in Western Basque (*ardi*), and the second part in Eastern Basque (*kukuso*). Lastly, I would also note that there are traces of the famous *erromako zubi* (literally, "bridge of Rome") rather than *ostadarra* in other dialects to say "rainbow."

Variants

The following are the most significant variants: *apaiz* rather than *apez* ("priest"), *bezela* instead of *bezala* ("like"), *bizki* instead of *biki* ("twin"), *ebi* instead of *euri* ("rain"), *elbi* instead of *euli* ("fly"), *eskubi* instead of *eskuin* ("right"), *igo* instead of *igon* or *igan* ("to go up"), *iltze* rather than *itze* ("nail"), *ipui* instead of *ipuin* ("tale"), *irentsi* rather than *iretsi* ("to swallow"), *labana* instead of *nabala* ("knife"), *osin* instead of *asun* ("nettle"), *pake* instead of *bake* ("peace"), *parre/farra* instead of *barre* ("laugh"), *sapai* instead of *sabai* ("loft"), *tximu* instead of *tximino* ("monkey"), *txindurri/txingurri* instead of *inurri* ("ant"), and *udara* instead of *uda* ("summer").

It seems that Iruñea and Vitoria-Gasteiz were the main focuses in creating the southern dialects. However, the Donostia-Hernani-Tolosa area gradually came between these two cities and formed the basis for the southern dialect in general. The influence of this dialect grew from the eighteenth century on throughout the Basque Country, and has been even more pronounced since the creation of Unified Basque in 1964.

6
Navarrese-Lapurdian Basque

Like the Navarrese and Central Basque dialects, Navarrese-Lapurdian Basque has few differentiating features. With regards to structure, nowadays it is largely standardized, although this standardization has been the result of a recent transformation. In 1657 the Zuberoan historian and writer Arnaut Oihenart, for example, explained at the end of his book of poetry how many words varied from place to place, mentioning Lower Navarre, Lapurdi, and the Lapurdi coast, as well as northern and southern Zuberoa.[1] He thus made a distinction between Lower Navarre and Lapurdi and, within Lapurdi, between the way of speaking on the coast (*kostatarra*) from the rest of the region. However, Oihenart believed there to be a single dialect in the whole of the Northern Basque Country: Aquitanian.

Oihenart's point of view seems to be more accurate than Bonaparte's, who wrote two centuries later. Bonaparte distinguished three Basque dialects in Lapurdi and Lower Navarre: Lapurdian, Western Lower Navarrese, and Eastern Lower Navarrese. One should remember, however, that Bonaparte was not completely sure about his decision, admitting that the two Lower Navarrese dialects could, in fact, be classified as a single dialect.[2] Several other observers also came to the same conclusion later on, such as Azkue for example.[3]

Likewise, in the mid-twentieth century Pedro Irizar found considerable standardization between Western and Eastern Lower Navarrese Basque when he studied their verb forms, and he published this reflection on the subject: "In view of the above, one wonders if it will be necessary to consider the existence of a single Low Navarrese dialect that comprises the two in Bonaparte's classification, as Azkue, who took these two for simple sub-dialects, advocated."[4]

Irizar, moreover, saw that the ways of speaking around Uztaritze (Ustaritz) and Hazparne, in Lapurdi, which Bonaparte had classified as Western Lower Navarrese, were in fact similar to the dialect in the rest of Lapurdi. As a consequence, he concluded that the boundary between Lapurdian and Western Lower Navarrese Basque was, in fact, vaguer than had been originally thought. In fact, Henri Guiter made the same argument a few years previously in a more transparent, direct way. He did not carry out studies in the area himself, yet based his argument on the information that Jacques Allières had published in his maps,[5] and reached the following conclusions: "There are clear, unbroken boundaries between Zuberoan and Lower Navarrese Basque. However, there are no boundaries between Lapurdian and Western Lower Navarrese Basque, or between Western and Eastern Lower Navarrese."[6]

This is, indeed, my opinion as well. I would not go so far, as did Guiter, to say that there are no boundaries between Lapurdian and Lower Navarrese Basque, but I do agree that the differences are not sufficient to justify talking about different dialects.

Let us examine, then, what Bonaparte based his judgment on when he made his classification. When Basque from the area is talked about, two features of language use are particularly noteworthy: the use of different second-person singular forms *zuka* and of *xuka*, depending on level of intimacy between speakers (with the latter reflecting a kind of intermediate intimacy somewhere between that of *zuka* and *hika*). In a few words, these verb forms are similar to *hitano*, with the suffixes *-zu* or *-xu* added instead of *-k*/*-n*. For example, the neutral form for "I am" is *ni naiz*, while the *zuka* form is *ni nauzu*, the *xuka* form is *ni nauxu*, and the *hitano* form is *ni nauk*/*naun*.

It is not easy to say exactly with whom and when these two forms of address are used, there being differences from one place to another.[7] As regards extension, though, *zuka* is used most widely: throughout the whole eastern Basque Country, Zuberoa, most of Lower Navarre, Aturrialdea (the area around the Atturi or Adour River) in Lapurdi, and the Erronkari and Zaraitzu Valleys in Navarre. By contrast, use of *xuka* is less extensive: it is common in most of Lower Navarre, Aturrialdea, and Zaraitzu. There are, moreover, a few traces of *xuka* use in a few local ways of speaking in eastern Lapurdi (specifically in the Hazparne area) and in the Aezkoa Valley of Navarre. The fact that *xuka* is used in a more reduced area than *zuka* demonstrates that it is more recent, and by noting how it has spread historically one can see that it clearly originates in Lower Navarre, and almost certainly in the Garazi area.

Obviously, the way of speaking changes considerably when these forms of address are used, but I do not believe that this, in itself, is sufficient to define a dialect. To put this another way, ways of speaking also change considerably when *hitano* is used, but the use of *hitano* or not has never been used, for example, to determine whether there are two Bizkaian dialects or two Navarrese dialects. And, ultimately, it was the use of these forms of address that led Bonaparte to distinguish between two Lower Navarrese dialects and to classify Zaraitzu Basque as Lower Navarrese; specifically, ways of speaking that used *xuka* were classified as Eastern Lower Navarrese and those without it as Western Lower Navarrese.

In Western Lower Navarrese Basque, moreover, Bonaparte distinguished three sub-dialects: that of Baigorri in Lower Navarre, Lapurdian, and that of the Aezkoa Valley in Navarre. He based his decision to classify these sub-dialects on the following reasons:[8]

- In the Baigorri sub-dialect, when the vowel *u* combined with the vowels *a* or *e*, *u* → *i* was the usual transformation (*burua* → *buria* "head"), the suffix *-a* was used in questions (*eginen duka?* "will you do it?"), and there was and is a difference between *izan* and *ukhan*: *izan* is used as the intransitive auxiliary verb and *ukhan* as the transitive (for example, *bizi izan naiz* "I have lived" as opposed to *ikusi ukhan dut* "I have seen it").
- In the Lapurdian sub-dialect, when the vowel *u* combined with the vowels *a* or *e*, *-i-* was placed between them, *burua* → *buruia*. This, in fact, was his whole reason for classifying this as a sub-dialect. Furthermore, he differentiated two groups within this sub-dialect: those of Hazparne and Uztaritze respectively. This was based on the fact that in Hazparne, the suffix *-a* was used in questions, and *izan* and *ukhan* were differentiated, while in Uztaritze this was not the case.
- Finally, in the Aezkoa Valley he found "absences," lacks of similarity with the other sub-dialects; there were no aspirations, the suffix *-a* was not used in questions, and no changes were made with *ukhan* or when /*u* + *a*, *e*/ were combined. He also mentioned features that connected Aezkoa Basque to Navarrese: *x-* at the start of words (*xan* for *jan* "to eat"), *g-* in demonstratives (*gau* for *hau* "this"), the lack of *-n* in past tense verb forms (*egon ze* for *egon zen* "he/she/it was"), and the variants *fan* for *joan* ("to go") and *ekendu* for *kendu* ("to take away" or "to remove").

These were, ultimately, the reasons for distinguishing a separate Lapurdian dialect: when the vowel *u* was combined with the vowels *a* or *e*, no changes took places (*burua*), and verb forms such as *naiz* and *gare* ("I am" and "we are") were used rather than forms such as *niz* and *gira*.

I will repeat what I said previously in chapters 3 and 4 on Navarrese and Central Basque: Bonaparte only took a few features into account, and he was excessively strict in his use of those factors. A good example of this is his assessment of Aezkoa Basque. There were many features that in reality distanced it from the forms of speech in the Northern Basque Country and that brought it closer to Navarrese Basque, but the mere use of verb forms such as *niz* led him to classify it together with the dialects of the Northern Basque Country.

Unifying Forces

In spite of what Bonaparte said, there has never been much difference between Lapurdian and Lower Navarrese Basque, and, as noted, these two ways of speaking have come to resemble one another more closely over recent years.

I will now examine some examples of this.

First of all, one should recall that there has always been a very close relationship between Lapurdi and Lower Navarre, and for many years they have shared the same civil, economic, and religious institutions. As a result, this close relationship has led to an increasingly standard form of Basque in the two territories. In addition to this, the countryside of Lapurdi and Lower Navarre is flat; there are no valleys or districts isolated by mountains. And this, too, makes linguistic unity and standardization easier.

On the other hand, no major urban center managed to exert any influential unifying force in this area because most such locations are relatively small; these include Uztaritze, the old capital of Lapurdi, and Donibane Garazi and Donapaleu, the main towns in Lower Navarre. Meanwhile, the one urban center that might have fulfilled such a role, Baiona, lost its Basque long ago with Gascon becoming the main language there. Because of this, historically market places became the main meeting places: specifically, those of Baiona, Hazparne, Donibane Lohizune, and Ezpeleta in Lapurdi and Donibane Garazi, Donapaleu, and Irisarri in Lower Navarre.

However, any discussion of the Northern Basque Country cannot ignore the reputation and influence of the way of speaking of the Lapurdi coast. For example, the notable seventeenth-century Counter-Reformation polemicists of the Northern Basque Country wrote very important works in the Coastal Lapurdian dialect: most importantly of all, in the book *Gero* (Later, 1643) by Axular (Pedro Agerre). As well as church activity and the excellence of the religious writers and their work, Donibane Lohizune and Ziburu (Ciboure) were also important economic and demographic centers, and because of this they also contributed to the growing influence of Coastal Lapurdian in the Northern Basque Country. In the eighteenth century, Pierre Urte from Donibane Lohizune bore witness to this in a grammar he wrote while living in England: "The best Basque in the Northern Basque Country is spoken in Lapurdi, above all in Donibane Lohizune and Sara, there being a distance of two leagues between the two towns. That is what everyone in the area says."[9]

Urte mentions Sara as well as Donibane Lohizune, and, in fact, Sara was to become the main point of reference. Fishing towns have always been affected by other places' ways of speaking, and, perhaps because of that, the Basque from Sara (located slightly inland) was considered purer and more authentic. However, the fact that the great writer Axular lived there was also a factor in the growing reputation of the Basque in Sara. Joanes Etxeberri, who was himself from Sara, wrote the following in his book *Laburdiri escuararen hatsapenac* (The basics of Lapurdian Basque, 1712):[10]

> There were two reasons this town had such a good reputation. On the one hand, its incomparable countryside and situation and, on the other,

> the beauty of its clear Basque, praised not only in Lapurdi but also in the other Basque areas in Spain and France. And, in fact, wherever I have gone I have always heard – as many other people must have heard – unanimous praise for the Basque of Sara.

However, Etxeberri and Urte were the last representatives of this linguistic renaissance. The economic situation in Lapurdi had long been unfavorable, and, after the eighteenth century, the Northern Basque Country as a whole declined quite drastically. Young people were forced to move away, and without young people the traditional way of life slowed down and lost impetus. This situation naturally also influenced linguistic evolution there. After the eighteenth century, no great writers stood out as they had done before; nor did any groups of writers, who used ways of speaking from specific areas and so promoted their use, emerge as they had done previously. In fact, with the decline of Coastal Lapurdian, everyone returned to their own regional way of speaking as a basis of their communication; and in many ways the renown these regional forms of speech later gained was down to their "words" rather than their "ways of doing things."[11]

The Church was the mainstay of Basque in the Northern Basque Country after the eighteenth century as well as its swiftest unifying force. In fact, the Basque-language *Herria* magazine was founded in 1945 with Church support, and its first editor, the priest Pierre Lafitte, also wrote the grammar *Grammaire basque (navarro-labourdin littéraire)*.

The title of this study, published in 1944, makes Laffite's objective clear: defining a model for educated speech and writing in Lapurdian and Lower Navarrese. And this grammar, together with the magazines *Eskualduna* and *Herria*, ultimately exercised a major influence on Basque in the Northern Basque Country during the twentieth century. Indeed, thanks to this influence, the Basque of Lapurdi and Lower Navarre were largely standardized as one dialect. When speaking about the importance of the Church in encouraging the development of Basque in the Northern Basque Country, one must mention the influence of the old seminary at Larresoro (Larressore) and the new seminary at Uztaritze, both in Lapurdi. Many priests from Lapurdi and Lower Navarre grew up and were educated at these seminaries and went on to use the way of speaking that they had learned there in their work.

In recent decades, there have been two significant developments as regards the state of Basque in the Northern Basque Country as a whole: namely, the use of Basque has diminished considerably, but, at the same time, the relationships between Basque speakers have become stronger and closer. Furthermore, efforts to promote Basque have become increasingly effective – through, for example, the ikastolas or schools where instruction is carried out in Basque, night schools with Basque classes for adults, and Basque-language

Bay of Biscay
Baiona
ATURRIALDEA
Bidarte
Milafranga
Getaria
Beskoitze
Donibane Lohizune
Arbona
Hazparne
Ahetze
KOSTARRA
Senpere
Uztaritze
AMIKUZE
Hendaia
THE WEST
Kanbo
Izturitze
Donapaleu
Etxarri
Azkaine
Ainhoa
Ezpeleta
Makea
Heleta
Domintzaine-Berroeta
Sara
Luhuso
THE EAST
Arüe-Ithorrotze-Olhaibi
Irisarri
OZTIBARRE
Lohitzüne-Oihergi
Pagola
Baigorri
Donibane Garazi
BAIGORRI
GARAZI
Luzaide
Navarrese-Lapurdian Basque Territory/Area
Province Boundary
Dialect Boundary
Overlapping Dialects

radio stations – and, thanks to these, a new common way of speaking has been sown and taken root. This common Basque promoted by the aforementioned initiatives has been combined with the previously existing Navarrese-Lapurdian Unified Basque, and today most young people from Lapurdi and Lower Navarre speak this standard dialect. Indeed, the same is also true for many young people from Zuberoa if they leave their home area. And there is already a name for this new way of speaking: *Iparraldeko batua* (Northern Unified Basque).

Navarrese-Lapurdian Sub-Dialects

Very few studies have been carried out on contemporary Lapurdian and Lower Navarrese Basque.[12] My own view of the situation, based on these works together with information I have gathered myself, is that in the early twenty-first century, Navarrese-Lapurdian is a single dialect, in which two sub-dialects can be distinguished. Following my customary practice thus far, I term these the Western and Eastern sub-dialects. The Western sub-dialect is spoken between the coast of Lapurdi and Ahetze, Senpere (Saint-Pée-sur-Nivelle), and Ainhoa; and the Eastern sub-dialect is spoken throughout the whole of Lower Navarre and eastern Lapurdi (specifically, Aturrialdea and the Hazparne area). Furthermore, there is an intermediate way of speaking between these two sub-dialects used in the area around Uztaritze. As is typical in such cases, innovations from both the bordering sides have been taken on in this area but, in itself, it does not have many differentiating factors. According to Irantzu Epelde,[13] when the vowel *u* combines with the vowels *a* or *e*, *ui*/*üi* is formed here: for example, *zuek* → *züik*, *nuen* → *nüin*, *duzue* → *duzüi*, *diozue* → *diozüi*, and so on.

As well as the two sub-dialects, there are also two marked ways of speaking that are still used to some extent today:

- *Amikuztarra*, from the Amikuze area of Lower Navarre. This is slightly different from the rest of Lower Navarre and was once close to Zuberoan Basque. Some towns in the north of Zuberoa are part of this area: Domintxaine-Berroeta (Domezain-Berraute), Arüe-Ithorrotze-Olhaibi (Aroue-Ithorots-Olhaïby), Lohitzüne-Oihergi (Lohitzun-Oyhercq), Etxarri (Etcharry), and Pagola (Pagolle).
- *Kostatarra*, or Coastal Lapurdian. Spoken on the Lapurdi coast in Hendaia (Hendaye), Biriatu (Biriatou), Urruña (Urrugne), Ziburu, Donibane Lohizune, and Azkaine (Ascain). This area is closely connected to both Gipuzkoa and Navarre.

I will now explain the criteria by which I classify the aforemtioned as sub-dialects. There are older innovations from the east, perhaps originating in Zuberoa, which spread from there to Lower Navarre, eastern Lapurdi, and the Erronkari, Zaraitzu, and Aezkoa Valleys in Navarre. They have not reached southwestern Lapurdi, however, and notably they have not influenced Coastal Lapurdian. Other innovations, though, are much more recent and probably originated on the Lapurdi coast. They have reached as far as southwestern but not eastern Lapurdi.

I will examine innovations from the Eastern sub-dialect in greater detail below, but by way of introduction I would highlight the following:

- From Zuberoa to the Uztaritze area, there has long been a tendency to introduce an *-i-* between *u* and *a*, and between *u* and *e*: *burua* → *buruia*, *duen* → *duien*. Later, a further step was taken: *-uia* → *-ia* (*buria*) and *-uie* → *-ie* (*diela*), but this was not adopted in Aturrialdea and in the Uztaritze area.
- Similarly, in second person plural verb forms, *-zue* → *-zi(e)* from the Uztaritze area to as far as Zuberoa, and also in eastern Navarre: *duzue* → *duzie*, *zaizue* → *zaizie*, *dakizue* → *dakizie*.
- In absolutive-ergative *izan* and **edin* verb forms, *-ai-* → *-i-* from Zuberoa to the Uztaritze area: *naiz* → *niz*, *zaitezte* → *zitezte*, *gaitu* → *gitu* (→ *gütü* in Zuberoa). In the same area, *-au-* → *-u-* in absolutive-ergative verb forms: *nau* → *nu*, *nauzu* → *nuzu*.
- In absolutive-dative verb forms, the transformation *-ai-* → *-au-* is a tendency in eastern Lapurdi and in many areas of Lower Navarre: *zait* → *zaut*.
- The consonant cluster *-st-* appears from Zuberoa to the Uztaritze area, although *-rtz-* has not completely disappeared. This is mostly to be seen in the variants *beste* ("other"), *bost* ("five"), *ostegun* ("Thursday"), and *ostiral* ("Friday") but also in *hertze* instead of *heste* ("intestine") and *ortzadar* rather than *ostadar* ("rainbow") throughout the dialect area.
- In dative plural verbs with the plural the suffix *-er* predominates from Zuberoa to the Hazparne area: for example, *laguner* instead of *lagunei* ("to the friends"). In the Hazparne area, however, *-eri* is also used, and to the west of Hazparne that is the only suffix used.
- Along with the general comitative or associative suffix *-kin*, the variant *-kilan* is also used from Zuberoa to the Uztaritze area: for example, *lagunarekilan* ("with the friend"). Today, however, *-kin* is becoming more frequent due to the influence of Unified Basque.
- *Nihaur* ("I myself") model emphatic pronouns are used from Zuberoa to eastern Lapurdi. In the Uztaritze area, the *neroni* and *nihaur* forms compete with each other, and only forms such as *neroni* are used to the west of that area.
- The diminutive suffix *-ño*, originating in Navarrese-Lapurdian Basque (*irriño* instead of *barretxoa* "giggle") is not established in Western Lapurdian Basque.

- The suffix *-gi* (*jargia* instead of *jarlekua* "seat") has spread throughout the eastern part of the Northern Basque Country but is unknown in southwest Lapurdi.
- The *zuka* and *xuka* forms of address are used in Zuberoa, most of Lower Navarre, and in Aturrialdea. There are also traces of *xuka* in Hazparne.
- The verbs *afaldu* ("to have dinner"), *bazkaldu* ("to have lunch"), and *askaldu* ("to have a snack") are conjugated in the absolutive from Zuberoa to the Uzaritze area: for example, *bazkaldu niz* ("I have had lunch"). In southwestern Lapurdi they are conjugated in absolutive-ergative.
- The interrogative suffix *-a* has spread from Zuberoa to the Hazparne area: for example, *ikusi duka?* ("have you seen [him/her/it]?") It is also known farther west, but is not common.
- *Ber* is used in clauses of time and condition from Zuberoa to the Uztaritze area: for example, *lana dugun ber, ez dugu herria utziko* "so long as we have work, we won't leave town."

In most of the Northern Basque Country the focus of the sentence (known as *galdegaia* in Basque) is placed before the auxiliary verb when wishing to emphasize the former: for example, *guk dugu irabazi* instead of *geuk irabazi dugu* in Unified Basque ("*we* have won," that is, with an emphasis on "we"). On the Lapurdi coast, however, this is unknown.

Turning now to the main innovations in the Western sub-dialect:

- The only suffix in the destinative ("for whom") is *-entzat*: for example, *lagunantzat* instead of *lagunarentzat* ("for the friend"). This suffix also exists in other areas, but in the Uztaritze area it coexists with *-endako*. Nowadays, however, *-entzat* is gaining in strength thanks to the influence of Unified Basque.
- There is a tendency to use absolutive-ergative instead of absolutive-dative-ergative verb forms, except for when the indirect object is *hari/haiei*: for example, *erran nau*, not *erran daut* ("he/she told me"). This area includes Arbona (Arbonne), Basusarri (Bassussarry), and Arrangoitze (Arcangues), and there are also traces of it in Zuraide (Souraïde). This has also spread to northeastern Gipuzkoa (the area between Lezo and Irun) and to northwestern Navarre (Urdazubi, Zugarramurdi, Bera, and Etxalar). It is also to be found in Lekeitio (Bizkaia), which is quite distant from this area.
- In absolutive-dative-ergative verb forms, *-*i*- is the root: for example, *diozkat* rather than *dizkiot*. In the Uztaritze area, both *-*i*- and **eradun* roots are used (*dio/dako*), but **eradun* is the only option in the eastern area.

On the Lapurdi coast, three more features are almost certainly the result

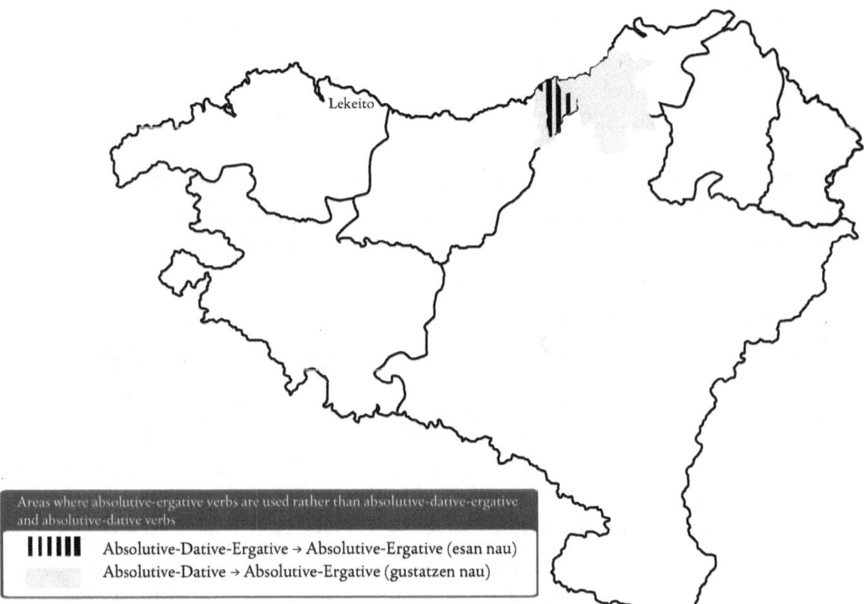
Lekeito
Areas where absolutive-ergative verbs are used rather than absolutive-dative-ergative and absolutive-dative verbs
Absolutive-Dative-Ergative → Absolutive-Ergative (esan nau)
Absolutive-Dative → Absolutive-Ergative (gustatzen nau)

of its connections with Gipuzkoa and Navarre:

- There is epenthesis with the vowel *i* in combination with the vowels *a*, *e*, and *o*: [*j*]: *herria* → *erriya* ("people," "country," or "town").
- Influenced by the vowel *i*, *n* → *ñ* and *l* → *ll* in many cases: *berdina* → *berdiña* ("same"), *ginen* → *giñen* ("we were"), *bila* → *billa* ("in search of"), *iluna* → *illuna* ("dark"), and so on.
- In plural *izan* verb forms, *-e-* is the root in the verb forms *ge* instead of *gara* ("we are") and *ze* instead of *zara* ("you are" in singular), as in Gipuzkoan Basque.

In southwestern Lapurdi the use of *-iten* to form verbal nouns has disappeared or almost disappeared: *izaten* rather than *izaiten* ("being") and *jotzen* rather than *joiten* ("hitting" or "playing").

There are also Eastern sub-dialect words in the vocabulary used. In most of western Lapurdi – above all in Coastal Lapurdian – the following words are unknown or uncommon: *ahar* instead of *liskarra* in Unified Basque ("fight" or "dispute"), *aiduru* instead of *zain* ("waiting"), *alta* instead of *ordea* ("however" or "but"), *apairu* instead of *otordua* ("meal"), *ardura* instead of *maiz* ("often"), *argizagi* instead of *ilargi* ("moon"), *askari* instead of *gosari* ("breakfast") and *atsalaskari* instead of *askaria* ("snack"), *azantz* instead of *hotsa* ("noise"), *bilo* instead of *ilea* ("hair"), *borta* instead of *atea* ("door"), *bortu* instead of *mendi garaia* ("high mountain"), *dailu* instead of *sega* ("scythe"), *ele* instead of *hitz* ("word") and *elekatu* instead of *hitz egin* ("to talk" or "to speak"), *engoitik* instead of *honezkero/hemendik aurrera* ("from now on"), *ereiaro* instead of *ekaina* ("June"), *hagun* instead of *aparra* ("foam"), *hazkurri* instead of *janaria* ("food"), *iguriki* instead of *itxaron* ("to wait"), *ikertu* instead of *aztertu* ("to investigate"), *jauzi* instead of *saltoa* ("jump"), *jin* instead of *etorri* ("to come"), *laket* instead of *atsegina* ("pleasant"), *larrazken* instead of *udazkena* ("Fall"), *lili* instead of *lorea* ("flower"), *maiasturu* instead of *zurgina* ("carpenter"), *osagarri* instead of *osasun* ("health"), *pot* instead of *musua* ("kiss"), *poxi* instead of *apurra* ("crumb"), *samurtu* instead of *haserretu* ("to get angry"), *so* instead of *begira* ("looking"), *ukan* instead of *eduki* ("to have"), *ukarai* instead of *eskumuturra* ("wrist"), *untsa* instead of *ongi* ("good" or "well"), *untsalaz* ("in the best case scenario"), *uzkaili* instead of *irauli* ("to turn over"), *zeinu* instead of *ezkila* ("bell"), and so on.

There are two words used in Lower Navarre and in eastern Lapurdi that are not heard in western Lapurdi: *elkor* instead of *gor* ("deaf") and *otto* instead of *osaba* ("uncle"). Moreover, *ebiakoitz* instead of *larunbata* ("Saturday") is used in Lower Navarre.

From the Uztaritze area to Zuberoa, furthermore, the *nihaur* ("I myself") type emphatic pronouns have come to mean *bakarrik* ("alone"): for example, *bera bizi da* instead of *bakarrik bizi da* ("he/she lives alone").

The following words, on the other hand, are used in the Western subdialect: *etxilar* instead of *ilarra* ("pea") and *unatu* instead of *nekatu* ("to get tired"); in much of Lapurdi, *ohantze* and *kafia* instead of *habia* ("nest"); and in Coastal Lapurdian *baratxe* instead of *emeki* or *poliki* ("slowly"), as in Zuberoa. The use of the following may be due to the proximity of Gipuzkoa: *atera(tu)* ("to take out"), which in the east is *ilki/jalgi*; *begira* ("looking"), which in the east is *beha*; *bota* ("to throw"), which in the east is *bota* and *aurdiki*; *dena* ("everything"), which in the east is *oro*; *errota* ("mill"), which in the east is *eihera*; *garbitu* ("to clean"), which in the east is *ikuzi/xahutu*); *gaur* ("today"), which in the east is *gaur* and *egun*; and *nere* and *ene* ("my").

With regard to variants, the proximity of Gipuzkoa can be seen in southwestern Lapurdi, in Coastal Lapurdian: *elkar* ("each other" or "one another") as well as *elgar*, *piper* ("pepper") instead of *biper*, *ttiki* ("small") as well as *ttipi*, *uso* ("dove") instead of *urtxo*, and *zein* ("which") as well as *zoin*. A variant from the area itself (and now also used in the Baztan Valley, Navarre) is *gan* instead of *joan/eraman* ("to go"/"to lead").

Navarrese-Lapurdian Basque Characteristics

As noted above, this dialect has very few distinguishing features. Here we discuss some of the most significant.

Rules

In most of the dialect area, palatalization after the vowel *i* is unknown; *in*, *il*, and *it* are pronounced as such, without becoming *iñ*, *ill*, and *itt*: for example, *edozoini* ("to anyone" or "to any"), *gainetik* ("off" or "over"), *etxezaina* ("porter"), *etxeraino* ("[up to] home/the house"), and so on. In the past, moreover, *ñ* and *ll* in loanwords from Spanish became *in* and *il*. This tendency also spread to Urdazubi and Zugarramurdi in Navarre, from where the following examples are taken:[14] *bainu* ("bath" from the Spanish *baño*), *bonbila* ("light bulb" from the Spanish *bombilla*), *botoila* ("bottle" from the Spanish *botella*), *gaztaina* ("chestnut" from the Spanish *castaño*), *koinatu* ("brother-in-law" from the Spanish *cuñado*), *oilo* ("oil" from the Spanish *óleo*), and *taila* ("size" from the Spanish *talla*).

Nowadays, however, avoiding palatalization is less and less common. According to Irantzu Epelde,[15] palatalization is left as it is in new loanwords taken from French: *kallatu* ("to curdle" or "to clot" from the French *cailler*) instead of *gatzatu*, *kanpaña* ("field" from the French *campagne*) instead of *landa*, *konpañia* ("company" from the French *compagnie*), *makiñuna* ("dealer" or "wheeler-dealer" from the French *maquignon*) instead of *tratularia*, *papilluna* ("butterfly" from the French *papillon*) instead of *tximeleta*, and *sua-*

ñatu ("to look after" from the French *soigner*) instead of *zaindu*.

With regard to palatalization, two parts of the dialect area are exceptions: western Lower Navarre (Amikuze, Oztibarre (Ostabarret), and part of the Garazi area) and, above all, the Lapurdi coast.

The use of *x-* instead of *tx-* at the start of words is another of this dialect's distinguishing features: *ximino* ("monkey"), *xingarra* instead of *urdaiazpikoa* ("ham"), *xirula* ("small flute"), *xistu* ("whistle"), *xoko* ("corner"), *xori* ("bird"), and so on. Loanwords have also been adapted in this way, as they have in Urdazubi and Zugarramurdi (Navarre):[16] *xanpiñona* ("mushroom" from the French *champignon*) instead of *perretxikoa*, *xantza* ("luck" from the French *chance*) instead of *zoria*, *xatoa* ("castle" from the French *château*) instead of *gaztelua*, *ximenea* ("chimney" from the French *cheminée*, Spanish *chimenea*), and so on.

Pronouns in the *nehor* rather than *inor* model are used (*nehork*, *nehori*, *nehun*, and so on). This used to be the case in Lower Navarre as well, but it seems the tendency originated in Lapurdi, perhaps in Coastal Lapurdian.

The diminutive suffix normally used in this dialect is *-ño*: for example, *baño* instead of *bakarra* ("only" or "sole"), *begiño* ("little eye"), *haurño* ("little child"), *irriño* instead of *barretxoa* ("giggle"), *ño* instead of *joan-etorri laburra* ("short round trip"), *mahaiño* ("small table"), *ñimiño* instead of *txikitxoa* ("very small"), *pausaldiño* instead of *atsedentxoa* ("short break"), *poxiño* instead of *apurtxoa* ("smidgeon"), and *xortaño* ("little drop"). A special word has also been created using this suffix: *amaño* rather than *inudea* ("wet nurse").

The foreign ending *-on* becomes *-oin* in most of the dialect area: *arrazoin* ("reason"), *botoin* ("button"), *garratoin* instead of *arratoi* ("mouse"), *gaskoin* ("Gascon"), *kantoin* ("canton"), *kartoin* ("cardboard"), *maratoin* ("marathon"), *meloin* ("melon"), *patroin* ("boss" or "patron"), *saboin* ("soap"), *sasoin* ("season"), *takoin* instead of *orpoa* ("heel"), *zitroin* instead of *limoia* ("lemon"), and so on. However, in some new loanwords *-on* is maintained, as in the French: for example, *balon* ("ball"), *bonbon* instead of *gozokia* ("candy"), *kornixon* ("gherkin" from French *cornichon*), and *marron* ("brown").

A distinguishing feature of this dialect is the ending *-aia* in old loanwords: *bisaia* instead of *aurpegia* in Unified Basque ("face"), *domaia* instead of *zoritxarra* ("misfortune"), *kuraia* instead of *kemena* ("courage," "energy," or "vigor"), *lengoaia* instead of *hizkuntza* ("language"), *piaia* instead of *joan-etorria* ("trip" or "journey"), *salbaia* instead of *basatia* ("wild"), *usaia* instead of *ohitura* ("custom" or "habit"), and so on. This rule is no longer productive, though, and *-adxa* [*a a*] is the transformation in new loanwords: for example, *afitxadxa* instead of *iragarkia* ("poster" or "flyer"), *brikoladxa* instead of *brikolajea* ("bricolage"), *depanadxa* instead of *konponketa* ("repair"), *ga-*

radxa instead of *garajea* ("garage"), *peadxa* instead of *bidesaria* ("tollbooth"), *rezikladxa* instead of *berregokitzea* ("recycling"), and *xomadxa* instead of *langabezia* ("unemployed").

Nowadays, thanks to Unified Basque, the ending *-aia* has spread throughout the Basque Country in words such as *bidaia* (trip" or "journey"), *eskifaia* ("crew"), *paisaia* ("landscape" or "scenery"), and *xantaia* ("blackmail").

Vocabulary and Variants

The following words are particular to this dialect, although not all of them are used throughout the dialect area: *altxagarri* instead of *orantza* or *legamia* ("leavening"), *auzapez* instead of *alkatea* ("mayor"), *azantz/harrabots* instead of *hotsa* or *zarata* ("sound" or "noise"), *babazuza* instead of *kazkabarra* ("hailstone"), *biziki* instead of *oso* ("very"), *buruil* instead of *iraila* ("September"), *elkor* instead of *gor* ("deaf"), *fitsik* instead of *ezer* ("nothing"), *gako* instead of *giltza* ("key"), *guri* instead of *bigun* ("soft" or "smooth"), *kalapita* instead of *iskanbila* ("disturbance"), *ortzantz* instead of *trumoia* ("thunder"), *otto* instead of *osaba* ("uncle"), *pairatu* instead of *eraman* or *jasan* ("to bear"), *parada* instead of *aukera* or *beta* ("opportunity"), *pittika* instead of *antxumea* ("kid" as in young goat), *sehi* instead of *zerbitzaria* ("maid"), *urririk* instead of *doan* ("free"), *urtzintz* instead of *usina* ("sneeze"), and *xingar* instead of *urdaiazpikoa* ("ham").

The following variants, however, are used throughout most of the dialect area: *ahantzi* instead of *ahaztu* ("to forget"), *arno* instead of *ardo* ("wine"), *ba* and *bai* ("yes"), *biper* instead of *piper* ("pepper"), *botoila* instead of *botila* ("bottle"), *buraso* instead of *guraso* ("parent"), *elgar* instead of *elkar* ("each other" or "one another"), *ereman* instead of *eraman* ("to take" or "to carry"), *eskuara* instead of *euskara* ("the Basque language"), *fruitu* instead of *fruta* ("fruit"), *giristino* instead of *kristau* ("Christian"), *hogoi* instead of *hogei* ("twenty"), *irrisku* instead of *arrisku* ("risk" or "danger"), *jakintsun* instead of *jakintsu* ("wise"), *kondatu* instead of *kontatu* ("to count"), *saindu* instead of *santu* (saint"), and *xin(a)urri* instead of *inurri* ("ant").

In at least a few local ways of speaking, the following words are also used: *aments* instead of *amets* ("dream"), *garratoin* instead of *arratoi* ("mouse"), *hainitz* and *hanitz* ("a lot [of]"), *hausko* instead of *hauspo* ("bellows"), *oseba* instead of *osaba* ("uncle"), and *pertsu* instead of *bertso* ("verse"). Furthermore, in clauses expressing cause *-(e)lakoan* rather than *-elako* is used in some local ways of speaking.

In sum, this dialect has few differentiating features, but it does have its own distinctive character. It is not clear where the dialect emerged, but it took as its model the way of speaking on the coast of Lapurdi, at least during the seventeenth century. Thereafter, in the centuries that followed, ways of speaking from inland Lapurdi and Lower Navarre also came to influence this dialect.

7
Basque in the Americas

People have long emigrated from the Basque Country to the Americas.[1] When Castile reached the continent and started to conquer it in 1492, it needed help from the Basques. Much of the transport to the Americas took place on Basque-built and crewed ships. Furthermore, the arms and tools needed to colonize the Americas were largely made in Basque ironworks. Thanks to all this, the Basque economy grew considerably during the sixteenth century. At the same time, many Basques themselves set off for the Americas: merchants, Churchmen, administrators, soldiers, and so on.

At the start of the colonization process, most Basques went to Mexico. In the late sixteenth century, however, Panama became the main market place and thus also began to attract Basques. Then Chile (in the seventeenth century) and Venezuela (in the eighteenth century) became the main destinations for Basque emigrants.

From the early 1800s through the rest of the nineenth century, most of the countries in the Americas proclaimed their independence and separated from Spain. Naturally, this slowed emigration down considerably, but not entirely. Chile and, above all, Uruguay and Argentina opened their doors to foreigners and many people from all over the Basque Country settled there. In fact, this era coincided with a harsh period in the Basque Country. Many young people began to leave the Northern Basque Country after the French Revolution of 1789 and beyond, either in search of work or just to avoid doing French military service. Emigration from the Northern Basque Country centered on Montevideo, Uruguay.

Life was similarly hard in the Southern Basque Country as a result, among other things, of two major civil wars in the nineteenth century: the First and Second Carlist Wars (1833–39 and 1872–76 respectively). The consequence of all this was that many young people also left the Southern Basque Country, either to avoid heavy taxation or being called up to do Spanish military service. Most of these emigrants went to Argentina. Principally from 1850 onward, the Argentinean government worked to promote the Pampas region, and workers were needed for livestock farming and the dairy and meat industries.

Basques also settled in Colombia and Peru, and, from 1840 onward, emigration to Mexico started up again, with emigration to Cuba also increasing considerably at the same time.

News of the gold discovery in California broke in 1848, encouraging many Basques to join in the Gold Rush. Initially, the Basques who went to California came from Mexico, Chile, Panama, and other countries they had already first migrated to; but soon after, they began to arrive directly from the Basque Country. Most of these direct arrivals were from the Northern Basque Country, obliged to emigrate because of the economic downturn in France. Naturally, given their rural backgrounds, when the gold ran out most of them started to work in livestock farming. Emigration to California increased around 1880, and Basque livestock farmers then began to move on to neighboring states. For example, they moved into Nevada and Idaho in the late nineteenth and early twentieth centuries respectively. Thereafter, they began to settle in other western states as well. There was a noticeable decline in emigration to the Americas after the outbreak of World War I in 1918. In Argentina, for example, farming on the Pampas had already been developed and land was now too expensive to buy for Basque immigrants. Furthermore, the modernization of farming meant that fewer workers were required. At the same time, the economic situation for Basques in Europe improved slowly after the war; with the exception, of course, for those in the Southern Basque Country during the Spanish Civil War (1936–39). Following the triumph of General Franco in the Spanish Civil War, many Basques fled the subsequent dictatorship to the Americas, with Venezuela, Argentina, Chile, Uruguay, and Mexico becoming the main places of refuge for these Basque exiles. In fact, in many cases Basque refugees settled in areas where there were already Basques. Meanwhile, people stopped migrating in large numbers to work in livestock farming in the Americas around 1960, although a few still emigrated to work in this sector into the 1970s.

American Basque

It is a widely held belief among Basques that there is a special type of Basque in America. Allegedly, all the dialects merged, and Basques from different areas met up there and learned each other's dialects in a natural way.

The first recorded mention of that special type of Basque dates from 1900 in a report drawn up at the International Conference on Basque Studies. A summary written by Telesforo Arantzadi was published in the Bilbao magazine *Euskalduna*:[2]

> Because the immigrants who find themselves together with one another do not exactly come from the same village, or the same valley, or indeed

> in many cases from the same dialectal province, each begins to speak according to his own dialect and ends up being influenced by the other dialects; from this the consequence for the colony is a kind of fusion of the dialects.

Pierre Lhande, meanwhile, drew a picture of *indianos* (Basque émigrés in the Americas) a few years later: "large moustache, darker complexion, short jacket generally replacing the smock, some thick gold ring on the finger, in sum, a certain distinctive accent and a mixture of dialects in the use of Basque, they are signs that do not lie."[3] Francisco Grandmontagne published *Los inmigrantes prósperos* (The prosperous immigrants) in 1933, and one of the stories he told in this work was to have far-reaching repercussions. Apparently, according to Grandmontagne, when Bonaparte was in Baiona he heard a way of speaking that was completely new to him; a man was mixing up all sorts of words. Bonaparte was unable to allay his curiosity and asked him where he was from. Apparently, he had been born in Aldude, in Lower Navarre, but had learned to speak the Basque he was then speaking in Buenos Aires, Argentina.

Grandmontagne almost certainly invented the story himself, but it came at a time when unifying Basque was very much under debate. In the 1930s, the renowned linguist Resurreccion Maria Azkue, the first head of Euskaltzaindia (the Academy of the Basque Language, created in 1919), proposed establishing what he termed *Gipuzkera osotua* (complete Gipuzkoan Basque) as a standard form of writing Basque. Yet the supposedly already existent American Basque alluded to in Grandmontagne's text seemed to be a challenge to this proposal. Indeed, for Grandmontagne, the "natural" Basque from the Americas was a better solution than the "artificial" Basque invented by linguists and language academies.[4]

Grandmontagne's tale was very well received by people who were against unifying Basque, including (among others) significant figures such as the Basque studies scholar Justo Garate, the writer Nikolas Ormaetxea "Orixe," and the dramaturge Antonio Maria Labaien;[5] and this is how the myth of a "naturally unified Basque" from the Americas came into being.

From Myth to Truth

It is easy to believe that when the speakers of different dialects came into contact with each other, this was reflected in and had some kind of consequence for the language they spoke. However, if we bear in mind the type and pattern of emigration that Basques took part in to the Americas, it is hard to imagine how all the dialects could so easily come together as one; and moreover one standard "American Basque" that spread through the Americas, from Chile to Montana. In fact, when one examines Basque emigration to the Americas more closely, one feature becomes clear: generally speaking, the Basques who emigrated joined people from their families or towns who had already settled there, in order to benefit from their help and protection. In fact, that is the way emigration typically functions all over the world.

During the first decade of the twentieth century, for example, Basques from the Northern Basque Country and from Navarre migrated to California, western Nevada, Arizona, Wyoming, and northeastern Montana. People from Bizkaia, on the other hand, settled in northern Nevada, eastern Oregon, and southern Idaho.[6]

There are also more exact examples of this: many of the Basques who settled in the Monterey-San Francisco area of California were from Etxalar, in Navarre; in Buffalo, Wyoming, Basques were mostly from Baigorri, Lower Navarre; in Fresno, California, many Basques were from Ezterenzubi (Estérençuby) in Lower Navarre; while most of the Basques from Bizkaia in Nevada, Oregon, and Idaho were from the Lea-Artibai and Busturialdea areas.[7]

Naturally, these migration and settlement patterns were reflected in language-use. For example, in the early 1950s Jon Etxaide wrote that, "In Idaho, one might say that Bizkaian Basque is spoken exclusively. However, most of the Basques in Montana are from Gipuzkoa [sic], and in Oregon and Utah the people are from the other side of the Bidasoa [River, meaning from the Northern Basque Country]. The Californians, on the other hand, mostly speak the soft, sweet Basque from Baztan."[8]

Toward the end of that same decade, a report by Castor Uriarte, representing Euskaltzaindia and read at the First National Basque Festival held in Sparks, Nevada, just outside of Reno, in 1959, and later published in the journal *Euskera*, observed that, "[in the] Basque emigration to the states of California, Nevada, Idaho, etc. . . . . it is admirable that they have maintained Basque . . . knowing that form of the village in our land in which their parents were born."[9]

An article from the same journal, published in 1973, included the following testimony: "Mr. Arrue said that a letter he had received from California told him that there was a radio program in Boise, Idaho, in Basque, but as the presenter spoke in Bizkaian Basque and the person who wrote the letter was from Navarre, it was incomprehensible to the latter."[10]

Despite Grandmontagne's assertion that an "American Basque" had been heard in Argentina, it would seem, as in the case of the United States, that there a similar pattern emerged. According to a 1955 edition of the journal *Euskalduna* (published in Argentina), "In Argentina we know of numerous cases of families living in the country whose second- and third-generation children speak Basque as if they had been born in Lapurdi or in Navarre."[11]

As these testimonies demonstrate, it was not inevitable that people from different parts of the Basque Country would somehow blend into one group in the Americas, and naturally people stuck to their original way of speaking when this was not the case.

As well as quotes like these, there is also even clearer evidence available. Terence Wilbur carried out a simple study in Bakersfield, California, in 1961 and found that there was no type of mixture in the way of speaking there; it was completely the Baigorri area way of speaking.[12]

Jon Joseba Etxabe carried out a similar study in Idaho in the 1980s and concluded that most of the Basque speakers in the state were from the Markina-Lekeitio-Gernika area of Bizkaia.[13] This was the same finding of the Aranzadi Science Association in its *Euskalerriko Atlas Etnolinguistikoan* (Ethnic and Linguistic Atlas of the Basque Country);[14] the association spoke with a collaborator from Idaho, and his way of speaking was from the same area of Bizkaia, with no features from other dialects.

There is, of course, a very obvious and distinctive dimension to the Basque spoken in the western United States: its traces of English, especially in the vocabulary. Etxabe, for example, finds many examples in Idaho: *anbrela* ("umbrella"), *drinka* ("drink"), *mauntena* ("mountain"), *nouna* ("known"), *nusa* ("news"), *raiterra* ("writer"), *singerra* ("singer"), *uikena* ("weekend"), *xipa* ("sheep"), *xopa* ("shop"), and so on. Many complete expressions have also been borrowed, such as "that's good," "that's nice," "you know," "you see," "anyway," and "maybe."[15] Etxabe's findings are confirmed by a later study that also lists a series of English loanwords in the Basque spoken in Elko, Nevada: *estorra* ("store"), *troka* ("truck"), *aiskrimia* ("ice cream"), and *postofiza* ("post office").[16]

It should also be pointed out, in this connection, that many "new" words and expressions have also been created or recovered, whether correctly or not, in the Basque Country in recent years: *aburu* ("opinion" or "guess"), *ahalbidetu* ("facilitate"), *azpiegitura* ("infrastructure"), *baldintza* ("condition"), *baliabide* ("means" or "resource"), *bideragarri* ("feasible"), *bilakaera* ("evolution" or "transformation"), *ekidin* ("to avoid"), *elebitasun* ("bilingualism"), *euskalki* ("Basque dialect"), *hedabide* ("means of communication" or "media"), *helegite* ("appeal"), *idazkari* ("secretary"), *kutsadura* ("infection" or "contamination"), *lorpen* ("achievement" or "conquest"), and so on. Naturally, these innovations are quite unknown to Basque speakers who live in the Americas (and, in fact, to many people who live in the Basque Country as well), and, from that point of view, Basque in the Americas is becoming archaic.

More Information about Basque Speakers Living in America

I noted above that chain migration patterns resulted in people from the same area in the Basque Country settling in the same area in the Americas, yet this was not always the case. However, even when Basques from different parts of the Basque Country settled in the same area, this did not necessarily lead to closer relations between the different groups. Indeed, in some cases, people stuck in their own small groups and lived only with the people from their home areas. To put it another way, what took place in the Basque Country also happened in the Americas; being from one particular area was more important than being a Basque speaker. In regard to Basque speakers in Argentina, for example, Douglass and Bilbao observe that:

> the Basque community of Rio de la Plata was not, in terms of internal organization, monolithic and undifferentiated. Old World Basque regional loyalties and animosities tended to be reproduced in the New World context. As early as the 1850s the considerable French colony of Buenos Aires conducted group activities independently of the Spanish Basques.[17]

According to Douglass and Bilbao, the Laurak Bat ("The Four [regions] Are as One") association was founded in Buenos Aires in 1876, and, in 1895, twenty-nine of its members from the Northern Basque Country left to find the Centro Vasco Francés (French Basque Center). The same year, apparently, some people from Navarre founded the Centro Navarro (Navarrese Center) in Buenos Aires.[18]

Similarly, the Asociación Vasco-Navarra de Beneficiencia (Basque-Navarrese Welfare Association) was founded in Havana, Cuba, in 1878, and people from the Northern Basque Country were forbidden from joining it.[19] In 1924, likewise, the Zazpiak bat ("The Seven [regions] Are as One") club was founded in San Francisco. Clearly the name of this association revealed its aim to bring Basques from all areas together, but this was not to be. There were quarrels between Basques from the North and those from the South, and, ten years after its foundation, the club disbanded.[20]

In the 1950s, Adrien Gachiteguy witnessed the Basques' lifestyle in Nevada close up and he, too, found the same problem there:

I believe that the lack of a specifically Basque organization in such large Basque colonies is due to the existence of two large groups of people: people from Navarre and Lower Navarre, on the one hand, and people from Bizkaia, on the other. They each have their own language – some Basque, some Spanish – and their own songs and character. It is as if they were living in the seventeenth century, in the time of the wars between France and Spain. The "Zazpiak bat" spirit has yet to enter the mentality, still less the feelings of these Basques.[21]

In a parallel way to events in the Basque Country, so attitudes began to change in the Americas around 1960, with Basques there starting to feel part of the Basque Country as a whole. The most significant development for Basques in the Western United States seems to have been the First National Basque Festival, held in Sparks, Nevada, in 1959. This was the first major occasion that Basques from all areas of the Basque Country (and, to some extent, of the Western US) got together, and it led to the creation of a series of annual festivals or "picnics" all over the West that are still popular today.[22] Moreover, in Reno in 1973 several Basque associations in the US merged to become North American Basque Organizations, Incorporated; with the aim of strengthening Basque unity and identity.

Mixed Ways of Speaking in America

Despite the above-mentioned obstacles, there have been and are mixed ways of speaking in the Americas. However, the issue is how to measure the extent and importance of this.

With regards to the areas concerned, it has been established that Basques had different objectives when they emigrated to the Americas, and people from all areas of the Basque Country did not necessarily settle in the same areas or socialize with one another. After reading some historical verses, for example, Koldo Mitxelena suggests that in 1761, most Basques in Lima, Peru, were from Gipuzkoa and Bizkaia due to the fact that elements from their respective dialects were to be found in the verse structures.[23] In the 1990s, meanwhile, Estibalitz Amorrortu studied Basque speakers in Elko, Nevada, where Bizkaian and Navarrese Basque are both spoken and interact.[24] It is clear, at the end of the day, that it is more appropriate to talk about "types of Basque in America" than about a generic "Basque in America," and each of them is made up of elements from different dialects rather than from all the dialects at the same time.

The importance of different ways of speaking usually depends on the extension of the area they are used in. In order to become significant and strong, they have to last over generations, and this is not characteristic of Basque in the Americas; the Basques who settled in the Americas have always had a deep sense of belonging and a strong connection to the Basque Country, but the language in itself has not been their priority when it comes to identity maintenance.

Most of the children of those Basques who first went to the Americas are Basque speakers. In many cases, these first-generation Basque-Americans married among themselves and Basque was still used to some extent at home. From the second generation onward, however, Basque-use declined. This generation began to marry outside the Basque community and one parent not being a Basque speaker often led to the language being lost. According to several studies, then, Basque was easily lost in the third generation. Naturally, there were always exceptions; in families involved in livestock ranching or running Basque boarding houses, for example, Basque was maintained for longer.[25] This tendency can be seen in Amorrortu's study of Basque speakers in Elko. Basque is used very little in everyday life and only in very specific situations: mainly at home, with relatives, with certain friends, over the telephone with relatives, and in Basque restaurants. Because of this, the mixed way of speaking in Elko does not have deep roots, and Amorrortu quotes the example of parents only using the Basque they already knew back in the Basque Country. Naturally, in mixed marriages between people from Bizkaia and from Navarre, there is a tendency to mix the two dialects, mostly by using words from both areas at the same time.

Here are some examples of this type of mixture quoted by Amorrortu:[26]

> *Okeri kosinerueri*
> "to these cooks"
>
> *Okin maistra okin*
> "with these (female) teachers"

Navarrese demonstratives can be seen in these two examples (*okeri, okin*), but they are positioned before the nouns, as in Western Basque. Of course, this mixture can also be seen in the vocabulary:[27] for example, the Navarrese *akitu* and Bizkaian *amaitu* can be found at the same time in order to say "to finish."

Looking at the future, it does not seem that mixed ways of speaking such as this have much future or chance of gaining strength, more than anything else because emigration from the Basque Country to the Americas ceased many years ago. Of course, there are an increasing number of initiatives being undertaken to revive Basque use in the Americas. In 1999, for example, an *ikastola* (Basque-language medium school) was founded in Boise, Idaho. Likewise, the Center for Basque Studies at the University of Nevada, Reno, is a significant sponsor of Basque culture. Yet the Basque encouraged in these places is the universal variety that is being used more and more: Unified Basque, which was created in 1964. Mixing that standard speech with English is what gives American Basque its character and personality. That, in fact, is what today's American Basque is.

Part II
Connections among the Dialects

Connections among the Dialects

There is a general, deeply held belief that every particular feature of the Basque language is linked to a particular dialect, but this is not necessarily so. Many features are to be found in more than one dialect, traversing the usual dialect boundaries and occupying wider areas. In some cases, this is evidence of relationships and connections from the past, but in other cases the reason behind a particular model is not clear.

The fact is that this type of feature is common. It would take too long to look at them all, and, for that reason, I will examine them in ten groups:

1. Common Features throughout the Whole of Basque Country
2. The Main Features of Central Basque
3. The Main Features of a Certain Part of Central Basque
4. The Main Features of Navarrese and Navarrese-Lapurdian Basque
5. The Features that Differentiate Western and Central Basque from that of the Northern Basque Country and Navarrese
6. The Main Features of Basque in the Northern Basque Country and Eastern Navarrese
7. The Main Features of Eastern Basque
8. The Main Features of Basque in the Northern Basque Country
9. The Main Features of Basque in the Southern Basque Country
10. The Main Features of Various Areas

Little or no attention has been paid to these features until now, and, because of this, they have been prone to erroneous speculation. It has often been asserted, for example, that the ablative suffix *-endako* (in, for example, *lagunarendako* "for the friend") and the associative *-ki* (*lagunareki* "with the friend") are distinguishing features of Navarrese Basque. And that using the genitive (*lagunaren ikustera joan da* "he/she has gone to see (his/her) friend") and *-en* in the future tense (*eginen* "will do," *izanen* "will be") are features of Basque in the Northern Basque Country. Many characteristics have also been incorrectly attributed to the Bizkaian dialect: the vowels *i* and *u* causing *a* → *e* (*dirua* → *dirue* "money"), the introduction of epenthesis between the vowels *i* and *a*, *e*, and *o* (*mendia* → *mendidxe* or *mendixe* "mountain"), and the suffix -*(i)e* in the second person plural absolutive (*zarie* instead of *zarete* "you are").

In fact, it is true that those characteristics are to be found in those places, but they are also to be found in other places, and that is what this section aims to show and clarify.

8
The Main Features of Basque across Several Dialects

I will first turn my gaze to the Basque Country as a whole, without specifying any particular or defined geographical or linguistic area.

Area and Causes

Here I will examine features wherever they are to be found, but specifically features that are not from a fixed, continual area. In other words, they crop up here and there: in some areas of Bizkaia, in some other parts of Navarre, and so on. They seem to be consequences derived from the language itself rather than things that have appeared in one particular place and then spread to a wider area, and they are not features that have spread due to relationships between different groups of people.

Features

I will concentrate on three main phonological features.

Firstly, in many ways of speaking, words that end in a vowel assimilate the article when it is added. In the Uribe Kosta area of Bizkaia, for example, this tendency is very strong. The following examples are from Getxo:[1] *basoak* → *basok*, *basoek* → *bások*, *basoari* → *basori*, *basoei* → *básori*, *basoaren* → *bason*, *basoen* → *báson*, and so on. When the article is removed, the singular and plural variants become the same. In these ways of speaking, then, it is the spoken accent that distinguishes between them. The same thing happens, by way of a comparison, in the Goierri area of Gipuzkoa.

In the Uribe Kosta area, furthermore, this same type of assimilation takes place with singular verb forms in the absolutive case, yet this is not such a common feature. The following examples are also taken from Getxo:[2] *etzea* (rather than *etxea* in Unified Basque) → *etze* ("house"), *basoa* → *baso* ("forest"), *iturria* → *iturri* ("spring"), *burua* → *buru* ("head"), and *alabea* (instead of *alaba*) → *alabe* ("daughter"). Beyond the Uribe Kosta area, this also happens in some parts of the Lea-Artibai area (Bizkaia), Basaburua in Navarre, as well as in some towns in the Imotz and Larraun Valleys, also in Navarre. There are also traces of this in other areas. For example, it can be found in Errezil, in central Gipuzkoa, when words end in the vowels *-i* or *-u*, but in no other cases: for example, *ogia* → *ogi* ("bread"), and *eskua* → *esku* ("hand").

As the assimilation of articles takes place in some towns but not in others, speakers of the language pick up on this difference immediately. In Ondarroa, for instance, it is very much in use, and people from neighboring towns might say say *Ondarru, herri berú* or in Unified Basque *Ondarroa, herri beroa* ("Ondarroa, the warm town") to make fun of the way Ondarroa people speak. Similar jokes are made about other ways of speaking. These sayings are attributed to the people of Orio, for example: *Oriyoko karamelok, merkek eta goxok / Oriyoko pikok, errial bikok* "The candies of Orio, cheap and sweet" / "The figs of Orio, one *real* for a pair" (*gustoa jateko moukok* "good for eating," the people of Orio themselves add).[3] Meanwhile, the people of Larraun, Navarre, parody the way of speaking in Lekunberri by saying: *Goizeko ordu batiin, Lekunberriko trinkitiin, atsoak eta guzi baltsiin* ("At one o'clock in the morning, at the party in Lekunberri, the old women and everyone waltzing").[4] These examples make it very clear that this feature can be found in any part of the Basque Country: Ondarroa, Orio, Lekunberri, and so on.

Secondly, in many places throughout the Basque Country, when the vowels *e* and *o* come together with the vowels *a*, *e*, and *o*, *e* → *i* and *o* → *u*, *etxea* → *etxia*/*etxie* ("house"), *besoa* → *besua*/*besue* ("arm"). This is more prominent in some ways of speaking than in others, and, as far as we know, it is most typical in Sakana, Navarre. For example, this also happens there when consonants disappear between vowels: *aberatsa* → *abiatsa* ("rich"), *egunero* → *egunio* ("every day"), *berandu* → *biandu* ("late"), *kalera* → *kalia* ("to the street"), *asto bat* → *astuat* ("one donkey").[5]

At the start of words, when consonants disappear between vowels and two vowels come togther, *e* → *i* also takes place. The following examples are from Urdiain, a village in the Sakana Valley: *edan* → *ean* → *yan* ("to drink"), *edozein* → *eozein* → *yozein* ("any" or "anyone"), *egon* → *eon* → *yon* ("to be"), *erantzi* → *eantzi* → *yantzi* ("to take off"), *eraztun* → *eaztun* → *yaztun* ("ring"), *erosi*/*egosi* → *eosi* → *yosi* ("to buy"/ "to boil"), and so on. This also happens in areas close to Sakana such as Imotz, Basaburua, and Larraun, as well as in Zuberoa, in the far eastern part of the Basque Country.

However, these two transformations do not follow the same model; *e* → *i* takes place in a wider area than *o* → *u*. For example, in the area around Gernika, Bizkaia, *kalea* → *kalie* ("street"), but *kanpoa* ("outside") remains as it is, without becoming *kanpua* or *kanpue*. The *e* → *i* transformation is almost certainly older, and that is why it is to be found in more places.

Finally, in participles with two or more syllables, the vowel *-i* disappears in many ways of speaking. Many authors have linked this with the Navarre syncope, but in fact there is no connection between the two. For instance, the following examples are from Mendata in the Busturialdea area of central Bizkaia:[6] *ekarri dau* instead of *ekarri du* in Unified Basque → *ekar deu* ("he/she has brought it"), *erosi beharko da* → *eros biko da* ("it will have to be bought"), *etorri da* → *etor de* ("he/she has come"), *ibili naiz* → *ibil nas* ("I have walked"), *ikusi dauenean* instead of *ikusi duenean* → *ikus dabenien* ("when he/she saw it"), and *ipini dot* instead of *ipini dut* → *ipin yot* ("I have put it").

This typically happens before the future tense suffix *-ko*: *ekarriko* → *ekarko* ("will bring"), *erosiko* → *erosko* ("will buy"), *etorriko* → *etorko* ("will come"), *ibiliko* → *ibilko* ("will walk"), *ikusiko* → *ikusko* ("will see"), and so on.

The Main Features of Central Basque

I will now focus on the Central Basque, which as noted above has been the key dialect in the development of Unified Basque.

Area and Causes

Certain features are found extensively throughout the central Basque Country. In most cases, when I use the term "central Basque Country" I do not include the following areas: the whole of Zuberoa, together with Erronkari and Zaraitzu (Navarre), in the east; and the Western Basque area together with, in some cases, Sakana (Navarre), in the west. Thus, there are similarities in the areas that lie outside this central area to both the west and east, in Bizkaia and Zuberoa respectively, because the dialects there show fewer innovations than in the dialect of the central Basque Country. Moreover, it would be very unusual for two separate areas, each at different extremes of the Basque Country, to use the same innovations. It is therefore more likely that innovations have taken place in the central area whereas the outlying areas have maintained older forms. Bearing in mind the areas involved and that these features have long been in place, it may well be that (at least in some cases) Iruñea, the Navarrese capital, was the source of these innovations. At the very least, Iruñea was once sufficiently influential to encourage the dissemination of these innovations.

Features

The features examined here are not all common to the same areas; some are more geographically extensive than others, as is usual in linguistic matters.

When the article is added to words ending in *-a*, *-a* + *a* → *-a* in the central Basque Country, *makila* + *a* → *makila* ("stick"). On the contrary, *-a* + *a* → *-á* takes place in Zuberoa, Erronkari, and, it seems, in an even wider area of the Northern Basque Country in the past (*makilá*). There is evidence of this in the sixteenth-century manuscripts of Joanes Leizarraga, from Beskoitze (Briscous) in Lapurdi.[7] In Zaraitzu, Navarre, it was *-ara* (*makilara*), and forms such as *-ea* are used in the western Basque Country (*makilea, makilia, makilie*).

Throughout the Basque Country, there is a tendency for *z* → *tz* and *s* → *ts* after *l*, *n*, and *r* in the middle of words: for example, Spanish *salsa* → *saltsa* ("sauce"), Spanish *pensado* → *pentsatu* ("thought"), and Spanish *cárcel* → *kartzela* ("jail"). But, as well as in the middle of words, there is also a tendency for this to happen at the start and end of words in a very wide area of the Basque Country: *hil tzituen* ("he/she/it killed them"), *omen tzen* ("apparently he/she/it was"), *han tzetorren* ("he/she/it was coming [there]"), *ohean tzela* ("when he/she/it was in bed"), *behar tzigun* ("he/she/it had to + verb + [to] us"), and so on. This innovation is not, however, used in either Erronkari and Zaraitzu, on the one hand, or the Western Basque area and most of Sakana, on the other. Furthermore, this feature is not used to the same degree in all areas.

The variants *-tik* ("from," as in *etxetik* "from the house") and *-gatik* ("because of," as in *egiteagatik* "for doing") predominate throughout the Basque Country, but the old forms *-ti* and *-gati* also still exist: *etxeti, egiteagati*. This older form exists mostly in western Bizkaia, the Aramaio Valley in Araba, the Goierri area of Gipuzkoa, Sakana and Larraun in Navarre, and Zuberoa.

This innovation probably originated in Iruñea, but, recently, it has been further strengthened and now the influence comes more from Gipuzkoa: as well as the old forms, *-tikan, -rikan, -gatikan, -gandikan* (*lagunengandikan* "because of the friends") and *-(e)nikan* as well (*ez du esan etorriko denikan* "he/she did not say he/she would come") have begun to be used more widely, as well as *-(e)larikan* (> *-(e)likan)* in some parts of Navarre (*lana zulikan, ez zen etortzen ahal* "she/he could not come because she/he had to work"). The whole of northern Gipuzkoa (including Mutriku, Elgoibar, and Soraluze) and northwestern Navarre are part of this area. It is used most prominently in the following areas of Navarre: Bortziriak, Malerreka, Bertizarana, and Basaburu Txikia.

The Goierri area in Gipuzkoa is outside this area, but, on the other hand, *-tio* (*etxetio*) and *-gatio* (*egiteagatio*) have come into use there.

In the central Basque Country the variant *-te* predominates in second person plural absolutive verb forms: *zarete, zaitezte, zaitezkete, zatozte, zoazte, zabiltzate, zaudete, zentozten, zeundeten*, and so on. On the peripheries of the Basque Country *-(i)e* replaces this. The following forms, for example, are used in Etxarri Aranatz, Navarre:[8] *zarié* instead of *zarete* ("you are"), *ziñién* instead of *zineten* ("you were"), *zettezie* instead of *zaitezte* (present imperative auxiliary, singular), *zettezkie* instead of *zaitezkete* (present imperative auxiliary, plural), *zuezie/ziyuezie* instead of *zoazte* ("you are going"), *zailtzie* instead of *zabiltzate* ("you are walking"), *zaudie* instead of *zaudete* ("you are"), and so on.

Verb forms like this are used throughout Sakana, except in the village of Irañeta. The same is true for the Western Basque area and was also the case in Zaraitzu and Erronkari when they were Basque-speaking areas.

A variant of the absolutive *-te* later spread to other verb forms as well: specifically, the third person plural (*dute*, *dakite*, *zaiote* instead of *zaie*, *diote/dakote*, and so on), and second person plurals in categories other than the absolutive (*duzute*, *diozute*, *nauzute*, and so on). This is used in a smaller area, which shows that it is more recent.

However, the third person *-te* variant is used in a wide area: Lapurdi, Lower Navarre, much of central Navarre, and northeastern Gipuzkoa. In Gipuzkoa, this is used in the area between Donostia and Hernani, on one side, and Irun. In Navarre, on the other hand, the following areas are not included: Zaraitzu and Erronkari in the east, and Araitz-Betelu, Larraun, and most of Basaburu Txikia (excluding Goizueta, Saldias, and Beintza-Labaien) and Sakana (except for Irañeta), in the west. In those ways of speaking *-e* is mostly used: *due/die/daue* (> *dabe*). Nowadays, however, *-te* is widely used due to the influence of Unified Basque.

The ending *-te* in the second person in categories other than the absolutive is used in a very reduced area in Gipuzkoa, between Donostia and Hernani, on one side, to Irun, on the other. In Navarre, it is used in Goizueta, Basaburu Nagusia, Imotz (but not in Muskitz) and in Irañeta in the Sakana Valley.

There is strong use of the plural infix *-zki-* in the central Basque Country; it also appears in absolutive-dative and absolutive-dative-ergative verb forms. Thus, forms such as *zaizkio* and *dizkidazu* are used in the central Basque Country.

In Zuberoa, *-(t)z* is used for forming plural in both categories: *záitzo* instead of *zaizkio* and *déitzo* instead of *dizkio*. In the Western Basque area, on the other hand, it is *-z*: *jakoz* instead of *zaizkio* and *deutsaz* instead of *dizkio*.

The pluralizing *-zki-* is less commonly used in absolutive-dative-ergative than it is in absolutive-dative verb forms. Erronkari and much of Navarre are excluded from this. In eastern Lapurdi, Lower Navarre, together with Aezkoa and Zaraitzu in Navarre, *-zki-* is used, but so is *-(z)t-*, depending on the dative. To put it another way, the area in which the pluralizing *-zki-* is used with absolutive-dative-ergative verb forms is made up of: western Lapurdi, Gipuzkoa (except for the Deba Valley) and, in Navarre, Araitz-Betelu, the western Larraun Valley, western Basaburu Txikia, Bortziriak, Etxarri Aranatz, and Ergoiena. It is also used in Burunda (Navarre), but only in certain verb forms.

Although the opposite has often been contended, the prefix *zit-* in past tense absolutive-dative verbs is new: *zitzaidan*, *zitzaigun*, and so on. In the Western Basque area, for example, forms such as *jatan* and *jakun* have always been used, and forms like *zéitan* and *zéikün* are used in Zuberoa. In a few other

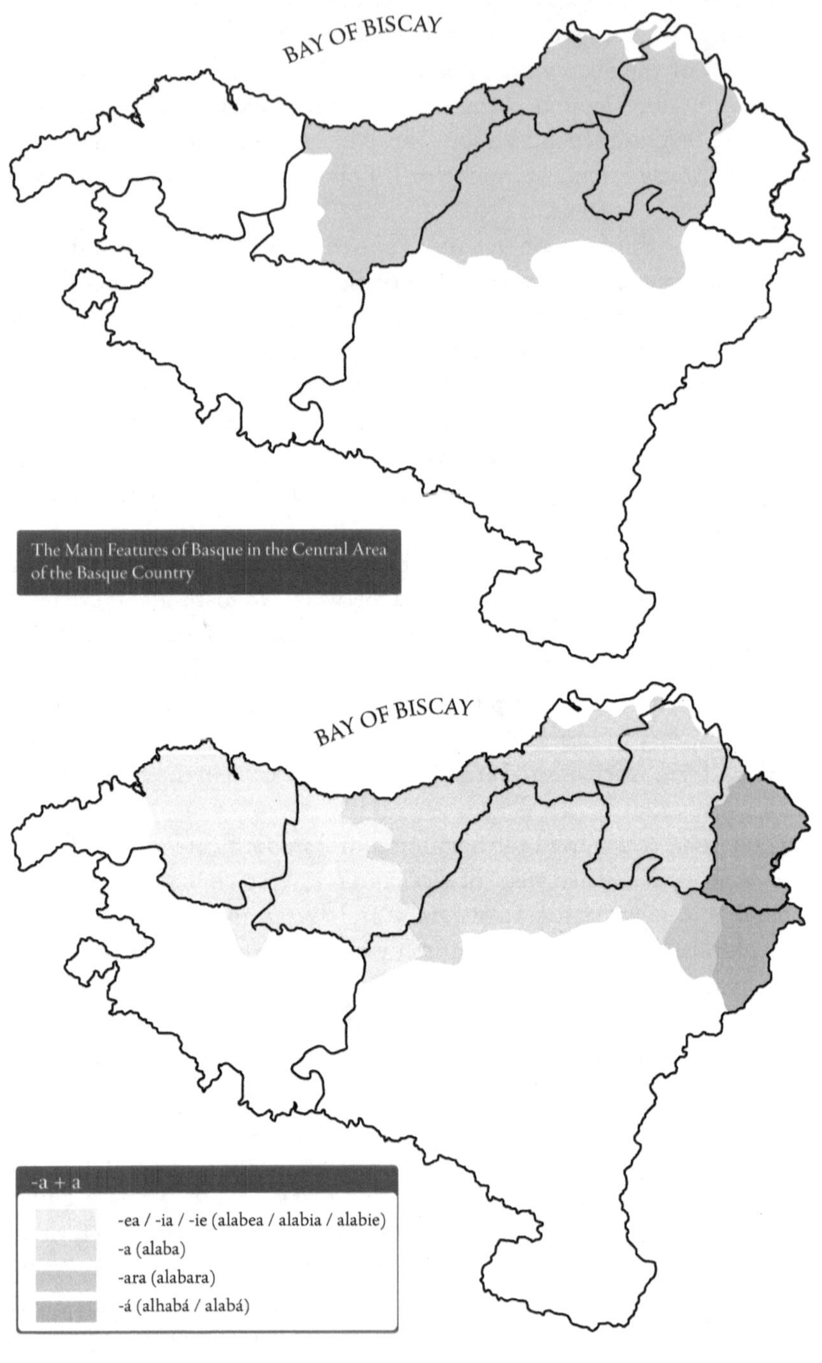
BAY OF BISCAY
The Main Features of Basque in the Central Area of the Basque Country
BAY OF BISCAY
-a + a
-ea / -ia / -ie (alabea / alabia / alabie)
-a (alaba)
-ara (alabara)
-á (alhabá / alabá)

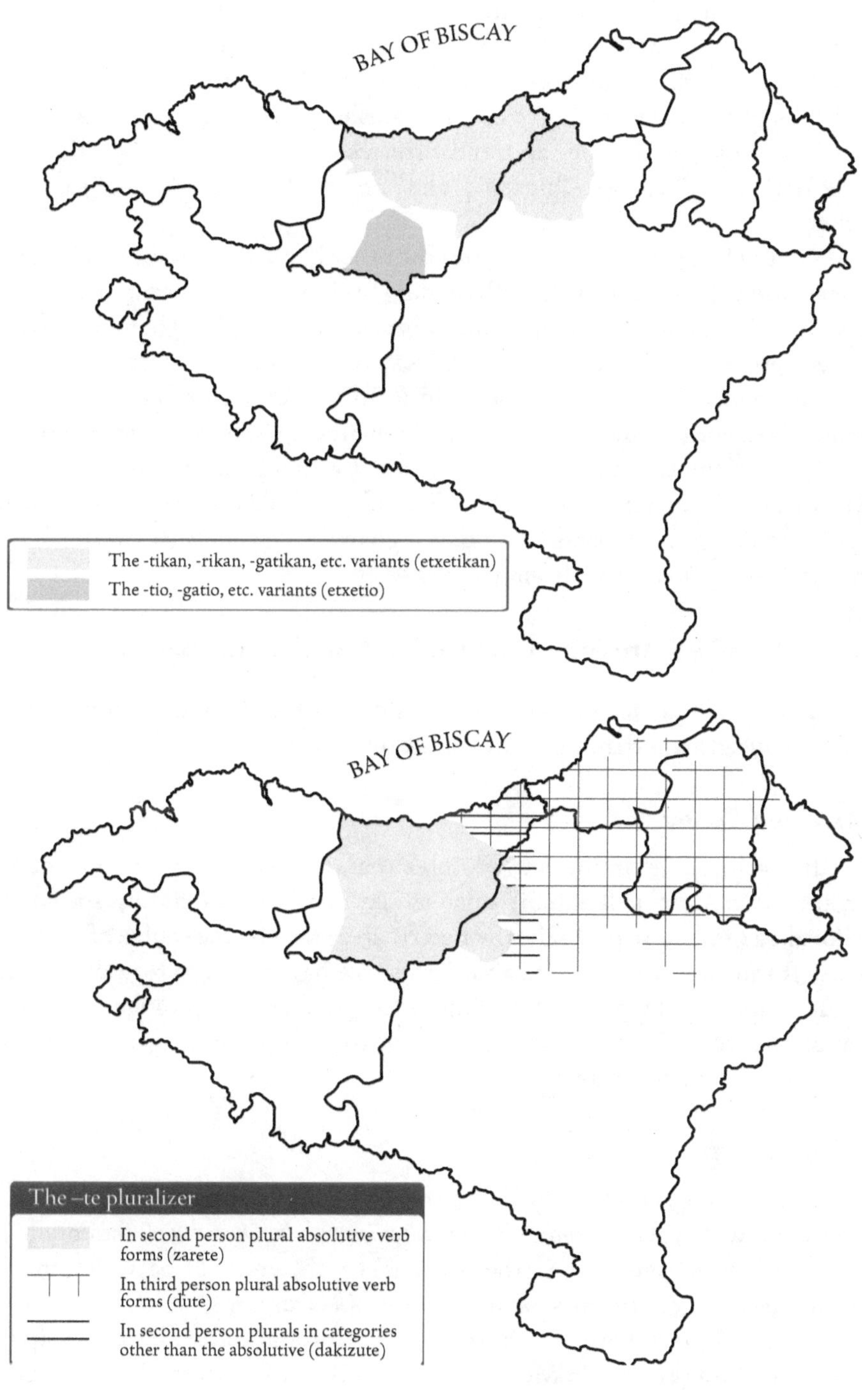
BAY OF BISCAY
The -tikan, -rikan, -gatikan, etc. variants (etxetikan)
The -tio, -gatio, etc. variants (etxetio)
BAY OF BISCAY
The –te pluralizer
In second person plural absolutive verb forms (zarete)
In third person plural absolutive verb forms (dute)
In second person plurals in categories other than the absolutive (dakizute)

places, verb forms without *zit-* have also been kept.

In the central Basque Country the suffixes *-ten/-tzen* are used in verbal nouns, and the separation between the two is clear: verbs ending in *-n* or *-{s, z, ts, tz} + i* take *-ten*, and all others take *-tzen*. Thus, one gets for example *edaten* ("drinking"), *ikusten* ("seeing"), *ikuzten* ("washing" or "cleaning"), and *irakasten* ("teaching") on the one hand, and *ateratzen* ("leaving"), *betetzen* ("filling"), *hartzen* ("taking"), *jotzen* ("hitting"), and *hiltzen* ("dying" or "killing"), on the other.

On the fringes of the territory, on the other hand, the variant *-ten* is more widely used. This is used with verbs ending in *-{l, n, r} + i*: for example, *ibilten* ("walking"), *ipinten* ("placing"), and *ekarten* ("bringing"). There are a few other options in the Western Basque area, as explained in Chapter 2. In Erronkari, meanwhile, *-tan* was the main form: *bordaltu* instead of *ezkondu* in Unified Basque ("to marry") → *bordaltan* ("marrying"). In most of the Northern Basque Country and in some areas of northwestern Navarre (most of Basaburu Txikia, Zubieta, Bortziriak, and Sunbilla), the old form *-iten* is still used: for example, *egoiten* ("being"), *emaiten* ("giving"), *eramaiten* ("carrying"), *erraiten* ("saying"), *izaiten* ("having"), and so on.

The Main Features of a Certain Part of Central Basque

I will now examine features that occur in the central Basque Country but in more reduced areas than those previously discussed.

Area and Causes

I will specifically examine four features that, although they are not found in the same areas, still exhibit some similarities. Geographically speaking, Gipuzkoa (and more precisely, the Beterri area) may be the source of some of these features. As I mentioned above, this area has long been regarded as the most Basque-speaking part of the Basque Country, and the prestige and admiration that come from this strength may be the reason for the growing use of these features in other areas.

Characteristics

When the vowel *i* combines with the vowels *a*, *e*, and *o*, sounds such as *y/dx/x* appear between them: *mendi + a → mendiya/mendidxe/mendixa* ("mountain"). This innovation is used in northern Gipuzkoa, the entire Deba Valley, much of Bizkaia, the Lapurdi coast, and two areas of Navarre.

In the Western Basque area, two types of pronunciation have appeared: in Mungialdea (but not in Mungia itself), in Busturialdea, the Lea area, Durangaldea, and the Otxandio-Oleta-Ubide-Legutio area, the epenthesis is *-dx-*: *mendidxe*. This also appears in the northern Nerbioi Valley in Basauri, Zaratamo, and Arrigorriaga, and it was also used to an extent in Bilbao. In the Deba Valley and the Artibai area, on the other hand, it is *-x-*: *mendixa/mendixe*. Something similar to this is also said in Azkoitia and also in Zumaia (both in Gipzukoa). Among young people in Zumaia, however, *-y-* predominates (*mendiya*), and that is also the case in northern Gipuzkoa, the Lapurdi coast, and Navarre. Elsewhere in Navarre, though, in Bortziriak, Sunbilla, and Arano, and in most of Sakana (except for Burunda), this epenthesis is used.

According to testimonies collected by Bonaparte,[9] another type of epenthesis was used in the central Basque Country in the mid-nineteenth century: when the vowel *u* combined with *a*, *e*, or *u*, *-b-* was usually placed between them: *esku + a → eskuba/eskube* ("hand"). This has fallen into considerable disuse since then and is now only used in a few small towns in northern Gipuzkoa (mostly in the Beterri area) and in the central Sakana Valley in Navarre. This disuse is the result of it being considered to be a "beggar's" (in other words, poor) way of talking. It is worth noting, however, that this is still very much in use in three towns in Sakana – Arbizu, Lakuntza, and Arruazu.[10]

In the central area, **-i-* is the main root in absolutive-dative-ergative verb forms: *diot*, *dizut*, *didazu*, *digute*, and so on. This is totally the case in the Central Basque area and also extends to the north of the Deba Valley (from Elgoibar to Deba) and much of Navarre. The area not included in Navarre comprises Burunda, Ergoiena, and Etxarri Aranatz, on one side, to Aurizberri and Erronkari on the other. In that area the root is **eradun*: for example, *dua* instead of *dit*, *duazu* instead of *didazu* and *duazai* instead of *didazue* are examples from Urdiain in the Burunda Valley.

In western Lapurdi, absolutive-ergative verb forms are mostly used (*erran nau* "he/she told me"), but when absolutive-dative-ergative is used (when the indirect object is third person), the root used is **-i-*. In central Lapurdi (and specifically in the Uztaritze area), **eradun* is the most frequently used root, but when the dative *nori* case is *hari/haiei* ("to him/her/it"/"to them"), **eradun* and **-i-* are both used: *dio/dako*. The same is true for Urdazubi, Zugarramurdi, and Baztan in Navarre. The opposite happens in the northern Erroibar Valley, and in the Bizkarreta-Gerendiain (Viscarret-Guerendiain), Mezkiritz, Esnotz, and Lintzoain (Linzoáin) areas. There **-i-* is the most frequently used root, and when *nori* is *hari/haiei*, **eradun* is used: *dire* instead of *dit*, *dizugu*, and the like, on the one hand, and *dako* instead of *dio*, and *dakote* instead of *die*.

In present tense *hitano* absolutive-dative-ergative verbs forms, *z-* is the absolutive characteristic in the central Basque Country: *dio → ziok/zion*, *dator → zatorrek/zatorren*, *dakigu → zakiagu/zakinagu*. This predominates in most areas

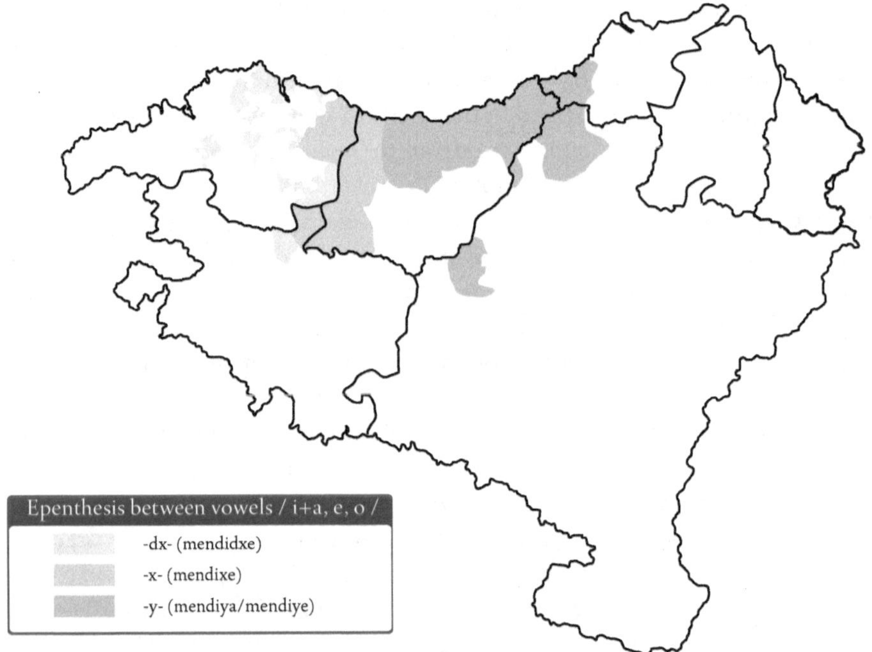
Epenthesis between vowels / i+a, e, o /
-dx- (mendidxe)
-x- (mendixe)
-y- (mendiya/mendiye)

of Lapurdi, Gipuzkoa, and Navarre. Outside this central area, the other options are as follows:

- Forms such as *y-/dx-/j-* in Western Basque and in Burunda: *juak/juan* instead of *zidak/zidan*, *jok/jon* instead of *zagok/zagon*, *jukat/jukanat* instead of *zaukaat/zaukanat*, *jakiai/jakinai* instead of *zakitek/zakiten*, for example, in Urdiain.
- *d-* is the characteristic in Zuberoa, most of Lower Navarre, northeastern Lapurdi, Erronkari, Zaraitzu, northern Erroibar, Baztan (*z-* is also used in the southern part of the area, in the Basaburua area) and in Lizarraga in Ergoiena and in Dorrao (Torrano). The same transformation has taken place in two towns in Gipuzkoa: Mutriku and Legazpi. These examples are from the Baztan Valley of Navarre:[11] *diekak* instead of *zioat*, *diok* instead of *zagok/zoak*, *dieilek* instead of *zabilek*, and *diekik* instead of *zakik*.
- *x-* is used in Aezkoa (Navarre), Elorrio (Bizkaia), and Oñati (Gipuzkoa). These verb forms are from the latter two towns: *xostak* instead of *zidak*, *xagok* instead of *zagok*, *xaton* instead of *zatorren*, and *xaukai* instead of *zaukatek*.

There is more than one option in intermediate forms of speech. In Urretxu and Zumarraga (Gipzukoa), for example, there are three types of pronunciation: *x-*, *dd-*, and *d-*.[12] In Urdazubi and Zugarramurdi (Navarre), on the other hand, *z-* is the most frequent form, but *d-* is used as well.[13]

Vocabulary

There are several words that have been created and strengthened in the central area: for example, *aditu* ("to hear") with *entzun* used only on the edges of the territory, *apar* ("foam"), which is *bits/pits* in the Western Basque area and *hagun* in the east, *atera* ("to leave"), which is *irten* in the Western Basque area and *jalgi/ilki* and similar forms in the east, *bota* ("to throw"), which is also *jaurti/urtuki/aurdiki* in the boundary areas, and *nazka/narda* ("disgust"), with just the variant *higuin* used in the boundary areas.

The Main Features of Navarrese and Navarrese-Lapurdian Basque

Some innovations in Lapurdi, Lower Navarre, and a wide area of Navarre have long demonstrated an unquestionable degree of homogeneity in the area as a whole.

Area and Causes

The connection between Navarre and Lower Navarre is well known because they were once part of the same country. The connection between Lapurdi

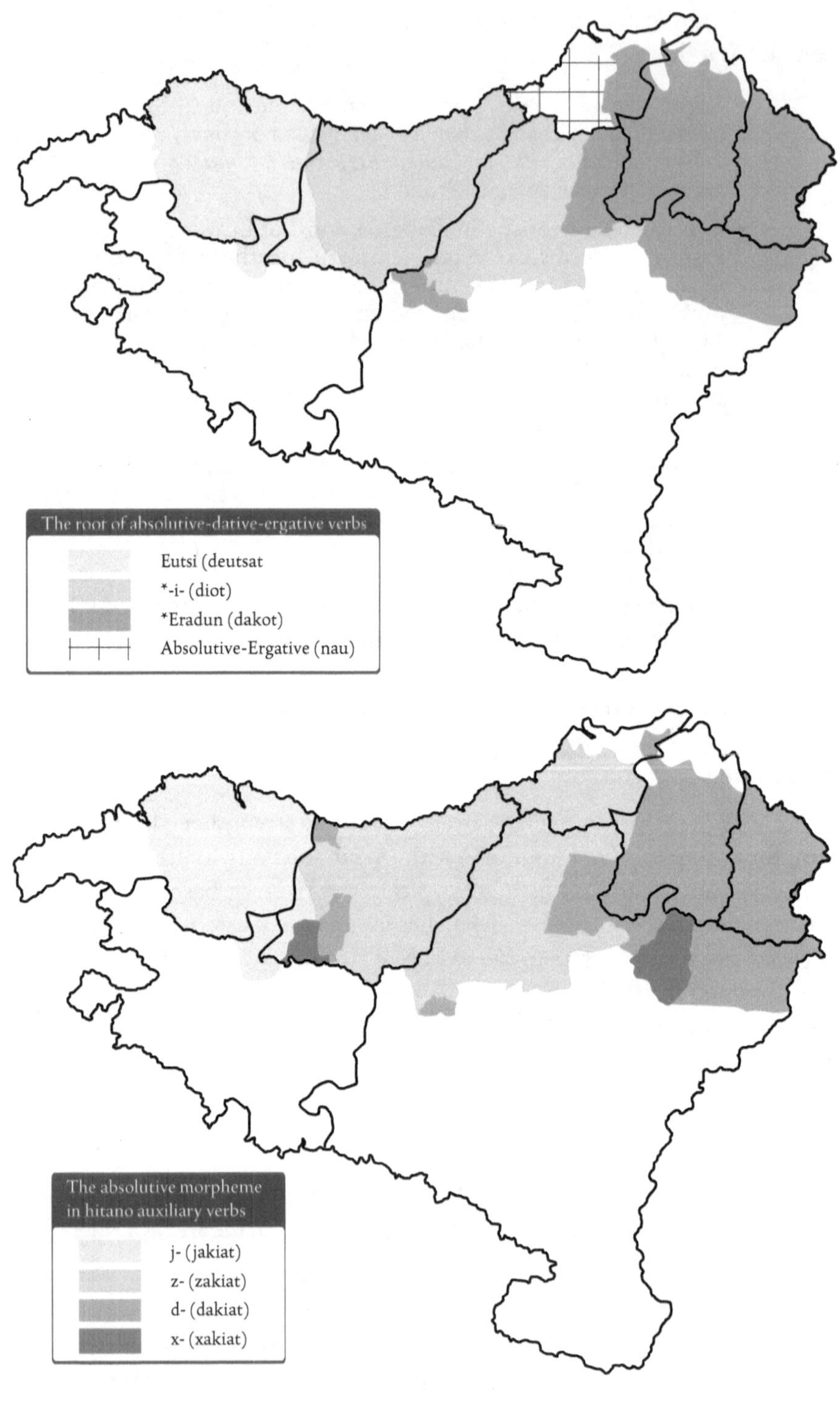
The root of absolutive-dative-ergative verbs
Eutsi (deutsat
*-i- (diot)
*Eradun (dakot)
Absolutive-Ergative (nau)
The absolutive morpheme in hitano auxiliary verbs
j- (jakiat)
z- (zakiat)
d- (dakiat)
x- (xakiat)

and Lower Navarre is also well known and still very much alive today. The connection I want to clarify here, though, is that between Lapurdi and Navarre. Historically, Navarre used the port of Baiona until, after the end of the First Carlist War in 1841, customs borders in Spain were moved to the official border between France and Spain in the Pyrenees (previously, the provinces making up the Southern Basque Country had formed a kind of free trade area, with Spanish customs borders beginning at their southern boundaries). After that, the relationship between Navarre and Lapurdi waned, but it never completely disappeared. Wool, olive oil, wine, and wheat were exported from Navarre to the other side of the international border. Cloth, meanwhile, was the main product imported into Navarre. Livestock, of course, went in both directions.

With regard to Navarre, these innovations did not spread to Zaraitzu and Erronkari; nor, to the west, did they reach Basaburua, Imotz, Larraun, Araitz-Betelu and Sakana. Some of the innovations did however reach as far as north-eastern Gipuzkoa, mostly in the Oiartzun-Hondarribia-Irun area.

Features

I will examine three features in particular:

Firstly, in the speech of many Western and Eastern dialects, and in Zuberoa and Erronkari as well, spoken emphasis is used to distinguish between singular and plural: for instance, *gizonák jan du* ("the man has eaten [it]")/ *gízonak jan dute* ("the men have eaten [it]") are examples from Lezo.[14] In Navarrese and Lower Navarrese Basque, however, this type of differentiating emphasis is not used.

Nowadays, in fact, the importance of this differentiating emphasis is lessening throughout the Basque Country. It is not taken into account in textbooks, and no efforts have been made to protect or promote this linguistic feature.

Secondly, in many ways of speaking in this area there is a tendency for *-aren* → *-ain* in the possessive-genitive *noren* singular case. However, there is no fixed model for this, and it crops up here and there. In Urdazubi and Zugarramurdi in Navarre, for example, it is normal for: *gizonaren* → *gizonain* ("of the man"), *amarendako* → *amaindako* ("for the mother"), and *jatekoarekin* → *yatekoaikin* ("with the food").[15]

Until very recently in Zuberoa, *-aen* has been the suffix in the singular genitive, but the newer *-ain* has now arrived there as well, mostly in cases expressing destination (*lagünaintáko* "for the friend") and the associative (*lagünaíki* "with the friend").

This transformation is at its strongest in the future tense, and this is used

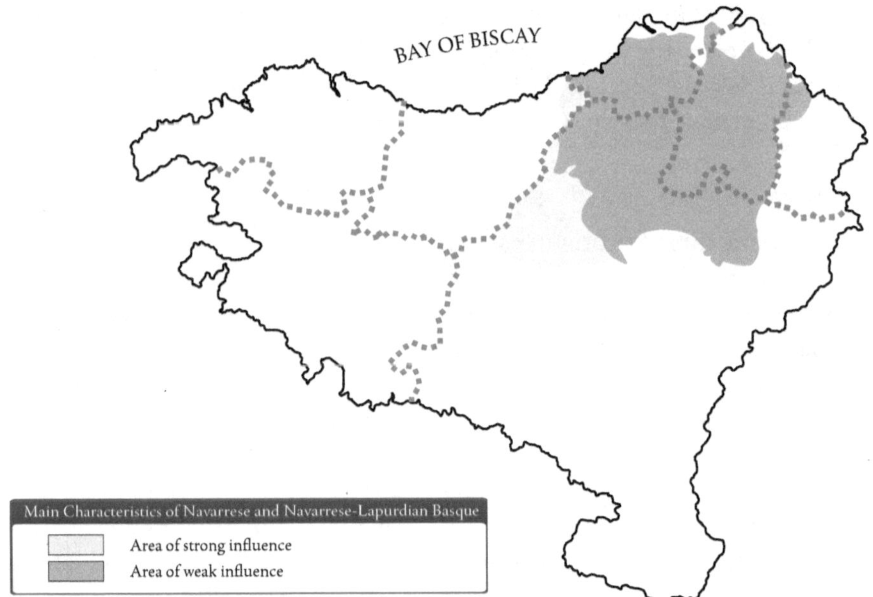
BAY OF BISCAY
Main Characteristics of Navarrese and Navarrese-Lapurdian Basque
Area of strong influence
Area of weak influence

in the widest area. In Goizueta, for example, *-an* is the suffix for nouns (*gizonan* instead of *gizonaren*), but *-in* is used in the future: *edanen* → *erain* ("to drink"), *egonen* → *egoin* ("to be"), *emanen* → *emain* ("to give"), *esanen* → *esain* ("to say"), *janen* → *yain* ("to eat"), and *joanen* → *yoin* ("to go").[16]

Finally, a third feature of the area is the suffix *-ki* in synthetic verbs; *izaki*, *joaki*, *ibilki*, *jakinki*, and *eramaki* are examples of this. This normally expresses two main meanings: cause or explanation, and precision.[17] Moreover, Txomin Sagarzazu gives the following examples of the former in Hondarribia:[18]

deus záki ez, ta emán in biartzen instead of
deus izan ez, eta eman egin behar zen in Unified Basque
"we had nothing, but we had to give it our all"

áurreko aldian bisíki, ta esta konturátu re instead of
aurreko aldean bizi, eta ezta konturatu ere
"I live right in front, and I didn't realize at all"

The meaning of precision is seen in this example from Sara in which the synthetic verb's meaning is the same:[19]

labórantza ere emen ez da ongi gaki instead of
nekazaritza ere hemen ez doa ongi
"farming is not so good here either"

Vocabulary

The following words are used in some parts of the area: for example, *airegaixto* instead of *tximista* ("lightning") in Unified Basque, *aitatxi* and *amatxi* instead of *aitona/amona* ("grandfather"/"grandmother"), *arras/raso* instead of *erabat* or *oso* ("completely" or "totally"), *esker mila/milesker* instead of *eskerrik asko* or *eskerrik hanitx* ("thanks"/"many thanks"), *gisu/kisu* instead of *karea* ("lime"), *horma* instead of *izotza* ("ice"), *hurbil* instead of *hur* ("close"), *pentze/euntze* instead of *larrea* ("meadow" or "pasture"), *solastu/jolastu* instead of *mintzatu* ("to speak"), and *xilko* instead of *zilborra* ("navel").

Variants

The use of *elkar/elgar* ("each other" or "one another") is characteristic of the area (*alkar* in the boundary areas). The following variants are also used in many areas: *kafia* instead of *habia* ("nest"), *uli* instead of *euli* ("fly"), and *uri* instead of *euri* ("rain").

The Features that Differentiate Western and Central Basque from the Northern Basque Country and Navarrese

The Basque Country can be divided into two main areas according to a considerable number of distinctive dialectal features: Western and Central Basque on one side; and that of the Northern Basque Country and Navarrese Basque on the other. Here I will explore these differences.

Area and Causes

Naturally, the boundaries demarcated by these differences are not always consistent, and there are also intermediate ways of speaking. In most cases, these intermediate forms are to be found on the Lapurdi coast and in several areas of Navarre: Bortziriak, Bertizarana, Basaburua, Imotz, Larraun, Aritz-Betelu, and Sakana. I will examine features from different eras that are both old – some dating from the sixteenth century – and more recent. The wide use of the older features may be connected with the break-up of the Kingdom of Navarre between the eleventh and thirteenth centuries. For example, during that process, Araba, Bizkaia, and Gipuzkoa turned toward Castile. Meanwhile, the reinvigoration of Gipuzkoan Basque may explain more recently introduced features. Specifically, the prestige of Gipuzkoan Basque began to grow in the eighteenth century, and thereafter its influence spread to Bizkaia, western Navarre, and the Lapurdi coast.

Features

Phonology

In many Western and Central ways of speaking, different spoken emphasis distinguishes different meanings in many word pairs. Many years ago, Koldo Mitxelena drew up a short list of words that vary in meaning depending on spoken emphasis as used in his home town, Errenteria (Gipuzkoa):[20]

arrantzá for *arrantza* ("bray" [of a donkey]) vs.
arrántza for arrantza (fishing)

ayéna for *aihena* ("vine") vs.
áyena for *haiena* (the demonstrative "[belonging to] those ones")

basúa for *oihana* ("forest") vs.
básua from the Spanish *vaso* ("glass")

datórrela ("upon coming") vs.
dátorrela ("come here")

eltzía for *eltzea* ("cooking pot") vs.
éltzia for *heltzea* ("arrival" or "seize")

iltzía for *iltzea* ("nail") vs.
íltzia for *hiltzea* ("death")

mendékua for *mendekua* ("revenge") vs.
méndekua for *mendekoa* ("subordinate")

onéna for *honena* (the demonstrative "[belonging to] this one") vs.
ónena for *onena* ("the best [one]")

zuéna for *zuena* ("what he/she/it had") vs.
zúena instead of *zeuena* (the pronoun "yours")

A longer list of these word pairs could be drawn up, although the words do vary from one way of speaking to another.[21] Jean-Baptiste Coyos also finds a few such word pairs in Zuberoa;[22] and Mitxelena finds another in Erronkari, Navarre: *éskia* for "hand" / *eskía* for "right hand."[23] However, there are too few examples to be able to draw any definite conclusions, and nowadays at least this differentiating spoken emphasis is only used in Western and Central Basque and, furthermore, is mostly used by speakers of a certain age. Just as singular and plural are distinguished using spoken emphasis, so are words with different meanings.

Ascending diphthongs are frequently used in Eastern dialect areas: *ja*, *je*, *jo*, *ju*, *wa*, and *we*. They also appear in loanwords in Western and Central dialect areas, in words such as *fwer.te*, and *ko.rrjen.te*. This can also be heard in a few Basque words: for example, *e.gwal.di* for *eguraldi* ("weather"), *e.gwa.rri* for *eguberri* ("Christmas"), and *e.gwer.di* for *eguerdi* ("midday"). They are, however, frequent in Eastern ways of speaking. The following are examples from the Baztan Valley in Navarre: *i.tsá.swa* for *itsasoa* ("ocean" or "sea"), *ó.tswa* for *otsoa* ("wolf"), *án.drjak* for *andreak* ("women"), and *gal.tzér.djek* for *galtzerdiak* ("socks" or "stockings").[24]

Noun Morphology

Inessive case features more or less define the different areas: for example, the use of either *-engan* (*lagunarengan*) or *baitan* (*lagunaren baitan*) to express "in the friend." These forms have been lost from many ways of speaking nowadays, and it is difficult to define the model for this. In most cases, the suffix for inanimate objects is used instead of that for living beings: *konfiantza handia dauka seme-alabetan* ("he/she has a lot of confidence in his/her children"). In Burunda, Navarre, on the border with both Araba and Gipuzkoa, *baitan* is used. In Baztan, on the other hand, *-engan* has been heard,[25] but this is probably something new. In a late eighteenth-century sermon, for example, that is still in use today in Baztan, *baitan* is used: *Iangoycoaren borondate saindua baitan / aren baitan escandalizatzen ez dena* ("In God's holy will" / "that which is not scandalized in Him").[26]

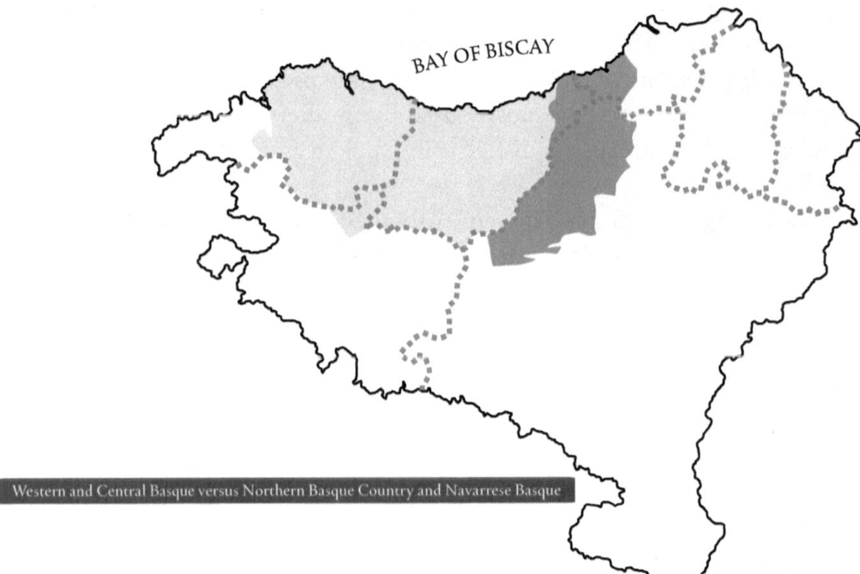

Western and Central Basque versus Northern Basque Country and Navarrese Basque

Undefined adverbs (*trankil egon* "to be calm") and the partitive (*isilik egon* "to be quiet") are used in most Western and Central dialect areas. In Eastern dialect areas, however, the absolutive case (and mostly in the singular) is used. The following examples are from Urdiain, Sakana, in Navarre, which is currently part of the Eastern dialectal area:

juxtu-juxtua pasatu dot hilabetia	instead of
justu-justua pasatu dut hilabetea	in Unified Basque
"I just about got through the month"	
ixil-ixila ibiltzen da	instead of
isil-isila ibiltzen da	
"he/she moves around very quietly"	

Thus, the form used there is *justua-justua* instead of *justu-justu* and *isil-isila* rather than *isil-isilik*. Nowadays, due to the influence of Unified Basque, the Western and Central tendencies are becoming more widely used.

Verbal nouns deriving from the verbs *eman* and *utzi* are used in the inessive case in Western and Central dialects, and the allative case in Eastern dialect areas. This can be seen in inessive/allative phrases such as *jaten eman / jatera eman* ("to feed") and *joaten utzi / joatera utzi* ("to let go"). A few other verbs also go in allative as one moves eastward: *saiatu/entseatu* ("to try"), *ausartu/menturatu* ("to dare" or "to venture"), *jarri/paratu* ("to put"), *usatu* ("to use"), *deliberatu* ("to decide"), and so on. Here, too, Western and Central dialect use has gained in strength over recent years.

In order to express the notion of "someone," "somebody," or, according to the context, "one or another," in the Western and Central dialect areas pronouns of the *baten bat* model are used, while in western Navarre the *bakarren bat* model is also used. These are both unknown in the Eastern dialect areas, where the *norbait* model is used.

The ending *-on* from foreign loanwords becomes *-oi* in Araba, Bizkaia, and Gipuzkoa: for example, *meloia* ("melon"). There is no single model in Eastern dialect areas: *-oin* is used in Navarrese-Lapurdian Basque (*meloina*), *-ú* in Zuberoan Basque (*melú*), and *-on* in most of Navarre (*melona*).

Two suffixes are used in Eastern dialect areas: *-go* and *-ka/-keta*. The former can be seen in words such as *artzaingoa* instead of *artzaintza* in Unified Basque ("sheepherding"), *ebasgoa* instead of *lapurreta* ("robbery"), *elkargoa* instead of *elkartea* ("association" or "club"), *nagusigoa* instead of *nagusitasuna* ("supremacy" or "prominence"), and *xapelgoa* instead of *txapelketa* ("championship"); and the latter in words such as *egurketa* ("lumbering"), *esneketa* ("milking"), and *urketa* ("water carrying").

Verb Morphology

The root *-u-* is used in **edun* verbs in the present tense in all Eastern dialect areas: *dut* (> *düt* in Zuberoa). There is no unity in other areas in this respect; *-o-* is used in Western Basque (*dot*), and *-e-* in Gipuzkoan Basque and in the neighboring areas of Navarre (*det*).

In most Western and Central dialect areas, the root *-a-* is used in third person singular *izan* verbs: for example, *dan*, *dala*, *dalako*, *zan*, *zala*, and *zalako*. In Eastern dialect areas, however, *-e-* is used. Let us be clear that this feature should not be confused with the coexistence of *-e-/-a-* in past tense verbs: *nintzen/nintzan*, *nuen/nuan*. The model in that case is very clearly different.

Verbs ending in *-n* have two very different future tense forms; in most Western and Central dialect areas, they take the suffix *-go* (*egingo*, *izango*), and *-en* in most Eastern dialect areas (*eginen*, *izanen*). The suffix *-go* is more and more common in the Southern Basque Country, including Navarre. In Burunda, for instance, *-en* (> *-in*) is often used by speakers of a certain age (*emain*), but young people only use *-ko* or *-go* (*emanko/emango*).

In Eastern dialect areas, the potential is expressed using the periphrastic imperfect participle form. The following examples of this are from Baztan:[27]

bein iarrite etziren xutiTZEN al *behin jarrita ez ziren zutitzen ahal* "once sat, they could not get up"	instead of
edozein gaTEN al da nere partez *edozein joaten ahal da nire ordez* "anyone can go in my place"	instead of

Synthetic verbs (*dezake*, *daiteke*) have not been completely lost in Western and Central dialect areas, but even when the periphrastic form is used, the perfect participle form is used: *ezin ziren zutiTU*, *JOAN ahal da*. This innovation did not reach Erronkari or Zaraitzu, and it is not frequent in Aezkoa either. It is unknown in Sakana.

In most Western and Central dialect areas, the structure 'participle + *ta*' predominates: *bazkalduta etorri gara* ("we have already had lunch"), *eginda dago* ("it is done"), *ikusita daukagu* ("we have seen it"). In northwestern Navarre and Lapurdi, however, 'participle + *a*' is the most common form, and the old form *-rik* has been kept in Zuberoa. Moreover, *-rik* is also often heard in Navarre and in Lower Navarre, but *-a* and *-ta* are also used there as well.

Eduki verb forms now completely predominate in Western and Central dialect areas: for example, *gogoan daukat* ("I remember"), and *ez daukazu lotsarik* ("you have no shame"). In most areas, **edun* is the auxiliary verb: *ekarri du* ("he/she has bought it").

Morphosyntax

The suffix *bait-* is used in many Eastern dialect areas to form relative clauses. This area includes Leitza, Navarre, from which the following example is taken:[28]

> *Tito Gaztelunan andrea, aisoarra baita, orren aman ama zen* instead of
> *Tito Gaztelunaren andrea, Aresokoa dena, horren amaren ama zen*
> "That person's mother's mother was Tito Gaztelu's wife, from Areso"

When used to express cause (*asko daki, asko ikusi baitu* "he/she knows a lot because he/she has seen a lot"), the suffix *bait-* has also reached Central dialect areas. In Gipuzkoa, these areas include the Beterri and Tolosaldea, as well as the eastern Goierri between Ordizia and Zaldibia. In Navarre, Etxarri Aranatz is on the boundary of this use, and it is unknown in Burunda.

In subordinate clauses, the suffix *-(e)nik* has gained strength in Western and Central dialect areas when the main verb is negative. Oiartzun (Gipuzkoa) is part of this area, and the following examples are from there:[29]

> *eztut uste egualdi txarra zenik* instead of
> *ez dut uste eguraldi txarra zenik*
> "I don't think it was bad weather"

This innovation has not yet reached Eastern dialect areas, where *-(e)la* is the only form used. This can be seen in the following examples from Larresoro, in Lapurdi:[30]

> *eztu iduri eri dela* instead of
> *ez du ematen gaixo dela*
> "he/she doesn't look like he/she is sick"
>
> *eztu erran jinen dela* instead of
> *ez du esan etorriko dela*
> "he/she didn't say he/she would come"

When the main clause uses verbs such as *uste* ("to believe"), *beldur izan* ("to be afraid"), *iduri* ("to seem" or "to look like"), and *badaiteke* ("it is possible"), *-(e)n* is a distinguishing feature of Eastern dialect areas. In Western and Central dialect areas, on the other hand, *-(e)la* is used. These examples are also from Larresoro:[31]

> *eztut uste erraiten den oi* instead of
> *ez dut uste esaten den hori*
> "I don't believe that (which is being said)"
>
> *baditake ezten hain gaztia* instead of
> *badaiteke ez den hain gaztea*
> "he/she/it is possibly not as young (as he/she/it looks like)"

-(e)la is used in clauses of manner and time in most Western and Cen-

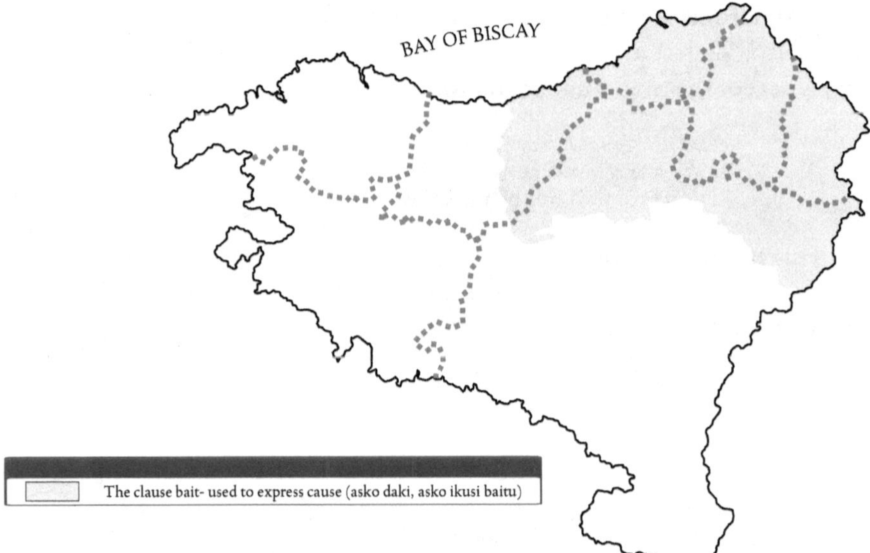
BAY OF BISCAY
The clause bait- used to express cause (asko daki, asko ikusi baitu)

tral dialect areas: for example, *gu gazteak giñela etzan olakorik* "when we were young there was nothing like that." In Eastern dialect areas, however, *-(e)larik* is almost always used: *gazteak ginelarik* "when we were young." In Eastern dialect areas, furthermore, this suffix has taken the place of *-(e)nean* as used in Western and Central dialect areas.

In causal clauses, 'verb + *eta*' and 'verb + *(e)la eta*' are used in Western and Central dialect areas. Lezo (Gipzukoa) is part of this area, and the following examples come from there:[32]

> *berua ikaragarriya, lau labe sien-ta!* instead of
> *beroa ikaragarria, lau labe ziren eta!*
> "a tremendous heat, because there were four ovens!"

> *jendiak saarronduak jartziai utzi, kontuik etzula ta* instead of
> *jendeak sagarrondoak jartzeari utzi, konturik ez zuela eta*
> "people stopped planting apple trees because that didn't bring them any money."

The causal variants *-kotz*, *-(e)lakotz*, and *-tekotz* are often used in Eastern areas: for example, *ordukotz* ("because it was time"), *nahi zuelakotz* ("because he/she/it wanted"), and *zu ikustekotz* ("in order to see you"). In most Western and Central dialect areas, those variants are unknown, and only *-ko*, *-(e)lako*, and *-teko* are used. Moreover, these forms are gaining strength due to the influence of Unified Basque.

In Western and Central dialect areas, there has been a considerable innovation with regards to syntax; the verb *egin* ("to do" or "to make") is used for giving emphasis. The following two sentences were recorded in Urdiain (Navarre) and are examples of *egin* being used as emphasis:

> *San Juango ermitia konpondu dai* instead of
> *San Juango ermita konpondu dute*
> "they have definitely fixed the San Juan hermitage"

> *Herrientxiek eztuka diruik,*
> *bea kaliek konpondu in tuai* instead of
> *Herriko Etxeak ez dauka dirurik,*
> *baina kaleak konpondu egin dituzte*
> "the city hall does not have any money,
> but it did manage to fix the streets"

Vocabulary

Many words used in Western and Central dialect areas are different from those used in the Northern Basque Country and in Navarrese Basque. These are some of the most significant word pairs from the two respective areas: *agindu/manatu* ("to order" or "to command"), *arotz/zurgin* ("carpenter"), *asko/anitz* and *asko* ("a lot"), *aukeratu/hautatu* ("to choose" or "to select"), *aurre/aitzin* and *aurre* ("front"), *atze/gibel* ("back" or "rear"), *barru/barne* ("inside"), *baso/oihan* ("forest"), *bertan/berean* ("right there"), *bi/bi* and *biga* ("two"), *dator/heldu da* ("he/she/it is coming"), *dirudi/irudi du* ("he/she/it seems" or "he/she/it looks like"), *errementari/arotz* ("blacksmith"), *eskerrak!/beharrik!* ("thanks!"), *eskuare/arrastelu* ("rake"), *ezer/deus* ("nothing"), *gogoratu/oroitu* ("to remember"), *kale/karrika* ("street"), *kirikino* (Central Basque *triku*)/*sagarroi* ("hedgehog"), *koipe/urin* ("fat," "grease," or "oil"), *laster/sarri* ("quick"), *morroi/mutil* ("servant" or "guy"), *nahikoa/aski* ("quite a bit [of]"), *ondo/ongi* (Northern Basque Country, *untsa*) ("good" or "well"), *hobeto/hobeki* ("better"), *oso/arrunt* ("whole"), *ostu/ebatsi* ("to steal"), *saguzar/gauenara* ("bat" as in the animal), and so on.

The following words are used in Western and Central dialect areas but not in Eastern dialect areas: *alkandora/alkondara* ("shirt"), *bigu(i)n* ("soft" or "smooth"), *eskerrik asko* ("thank you"), *gurpil* ("wheel"), *igurtzi* ("to spread"), *iritzi* ("opinion"), *ipui(n)* ("tale"), *itxaron* ("to wait"), *jaso* ("to receive"), *kanpai* ("bell"), *kare* ("lime"), *makal* ("poplar"), *malko* ("teardrop"), *trumoi* ("thunder"), *ugari* ("abundant"), and so on. And these words are used in Eastern dialect areas but are unknown among their Western and central counterparts: *aretxe* ("calf"), *atxiki* ("to attach"), *azkar* instead of *indartsu* ("strong"), *barratu/barreiatu* ("to spread"), *bederen* ("at least"), *hedatu* ("to arrive"), *hiruetan hogei* and *lauetan hogei* ("sixty" and "eighty"), *idortu/xukatu* ("to dry [up]"), *igorri* ("to spend [time]"), *irri* ("to laugh"), *kukuso* instead of *arkakuso* ("flea"), *mintzatu* ("to speak"), *neskato* instead of *neskame* ("maid"), *tenore* ("time" or "moment"), and so on.

Variants

Several variants also distinguish the two different areas: *aitatu/aipatu* ("to mention"), *atxur/aitzur* ("hoe"), *belarri/beharri-begarri* ("ear"), *bildur/beldur* ("fear"), *burruka/borroka* ("fight" or "struggle"), *erruki/urriki* ("pity," "compassion," or "mercy"), *esan/erran* ("to say"), *heste/hertze* ("intestine"), *ikutu/ukitu-hunkitu* ("to touch"), *itxi/hetsi-hertsi* ("to close"), *izu/izi* ("fear," "terror," or "fright"), *kirten-kerten/gider-kider* ("handle"), *orain/orai-guai* ("now"), and so on. The following are from Eastern dialect areas: *apez* instead of *apaiz* ("priest"), *eskuin* ("right"), which is *eskubi* in Central Basque and *eskuma/eskoi* in Western Basque, *iretsi* instead of *irentsi* ("to swallow"), *itze* instead of *iltze* ("nail"), and so on.

The Main Features of Basque in the Northern Basque Country and Eastern Navarrese

I will now examine some features that have disappeared in Western, Central, and Western Navarrese Basque, but that remain in use in the Northern Basque Country and in Eastern Navarrese, although they are also the consequence of several other factors.

Area and Causes

In some places, there are various options or the features originated in eastern areas. In Navarre, this includes the area between Esteribar and Erronkari, as well as most of the Baztan Valley.

Features

Singular and plural are differentiated in the ergative in eastern areas: *-ak* in the singular and *-ek* in the plural. Thus, the model is usually *gizonak erran du* ("the man has said") and *gizonek erran dute* ("the men have said"), as it is in the Baztan Valley. In other areas, by contrast, the *-ak* form was always used, both in the singular and in the plural. Recently, however, Unified Basque decided to separate the two forms and the consequences are clearly seen in the spoken language.

In Western and Central Basque, the suffix *-(e)tatik(an)* is used in the undefined and plural ablative: *etxetatik* ("from the house"), *etxeetatik* ("from the houses"). In Eastern Basque, however, the older form *-(e)tarik* has been kept, becoming *-(e)taik* in the spoken language: *etxetaik, etxeetaik*. In demonstratives, similarly, *-(e)ta(r)ik* is the form used in Eastern Basque. Baztan is part of this area, and the following examples are from there:[33] *unteik* instead of *honetatik* ("from this [one]"), *ortaik* instead of *horretatik* ("from that [one]" – near, not far away), *artaik* instead of *hartatik* ("from that [one]" – over there, in the distance), *oketaik* instead of *hauetatik* ("from these [ones]"), *oietaik* instead of *horietatik* ("from those [ones]" – near, nor far away), and *etaik* instead of *haietatik* ("from those [ones]" – over there, in the distance).

In nouns for animate beings, similarly, *-gandik(an)* now predominates in most Western and Central dialect areas: *lagunarengandik* ("from the friend"). In a few Eastern dialect areas and in western Bizkaia, on the other hand, the old form *-ganik* has been kept: *lagunarenganik*.

The completive form used with verbal nouns goes in the possesive in Eastern dialect areas: *lagunaren ikustera joan da* ("he/she has gone to see the friend"). It seems that this used to be an option throughout the Basque Country, but the absolutive has always been more frequently used in Western and Central dialect areas: *laguna ikustera* ("to see the friend"). This form long ago became the most frequent form in the Southern Basque Country. Nowadays, for example, the absolutive is normally used in Baztan, which was not formerly the case.

Participles and verb roots are differentiated in Eastern dialect areas, and the verb root is used in the potential, the imperative, and the subjunctive. Thus, *sartu da* ("he/she/it has come in") is the indicative and *sar daiteke* ("he/

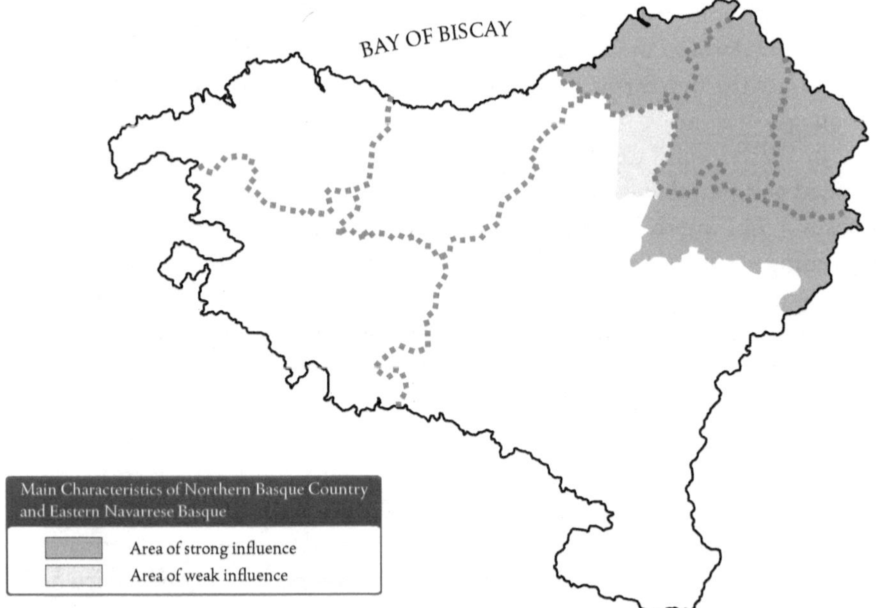
BAY OF BISCAY
Main Characteristics of Northern Basque Country and Eastern Navarrese Basque
Area of strong influence
Area of weak influence

she/it can come in"), *sar hadi* ("come in"), and *sar dadin* ("so that he/she it might come in") are the other forms. This form is now only maintained in Eastern dialect areas. According to old texts, the verb root was once used in the whole of the Basque Country. Nowadays, however, except for a few examples, such as *hor konpon!* ("that's just too bad!" or "tough!"), this form has been completely lost in Araba, Bizkaia, and western Gipuzkoa. In some areas of western Navarre and eastern Gipuzkoa this form is still used, but there are no fixed areas in which the verb root and the participle are exactly separated.

Making the verb agree with the dative is optional in Eastern dialect areas. It has always been normal and correct to use sentences such as *lagunari erran dut* ("I have told my friend"). In other areas, however, *lagunari esan diot* has always been the only option. Recently, due to schooling in Unified Basque and literary campaigns, making them agree has become much more common. This, for example, is the option I have heard young people in Baztan using, while until recently there were two possibilities.

As well as the general comparative structure *baino* ("than"), and so on — *ago, ago ezik/eze(n) ez* has also been adapted from French and is often used in Eastern dialect areas. This example is from Uztaritze, Lapurdi:[34]

> *naio tu baxerak garbitu, ezin ez eta xukatu* for
> *ontziak garbitu baino nahiago du lehortu* in Unified Basque
> "he/she prefers drying to washing the dishes"

Vocabulary

The following words are used in most of the Eastern dialect area: *ahalke* instead of *lotsa* ("shame"), *emazte(ki)* instead of *emakume* ("woman"), *haurride* instead of *neba-arrebak* ("sibling"), *kario* instead of *garestia* ("expensive"), *oren* instead of *ordua* ("hour" or "time"), *(b)urtxintxa* instead of *katagorria* ("squirrel"), *usu* instead of *maiz* ("often"), *xahutu* instead of *garbitu/eralgi/hondatu* ("to clean"/"to spend"/"to ruin"), and so on. There are also words that were previously used more widely and that are now only used in this area: for example, *egun* instead of *gaur* ("today"), *ene* instead of *nire* ("my"), and *eri* instead of *hatz* ("finger").

Variants

The following are used in these areas: *berant* instead of *berandu* ("late"), *gatu* instead of *katu* ("cat"), and *zilo* instead of *zulo* ("hole").

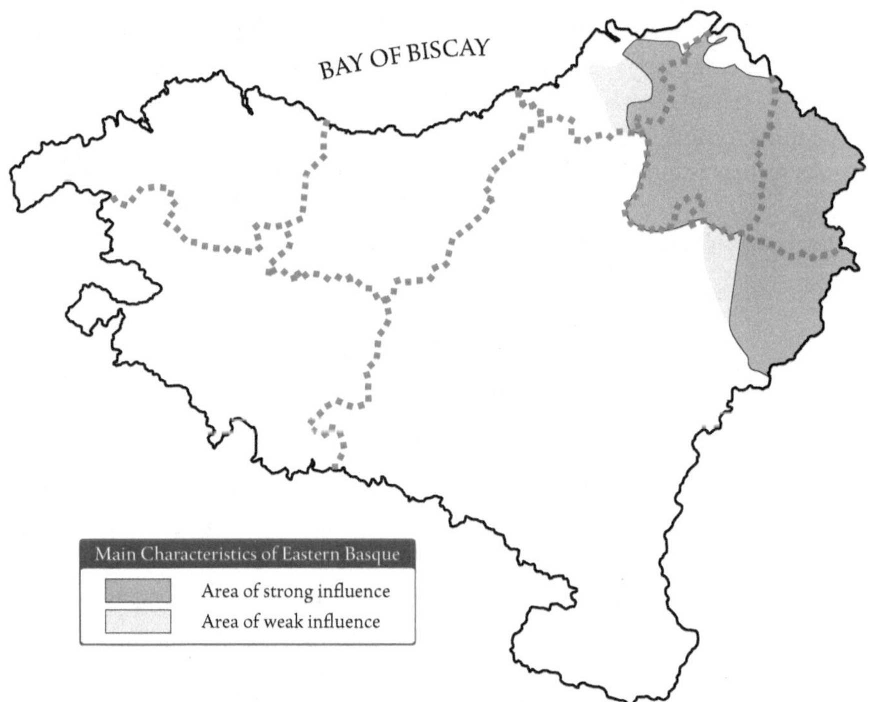
BAY OF BISCAY
Main Characteristics of Eastern Basque
Area of strong influence
Area of weak influence

The Main Features of Eastern Basque

As regards Eastern Basque, it should be noted that is was historically an important source of innovations.

Area and Causes

Zuberoa, Lower Navarre, and eastern Lapurdi in the Northern Basque Country, together with the two Navarrese valleys of Erronkari and Zaraitzu, are generally included in this area. Central Lapurdi and the Aezkoa Valley in Navarre are also sometimes included. These are innovations that originated long ago in Zuberoa or perhaps in Lower Navarre. It should be underlined that Erronkari, Zaraitzu, and the Aezkoa Valley in Navarre have long been connected to the Northern Basque Country.

Features

Phonology

When the vowel *u* combines with the vowels *a* and *e*, *-i-* was usually introduced in Eastern dialect areas: *buru + a → buruia* ("head"), *du + ela → duiela*. This took place throughout the whole Eastern dialect area with the exception of Zaraitzu in Navarre. Nowadays, however, this has been maintained in central Lapurdi. It also existed in the southern Erronkari Valley, where it became *-iua* in Bidankoze (Vidángoz) (*buriua*) and *-ioa* in Garde (*burioa*). In Zuberoa, northern Erronkari, Lower Navarre, and eastern Lapurdi, another step was later taken: *buruia → buria* and *duiela → diela* (*→ dila*).

In absolutive-ergative *izan* and **edin* verb forms, *-ai- → -i-*: *naiz → niz, zaitez → zite, gaitu → gitu*.

In absolutive-ergative verb forms, similarly, *-au- → -u-*: *nauzu → nuzu, nauk/naun → nuk/nun, haut → hut, nau → nu, naute → nute*.

Morphohology

The variant *-er* is used in the dative plural: for example, *gizoner* instead of *gizonei* ("to the men"), and *laguner* instead of *lagunei* ("to the friends").

The suffix *-gia* is used for places: for example, *etzangia* ("a place to lie down"), *hedagia* ("a place to dry clothes"), *idorgia* ("a drying place"), *jargia* instead of *aulkia* ("chair"), and *sargia* instead of *sarrera* ("entrance").

The main distinguishing feature of Eastern dialectal forms of speech is the use of *zuka* and *xuka* (see chapter 1 for a detailed explanation). The following examples of *zuka* are from Gabadi in Amikuze, Lower Navarre:[35]

han egoiten nüzü televizionari so instead of

han egoten nauzu telebistari begira
"I'm here watching TV"

etzü hiru emazte bezik ezautzen eztüztanak instead of
ez dituzu hiru emazte baizik ezagutzen ez ditudanak
"there are not three women, they are the ones that I don't know"

Thus *nauzu* = *naiz* ("I am"), and *dituzu* = *dira* ("they are").

Bonaparte incorrectly classified Luzaide Basque alongside that of Baigorri. It is in fact like the Basque from Garazi, as the use of *xuka* demonstrates. The following examples are from there:[36]

haurrak Eguerritako bakantzen bea diaudexu instead of
haurrak Eguberrietako oporren zain daude
"the children are waiting for the Christmas holidays"

akidura hunekin enuxu xutik egoiten al instead of
neke honekin ez naiz zutik egoten ahal
"I'm so tired I can't stand up"

In much of the Eastern dialect area, the root **iro* is used to form the potential, along with the more generally used **ezan*: *dirot*, *dirok/diron*, *diro*, *dirogu*, *dirozu*, *dirozie*, *dirote*. However, this form is beginning to disappear. These examples are from Beskoitze in Lapurdi:[37]

hoi eztioiat erran instead of
hori ez zezakeat esan
"I can't say that"

lephua paria niok instead of
lepoa joka nezakek
"I would bet my life on it"

In *bai/ez* ("yes/no") clauses, the suffix *-a* is used, as well as an interrogative intonation. These examples are from Hazparne, Lapurdi:[38]

zapeta horiikin yoan beaiza? instead of
zapata horiekin joan behar haiza?
"Do you have to go in those shoes?"

yende horiikin beauka musian ai izan? instead of
jende horiekin behar duka musean ari izan?
"Do you have to play *mus* [a card game] with those people?"

Vocabulary

There are many words that are specific to Eastern Basque: *ahar/akar* instead of *liskarra* ("fight" or "dispute"), *alta* instead of *ostera* ("on the other hand"), *apairu* instead of *jatordua* ("lunchtime"), *ardura* instead of *maiz* ("often"), *ar-*

gizagi instead of *ilargi* ("moon"), *askari* instead of *gosari* ("breakfast") and *atsalaskari* instead of *askaria* ("snack"), *bilo* instead of *ilea* ("hair"), *borta* instead of *atea* ("door"), *bortu* ("mountain summit"), *dailu* instead of *sega* ("scythe"), *ele* instead of *hitza* ("word") and *elekatu* instead of *hitz egin* ("to speak" or "to talk"), *engoitik* instead of *honezkero/hemendik aurrera* ("by now"/"from now on"), *gora* instead of *garai* ("high"), *hagun* instead of *aparra* ("foam"), *iguriki* instead of *itxaron* ("to wait"), *ikertu* instead of *aztertu* ("to investigate"), *ilki/jalgi* instead of *irten* ("to go out"), *larrazken* instead of *udazkena* ("Fall"), *lotsa* instead of *beldur* ("fear"), *oro* instead of *dena* ("everything" or "all"), *ukarai* instead of *eskumuturra* ("wrist"), and so on. There is also *jaugin* instead of *etorri* ("to come") and some forms that derive from this: *haugi* instead of *hator* (literally "come!" in the singular *hitano* you form), *zauri/xauri* instead of *zatoz* ("come!" in the singular you form), *zauzte* instead of *zatozte* ("come!" in the plural you form), and *daugin* instead of *datorren* ("that is coming").

The Main Features of Basque in the Northern Basque Country

I will now examine the principal features of Basque in Iparralde or the Northern Basque Country. Two main features characterize the Basque spoken here: on the one hand, the increasing similarity between Lapurdian and Lower Navarrese; and on the other, the distinctive nature of Zuberoan Basque. That said, there are still common features throughout the Northern Basque Country.

Area and Causes

The influence of French spread and deepened throughout the Northern Basque Country particularly during the twentieth century. It spread because it now affected the whole of society (rather than just being the preserve of its upper echelons), and it deepened because it now influenced every part of the language; in other words, in addition to vocabulary, phonology, morphology, and syntax were also affected. I will mention several dimensions of this influence, but I will also examine the numerous common internal features of Basque. The borders imposed by the French public administration after the French Revolution halted or at least hindered relationships between Basque speakers, and this also had important consequences for the language. Nowadays, in fact, although Basque dialects are becoming more homogeneous among themselves, the border between the Northern and Southern Basque Country is becoming stronger and stronger in a linguistic sense.

However, the differentiation of many characteristics has not been caused by an exact administrative border because, for example, the relationship between northern Navarre and the Northern Basque Country, above all in vocabulary, is still very apparent. I have already mentioned on more than one occasion that people from the Navarrese side of the Pyrenees used to go to markets in the Northern Basque Country rather than to Iruñea, the capital of Navarre. In this regard, the testimony recorded by Iñaki Camino in his study of the Aezkoa Valley in Navarre is highly significant: "Donibane Garazi used to be what Iruñea is nowadays."[39] In other words, the main town and meeting place for the people of Aezkoa used to be Donibane Garazi in Lower Navarre.

In fact, I have categorized Basque from Luzaide in Navarre as Northern Basque – that of the Northern Basque Country – even though there is a difference between younger and older people's ways of speaking; in short, the latter's speech is moving toward that of the Southern Basque Country. There have also been decisive changes in the Navarrese towns of Urdazubi and Zugarramurdi and I have classified them as now possessing intermediate ways of speaking, along with Baztan.

Features

Phonology

Throughout the Northern Basque Country, *o* → *u* in front of the nasal consonants *m*, *n*, and *ñ*, and this tendency grows stronger the further east you go: *ontsa* instead of *ondo* → *untsa* ("good" or "well"), *hondar* → *hundar* ("sand" or "rubble" in one sense, or "bottom" or "end" in another), *ontzi* → *untzi* ("container" or "boat") and similar words, and demonstratives such as *hunek*, *huni*, *huntan*, and *hunekin* are the most frequent. There are also traces of this transformation in northwestern Navarre, in the area between Baztan and Bortziriak.

Many words that end in *-e* in French or in consonants in Basque have *-a* added to them in the Northern Basque Country. This makes many words look different in the Southern and Northern Basque Country as reflected in the following list of word pairs with the same meaning that derive from Spanish and French respectively (Southern/Northern variants): *aboga(d)u/abokata* ("lawyer"), *aperitibo/aperitifa* ("aperitif"), *disko/diska* ("record"), *ekipo/ekipa* ("team"), *grupo/grupa* ("group"), *jefe/xefa* ("boss"), *kilometro/kilometra* ("kilometer"), *minutu/minuta* ("minute"), *plastiko/plastika* ("plastic"), *presidente/presidenta* ("president"), *sindikatu/sindikata* ("labor union"), *telefono/telefona* ("telephone"), *txeke/xeka* ("check"), *txokolate/xokolata* ("chocolate"), and so on.

Many pronunciations derived from French are used in the Northern Basque Country. Irantzu Epelde, for example, mentions [*v*] (*divorzatu* "to divorce"), [*z*] (*ezterilizatu* "to sterilize") and [ʒ] (*kondxelatorra* "freezer").[40] Because French has more vowels than Basque, the following are new incorporations: [*y*] (*otobüza* "bus"), [ã] (*tãzionia* "tension"), [e with tilde] (*eternet* "Internet"), [œ]the suffix *-eur* (*azpirat r* "vacuum cleaner"), and so on. However, the guttural *r* is the most frequent and the most deeply rooted of these: *garrasi* → *gaRaxi* ("scream"), *gorri* → *goRi* ("red"). This pronunciation is a fairly recent feature. According to Roger Gimet, it came into use in the mid-twentieth century and mainly in Donibane Lohizune.[41] Nowadays, it is not used by very old speakers, especially those who speak Zuberoan Basque, and naturally it has not reached the Navarrese towns of Urdazubi, Zugarramurdi, or Luzaide either. Patxi Salaberri Zaratiegi and Peio Kamino record the following testimony from an inhabitant of Luzaide: "The people from Donibane [Garazi] speak *geka* [guttural r] Basque; older people did not used to, but nowadays all the young people do."[42]

Morphology

The variant *–rat* (instead of *–ra* in Unified Basque) in the allative is a distinguishing feature of the Northern Basque Country, with common examples of this including *herrirat* ("to the village/town"), *herritarrenganat* ("to the people/citizens"), and *herritarren ikusterat* ("to see the people/citizens"). Nowadays, furthermore, the variants *-ra* and *-rat* mean the same thing, although they used to have different meanings. As regards Navarre, some traces of this can also be found in Baztan, and even more so in Bera, Etxalar, Urdazubi, Zugarramurdi, and Luzaide.

In the Northern Basque Country, it is common to express direction using the *-rat/-ri buruz* structure. The following examples are from Beskoitze, Lapurdi:[43]

> *zahartziaai buuz zentzatzen tuk* instead of
> *zahartzaroa hurbil denean zentzatzen dituk*
> "you change your ways when you approach old age"
>
> *noat ari iz, ore, ilhunaai buuz?* instead of
> *nora hoa, orain, iluna gertu denean?*
> "where are you going now, when it will soon be dark?"

In the comitative or associative case, the variant *-kilan* is used in most of the Northern Basque Country except for western Lapurdi: for example, *elgarrekilan* instead of *elkarrekin* ("together"). Recently, *-kin* has started to prevail and *-kilan* is beginning to disappear due to the influence of Unified Basque.

In the same area, emphatic pronouns such as *nihaur* ("I myself"), *hiaur* ("you yourself" in the *hitano* or intimate singular form), *guhaur* ("we ourselves"), and *zuhaur* ("you yourself" in singular) have become widely used, having the same meaning as forms such as *neu/neroni* in the Southern Basque Country. These pronouns have also come to mean *bakarrik* ("alone" or "only"), as Beñat Oihartzabal's examples show:[44]

nihaur bazkaldu niz instead of
bakarrik bazkaldu dut
"I had lunch alone"

Xan beti bera da instead of
Xan beti bakarrik dago
"Xan is always alone"

Nowadays, in fact, younger people only use these emphatic pronouns to express the idea of *bakarrik* or being/doing something alone. This emphatic pronoun is also clearly being lost in Gipuzkoa and in Navarre, while in Bizkaia, by contrast, the opposite is happening because there emphatic pronouns have started to often replace ordinary pronouns.

With regards to verb morphology, there is a structure in the Northern Basque Country that has been borrowed from French: namely, to express events in the past, present tense auxiliary verbs are often used. The following examples are from Larresoro in Lapurdi:[45]

mainuetan asi niz atzo instead of
bainuetan hasi naiz atzo
"I started swimming yesterday"

yoan den astian ikusi duu elgar instead of
joan den astean ikusi dugu elkar
"We saw each other last week"

Thus, the form used is, in Unified Basque, *hasi naiz* ("I have started") and not *hasi nintzen* ("I started"); *ikusi dugu* ("we have seen") and not *ikusi genuen* ("we saw"). This tendency is quite new and has not reached Urdazubi, Zugarramurdi, or Luzaide in Navarre.

The verbs *afaldu* ("to have dinner"), *askaldu* ("to have a snack"), and *bazkaldu* ("to have lunch") are intransitive in most of the Northern Basque Country. On the other hand, when verbs are conjugated with *ari* (to be engaged in or doing something) or with *nahi* (to want to do something), they are conjugated depending on whether they are intransitive or transitive in many areas of Lapurdi and Lower Navarre. For example, *bazkaldu gira* ("we have had lunch"), *jaten ari dute* ("they are eating"), and *joan nahi niz* ("I want to take it") are common similar structures and the norm in those areas.

In connection with this, I should mention that the verb *joan* (meaning "to go" in Unified Basque) is used in many areas to mean *eraman* ("to carry," "to wear," "to take," and so on) with transitive auxiliary verb forms: *joan dut* instead of *eraman dut*. This also happens in Baztan.

Morphosyntax

It is common for participles to be used on their own in relative clauses in the

Northern Basque Country. The following example is from Amikuze, Lower Navarre:[46]

ina'una nik manatü lana? instead of
egina al dun nik agindu [agindutako] lana?
"have you done the work that I told you to?"

This one, meanwhile, is from Beskoitze, Lapurdi:[47]

gaskoinetik jin hitzaakin ordaintzen bitute instead of
gaskoinetik etorri [etorritako] hitzarekin ordaintzen baitute
"because they substitute it with a word [that comes] from Gascon"

The suffix for expressing time *-(e)ino* has been kept in the Northern Basque Country. The following example is from Hazparne, Lapurdi:

gerlak irauten dino, gure sustengua ukain dute instead of
gerrak irauten duen bitartean, gure laguntza edukiko dute
"so long as the war lasts, they will have our help"

In *bai/ez* ("yes/no") questions, the suffix *-(e)netz* is used in the Northern Basque Country. This example is from Beskoitze:[48]

pedofiliaaik bazenetz ee ez ginakian instead of
pedofiliarik ba ote zen ere ez genekien
"We didn't know if he was a pedophile or not"

In clauses expressing time and condition, *ber* is used in most of the Northern Basque Country except in western Lapurdi. The following examples are from Hazparne:[49]

arno xorta baden ber, nik edanen dut instead of
ardo tanta bat baldin bada, nik edango dut
"If there is a drop of wine left, I will drink it"

mutüa ezten ber, bearko du zerbit erran instead of
mutua ez baldin bada, beharko du zerbait erran
"unless he/she is mute, he/she will have to say something"

In neutral clauses in which nothing needs to be emphasized or underlined, *ba-* is added to verbs in the Northern Basque Country. Thus, *gizonak bi seme bazituen* ("the man had two sons") is a neutral clause in which nothing is emphasized or underlined. On the other hand, *gizonak bi seme zituen* is a marked clause, meaning that the person had "*bi seme*" ("two sons") and not, for example, "*bi alaba*" ("two daughters").[50]

This is also common in some areas of northern Navarre, and the following examples are from Baztan:[51]

uden badire iende aunitz instead of
udan jende asko dago

"in summer there are a lot of people"

norat bagoazi? instead of
nora goaz?
"where are we going?"

denek badakite eskuaraz mintzetzen instead of
denek dakite euskaraz mintzatzen
"everyone can speak Basque"

aserre baño beldur geiago badu instead of
haserre baino beldur gehiago du
"he/she is more afraid than angry"

arbol aunitz badire instead of
zuhaitz asko daude
"there are a lot of trees"

In order to emphasize and underline the focus of a sentence (known in Basque as the *galdegaia*), the participle goes after the auxiliary verb in most of the Northern Basque Country except for the Lapurdi coast. The following examples are from Sohüta in Zuberoa (focus emphasized in italics in English:[52]

hartakotz da Lígiko zübín harríbat mentx instead of
hargatik da Ligiko zubian harri bat falta
"because of that, on *the Ligi bridge* there is a stone is missing"

Kakuétan da sórtzen Máuleko üháitza instead of
Kakuetan da sortzen Mauleko ibaia
"*the origin* of the Maule River is in Kakueta"

Undeveloped Rules

As in Western Basque, the ending **ani* has become -*ain* in the words *arrain* ("fish"), *usain* ("smell"), and *zain* or *artzain* ("shepherd").

Vocabulary

Many words are particular to the Northern Basque Country, although several of them are also known and used in northern Navarre. The following are the most frequent:

A *abantxu* instead of *ia* ("almost" or "nearly"), *agorril* instead of *abuztua* ("August"), *aizturrak* instead of *guraizeak* ("scissors"), *alimaleko* instead of *sekulakoa* ("perennial" or "excellent"), *andana* ("a lot of"), *andereder* instead of *erbinudea* ("weasel"), *artatu* instead of *zaindu* ("to look after"), and *atxeman* instead of *aurkitu* or *harrapatu* ("to catch").

B *baitezpada* instead of *nahitaez* or *ezinbestean* ("inevitably"), *beha* instead of *begira* or *zain* ("to watch over"), *bereter* instead of *mezalaguna* ("acolyte"), *Besta Berri*, which in the Southern Basque Country is *Korpus Eguna* ("Feast of Corpus Christi"), and *bihi* instead of *alea* ("grain").

E *eihera* instead of *errota* ("mill"), *emeki* instead of *poliki* ("slowly"), *emendatu* instead of *gehitu* ("to add" or "to increase"), *erasiatu* instead of *errieta egin* ("to quarrel"), *eskuzarta* instead of *txaloa* ("applause"), *estakuru* instead of *aitzakia* ("excuse"), and *estekatu* instead of *lotu* ("to tie" or "to fasten").

F *ferekatu* instead of *laztandu* ("to hug" or "to embrace").

G *gisako* instead of *jator* ("native," "local," "real," and so on).

H *hauts* instead of *errauts* ("ash") and *errauts* instead of *hauts* ("dust"), *herra* instead of *gorrotoa* ("hate"), and *higitu* instead of *mugitu* ("to move").

I *ihardetsi* instead of *erantzun* ("to answer"), *ilar* instead of *indaba* ("bean") and *ilar biribil/ilar xehe/etxilar* instead of *ilarra* ("pea"), *iskilinba* for a kind of needle or pin, and *izari* instead of *neurri* ("measure"), with *izartu* instead of *neurtu* ("to measure").

J *jin* instead of *etorri* ("to come").

K *kausitu* instead of *aurkitu* ("to find"), *kofoin* instead of *erlauntza* ("beehive"), and *koskoil* instead of *barrabila* ("testacle").

L *laborari* instead of *nekazaria* ("farmer"), *laket* instead of *atsegina* ("pleasant"), *larderia* instead of *beldurra* ("fear"), *lili* instead of *lorea* ("flower"), and *lursagar* instead of *patata* ("potato").

M *mihise* instead of *maindire* ("bedsheet"), and *mozkin* instead of *etekina* ("gain" or "profit").

O *ogi* instead of *gari* ("wheat"), *ohoin* instead of *lapurra* ("thief"), *orga* instead of *gurdia* ("cart" or "wagon"), *osagarri* instead of *osasun* ("health"), *ostadar/ortzadar* ("rainbow"), and *otoi* instead of *arren* or *mesedez* ("request").

P *papo* instead of *bularraldea* ("chest"), *patar* instead of *aldapa* or *malda* ("slope"), *pipatu* ("to smoke") and *pot* instead of *musua* ("kiss").

S *selauru* instead of *bihitegia* ("granary" or "barn"), and *suntsitu* instead of *desegin* ("to undo" or "to come apart").

T *trufa* instead of *iseka* ("mockery").

U *ukaldi* instead of *zartakoa* ("slap"), *ukan* instead of *eduki* ("to have"), *untsa* instead of *ondo* or *ongi* ("good" or "well"), *untsalaz* ("in the best case scenario"), *urrats* instead of *pausoa* ("step"), and *uzkaili* instead of *irauli* ("to turn" or "to turn over").

Naturally, many loanwords have been taken from French in recent years and I will not cite them all here. However, I will mention a few consequences that have arisen from this outside influence: for example, the use of *baina* ("but" in the sense of "although" in Unified Basque) to mean *baizik* ("but [rather]"), for example in *ez enetzat, baina amarentzat* ("not for me, but for [my] mother"); *beti* ("always") to mean *oraindik* ("still"), for example in *beti badu euria* ("it's still raining"); *galdegin* ("to ask [something]") to mean *eskatu* ("to ask for"), for example

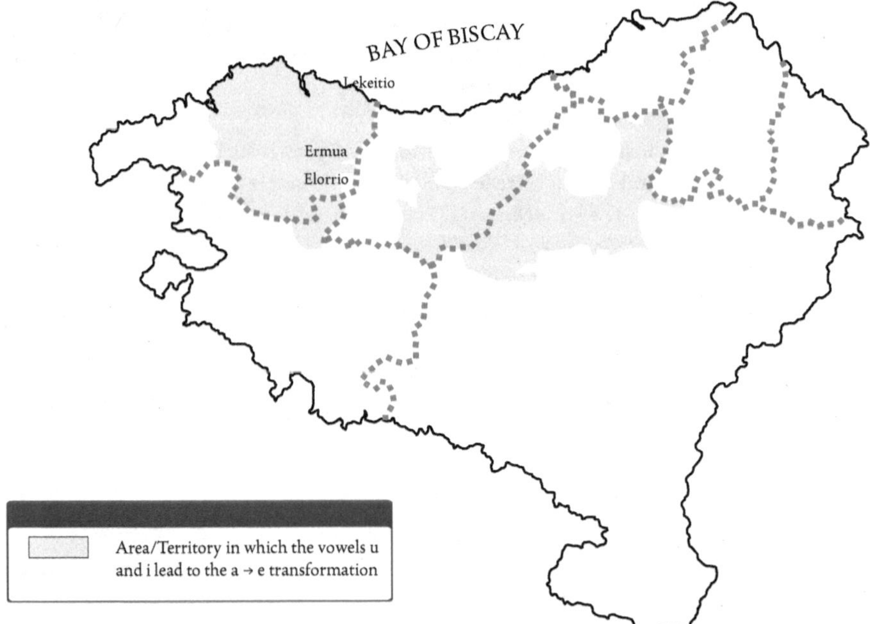
BAY OF BISCAY
Lekeitio
Ermua
Elorrio
Area/Territory in which the vowels u and i lead to the a → e transformation

in *liburuaren ekartzeko galdegin dakot* ("I asked him/her to bring the book"); and *gehiago* ("more") to mean *dagoeneko* ("any more"), for example in *ez da gehiago Azkainen bizi* ("he/she doesn't live in Azkaine any more"). Likewise, the verb *egon* ("to be" somewhere, as in a location, or to possess a transient property), as opposed to *izan* ("to be" as regards possessing standing properties), is used very little in the Northern Basque Country due to the influence of French, which only has one verb for "to be" (*être*): thus, for example, *akitua da* ("he/she is tired") *bakarrik da* ("he/she is alone"), and similar forms are the norm there; on the other side of the border, however, *nekatuta dago* ("he/she is tired"), *bakarrik dago* ("he/she is alone"), and similar forms using *egon* are the norm. Similarly, *maite* ("to love") is used in the Northern Basque Country in a similar way to its use in French, namely in the sense of "to like" (expressed as *gustatu* in the Southern Basque Country): for example, *ez du biziki maite mendian ibiltzea* ("he/she doesn't like hiking too much").

Variants

The following are the most significant: *barda* instead of *bart* ("last night") in Unified Basque, *eihar* instead of *ihar* ("dry"), *gasna* instead of *gazta* ("cheese"), *gerla* instead of *gerra* ("war"), *hetsi* instead of *itxi* ("to close"), *hunkitu* instead of *ukitu* ("to touch"), *jinko* instead of *jainko* ("God"), *katixima* ("catechism"), *libro* instead of *libre* ("free"), *zoin* instead of *zein* ("which") and *zonbait* instead of *zenbait* ("some"), *zonbat* instead of *zenbat* ("how much" or "how many"), and so on. *Ttipi* instead of *txiki* ("small"), which was formerly used to be used in a much wider area, is still used in the Northern Basque Country. Some of the variants mentioned are also known in northern Navarre.

The Main Features of Basque in the Southern Basque Country

There are not many distinctive features from the Southern Basque Country, but they are significant. After the vowels *u* and *i*, *a* → *e* is frequent in many areas of the Southern Basque Country. This area includes Bizkaia, the Basque-speaking part of Araba, southern Gipuzkoa, and a large part of Navarre. This happens in all of Bizkaia except for three towns: Lekeitio, Ermua, and Elorrio. Mundaka has also been an exception until very recently, but its way of speaking has now come to resemble that of its neighboring town Bermeo.

In Gipuzkoa, it is common in the Goierri, and the area to the south of Tolosa, and even more so in Azkoitia and Azpeitia. Three towns from the Upper Deba Valley are also included: Arrasate, Aretxabaleta, and Eskoriatza. However, this is no longer the rule among younger speakers, and they have started to leave *-a* as it was once more.

Finally, in Navarre, two northern areas are excluded from this rule: from

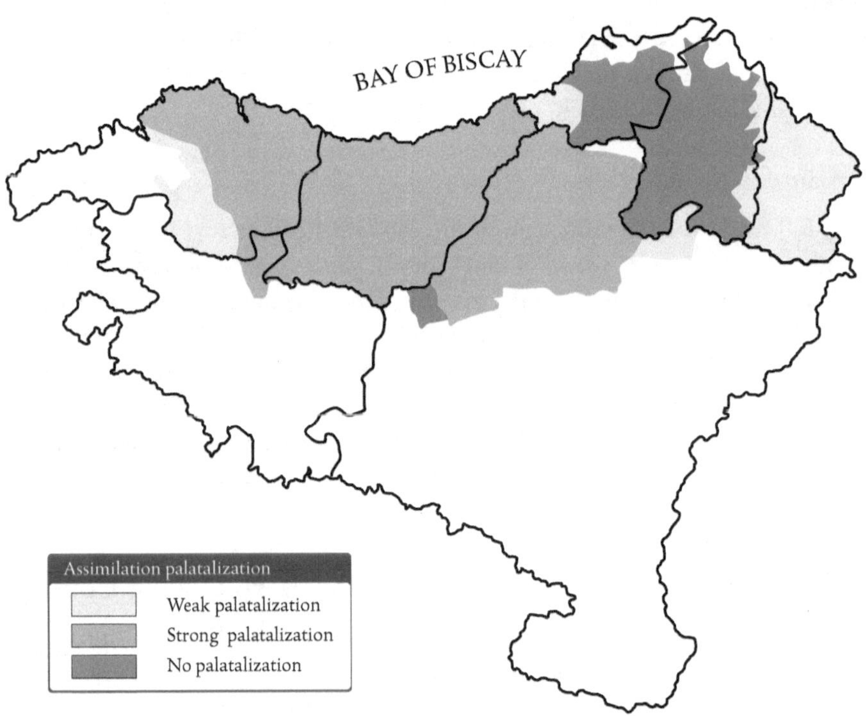
BAY OF BISCAY
Assimilation palatalization
Weak palatalization
Strong palatalization
No palatalization

Aurizberri (Erroibar) to Erronkari on the one hand, and in the Bortziriak, Malerreka, and Bertizarana areas on the other, as well as in several neighboring towns: Arano, Goizueta, Saldias, and Beintza-Labaien, Basaburu Txikia, and Oronoz-Mugairin in Baztan. It does not happen in Urdazubi or in Zugarramurdi either.

However, this transformation is not used with equal force in all places in the area.[53] In some areas, the tendency is weaker and it is more a case of the article changing: *begia* → *begie* ("eye"), *dirua* → *dirue* ("money"). This is most common in southern Gipuzkoa, although sometimes it can also be seen in other areas as well: in *eduki* verb forms (*daukat* → *dauket, daukazu* → *daukezu*) and in a few words such as *behintzet* instead of *behintzat* ("at least"). The article is also changed in the neighboring Navarrese area of Burunda, although not at the end of words: for example, *begiek* and *begien*, but then *begia* is used.

It is stronger in some other areas, and also used in the middle of words: *ikasi* → *ikesi* ("to study"), *ukatu* → *uketu* ("to touch"). It also happens in suffixes: *-ka* → *-ke* (*harrika* → *harrike* "throwing stones"), *-garri* → *-gerri* (*izugarri* → *izigerri* "tremendous"), *-garrena* → *-gerna* (*bigarrena* → *bigerna* "second"), *-la* → *-le* (*ditugula* → *ditugule*), and *-lako* → *-leko* (*dituelako* → *dittuleko*). And it occurs too in *izan* auxiliary verb forms, the quantifiers *bat/batzuk* ("one"/"some"), and also in the coordinating conjunction *(e)ta*: *etorri da* → *etorri de* ("he/she/it has come"), *lagun bat* → *lagun bet* ("one/a friend"), *lagun batzuk* → *lagun betzuk* ("some friends"), *Iñaki eta biok* → *Iñaki te biok* ("Iñaki and me"), *ikusita daukat* → *ikusitte dauket* ("I have seen it"). This is most common in western Bizkaia and, above all, in central Navarre.

As in the case of French in the Northern Basque Country, so in the Southern Basque Country some pronunciations have been taken from Spanish, as in, for example, *gozada* ("pleasure" or "absolute delight") and *zona* ("zone"). However, /x/ is the most common example of this, and this has spread throughout the entire Southern Basque Country, including Urdazubi, Zugarramurdi, and Luzaide in Navarre. This can be heard in loanwords such as *jeografia* ("geography"), *jenetika* ("genetics"), *rejimena* ("regime," "diet," or "system"), *garaje* ("garage"), and so on.

In the late nineteenth century, Bonaparte recorded absolutive-dative-ergative verbs being used instead of absolutive-ergative in southeastern Navarre.[54] This has since spread to most of the Southern Basque Country. The following examples are from Pasaia in Gipuzkoa:[55]

oan dala urte batzuk ikusi zian eta esantzian for
orain dela urte batzuk ikusi zidan eta esan zidan
"a few years ago he/she saw me and told me"

bi illabeteta bialtzen siguten kalea, "fija" ez isatiatik for
bi hilabetetara bidaltzen ziguten kalera, "fija" ez izateagatik

"they're going to fire us in two months, for not having a permanent job"

Thus, in these examples, *ikusi zidan* is said and not *ikusi ninduen* and *bidaltzen ziguten* rather than *bidaltzen gintuzten*.

Vocabulary

Leaving aside many words taken from Spanish, other words are particular to the Southern Basque Country: *aurpegi* ("face"), which is *begitarte* or *bisaia* in Northern Basque; *erabaki* ("to choose"), which is *deliberatu* in Northern Basque; *erantzun* ("to reply"), which is *ihardetsi* or *arrapostu* in Northern Basque; *gari* ("wheat"), which is *ogi* in Northern Basque; *jai* ("festival"), which is *besta* in Northern Basque; *urdai* ("pork"), which is *xingarra* in Navarrese-Lapurdian and *txinkhorra* in Zuberoan; *zergatik* ("why"), which is *zertako/zendako* in Northern Basque, and so on. The verb *jaio* ("to be born") is also typically a Southern Basque term nowadays, although it was once more widely used.

The Main Features of Various Areas

Finally, I will examine features that make up special areas. Because they are significant, I believe they are best addressed in a special section. Here, specifically, I am referring to four features: palatalization; the comitative or associative suffixes *-ki/-kin*; the benefactive suffixes *-entzat/-entzako/-endako*; and the prolative suffixes *-tako/-tzat*.

There are two types of palatalization in Basque. One of them is defined as being "expressive" and implies agreeableness or smallness in size: for example, *hezur* ("bone") → *hexur* ("little bone"). The second is "assimilation palatalization," which is caused by the vowel *i* and does not result in any change of meaning: *ahalegina* → *ahalegiña* ("effort"), *iluna* → *illuna* ("dark"), *ditugu* → *dittugu*. This occurs when the vowel *i* combines with the consonants *s*, *ts*, *n*, *l*, *t*, *ld*, *lt*, *nd*, and *nt*.[56]

From a dialectological point of view, the latter has little influence; it exists, to a greater or lesser extent, in all the dialects except for Western Basque. Except for a few isolated, fossilized examples, expressive palatalization does not exist in Western Basque. Some examples of this are *pittin* instead of *apurra* ("bit"), *txanka* instead of *hanka mehea* ("thin/slim leg"), *txatal* instead of *ataltxoa* ("little piece"), *txatxar* instead of *txiki-txikia* ("very small"), and *txuringa* instead of *zurixka* ("whitish"). There are not even many examples of this in children's speech, in which such palatalization is usually common, in Western Basque: *txatxa* instead of *sagarra/madaria* ("apple"/"pear"), *txatxur* instead of *hagina* ("tooth"), *txintx egin* instead of *zintz egin* ("to blow one's nose"), and so on.

In contrast, there are many consequences arising from palatalization caused by the vowel *i*. There are, on the one hand, conservative areas in which this type of palatalization has not been adopted: for example, most of Navarrese-Lapurdian Basque, including that of Aezkoa and Burunda. In such areas, furthermore, there is a tendency to avoid palatalization in loanwords. In Urdiain in Burunda, for example, I have recorded the following examples taken from Spanish: *caño* instead of *hodia* → *kainu* ("pipe" or "tube"), *cuchillo* instead of *ganibeta* → *kutxilo* ("knife"), *cuñado/cuñada* → *goinatu/goinata* ("brother-in-law"/"sister-in-law"), *daño* instead of *mina* → *dainu* ("pain" or "hurt"), *guiño* instead of *keinu* → *gainu* ("wink"), *ladrillo* instead of *adreilua* → *ladrilu* ("brick"), *silla* instead of *aulkia* → *sila* ("chair"), and so on. The same thing is to be found in all the other areas in which palatalization does not take place, although recent loanwords are used with their imported palatalization: *tortilla* ("omelette"), for example, in Urdiain, Navarre.

Palatalization occurs in other areas, but it is weak. In those areas, palatalization only happens with *n* → *ñ* and *l* → *ll*, and, for this to happen, the semi-vowel *j* has to appear between the letters *n* and *l*, in other words, /*j* — *V*/. The following examples are from northern Baztan:[57] *arraina* → *arrañe* ("fish"), *ezpaina* → *ezpañe* ("lip"), *erdoila* → *erdolle* ("rust"), and *otsaila* → *otsalle* ("February"); but *zikine* instead of *zikina* ("dirty") and *biletu* instead of *bilatu* ("to look for"), for example, are left unchanged. Of course, in the last two examples, the complete vowel *i* appears before *n* and *l*, rather than the semi-vowel *j*. In spite of some differences, the same kind of palatalization that occurs in northern Baztan also happens in very similar ways in Esteribar and Erroibar in Navarre, Zuberoa, and neighboring areas of Lower Navarre, such as Amikuze, Oztibarre, and, sometimes, Garazi. There is also a slight tendency toward palatalization in one area of western Bizkaia: the Txorierri Valley, Zeberio, Orozko, the Arratia Valley, and the southern Nerbioi Valley (Arrankudiaga and Arakaldo).

There are also areas in which there is considerable palatalization. Although there are local differences, these include the Central Basque area, most of the Western Basque area, and the area corresponding to Western Navarrese Basque. In those areas, as well as *n* → *ñ*, *l* → *ll*, and *t* → *tt*, the changes *ild* → *illdd*, *ilt* → *illtt*, *ind* → *iñdd*, and *int* → *iñtt* also appear, and there is no need for the consonant to appear between the semi-vowel *j* and another vowel. This area includes Aramaio in Araba, from which the following examples come:58 *dabil* → *dabill* ("he/she is walking"), *badakit* → *bakitt* ("I know [it]"), *ofizina* instead of *bulegoa* → *ofisiña* ("office"), *kozineroa* instead of *sukaldaria* → *kosiñerue* ("cook"), *albañila* instead of *igeltseroa* → *albañille* ("construction worker"), *indar* → *iñdder* ("strength"), *egin dot* → *eiñddot* ("I have done it"), *hil da* → *illdda* ("he/she has died"), *zinturoi* instead of *gerrikoa* → *siñtturoi* ("belt"), and so on. Nowadays, however, *illdd, illtt, iñdd,* and *iñtt* are less and less frequent among younger speakers.

Naturally, the situation changes considerably from one area to another. In Gipuzkoa, for example, there is palatalization with the letter *t* in many towns such as Zarautz, Orio, Igeldo, Donostia, Pasaia, Zegama, and Azpeitia.

Similar features can be seen in several other areas of the Basque Country. In the Anue Valley in Navarre, *t* is not palatalized, and people there find the way people speak in neighboring Ultzama funny. Indeed, they have a saying that makes fun of their neighbors: "*ezttuk eta baittuk, gu ultzamarrak gaittuk*" ("it is and it isn't, [but] *we* are from Ultzama").[59] Similarly, Zarautz and Getaria in Gipuzkoa are neighboring towns, yet there is more palatalization in the latter than in former. In Getaria, the word *bina* ("two each") is pronounced *biña* (in other words, pronouncing the *ñ* or /eлe/), while in Zarautz it is pronounced *bina* (with the *n* pronounced / зп/). This is the origin of the Getaria expression: *Tautalak, bina-bina* (*tautalak* is their nickname for people from Zarautz, so meaning "Zarautz people, two-by-two"). In the Bortziriak area, similarly, the letter *t* is not palatalized in Etxalar, and the people from there realize that. On the Lapurdi coast, the letters *n* and *l* are often palatalized, but *t* is never palatalized.

Finally as regards palatalization, *s* → *x* and *ts* → *tx* are general tendencies when they are between *i* and another vowel: for example, *isilik* → *ixilik* ("quietly" or "silently") and *itsusi* → *itxusi* ("ugly").

The comitative or associative suffix *-ki* is used in much of Zuberoa and Navarre, although this also coexists with *-kin* in most places. This example is from Arbaila in Zuberoa:[60]

> *ezkontü zen Urdiñarbéko emázte batéki* for
> *ezkondu zen Urdiñarbeko emakume batekin*
> "he married a woman from Urdiñarbe"

In Navarre, the western areas are the exception: the Northwestern Navarrese sub-dialect and those of Baztan and Burunda, as well as Araitz, Larraun, Basaburua, and Imotz, which look toward Gipuzkoa. In recent years, the influence of Unified Basque has tended to replace use of *-ki* with that of *-kin.*

The benefactive suffixes that express destination (something akin to "for") *-entzat* (and *-entzako*) are used in some areas, while *-endako* is used in others. In some areas, for example in much of Lapurdi, they are widely used. In Zuberoa, Navarre, and most of Lower Navarre *-endako* predominates. This is also used in much of the Deba Valley and some forms of speech in Durangaldea, as well as in some western parts of the Goierri: for example, in Legazpi, Zerain, Segura, and Zegama. In Navarre, *-entzat/-entzako* is used in the western areas: for example, in Bortziriak, Araitz, and Larraun. In Basaburua and Imotz, likewise, *-entzat*/*-entzako* is the most frequent form, but *-enda* is also known. In recent years, however, *-entzat* has been reinforced due to the influence of Unified Basque.

The suffix expressing destination is connected to the prolative, and, once more, there are two options: *-tako* and *-tzat*. A third option, the suffix *-tako*, is however used in fewer areas and mostly in Zuberoa and Navarre. The following testimony is from Urdiain, Navarre:

> *leno azkenekuek saritako kotxia're jasotzen ziken* instead of *lehenago azkenekoak [sailkapeneko azken txirrindulariak] saritako automobila ere jasotzen zian*
> "before, even the last cyclists in the race won a car"
>
> *eskualdunetako dukau geure bua instead of euskalduntako daukagu geure burua*
> "we think of ourselves as Basques"

However, this declension has been lost in much of the Basque Country. In Gipuzkoa, it is common to hear *lagun bezala daukat* ("I consider him/her a friend"), and the instrumental declension is often used in Navarre: *ez nazazu tontoz hartu* ("don't take me for a fool"). In Lapurdi and Lower Navarre, meanwhile, the suffix expressing destination has replaced this. This example is from Uztaritze, Lapurdi:[61]

> *aberatsaantzat dauka bee buruia* for *aberatsarentzat dauka bere burua*
> "he/she considers himself/herself rich"

Endnotes

Chapter 1. Unifying and Separating Forces within Basque

1. Saussure, *Cours de Linguistique générale*, 28.
2. See Barandiaran, "Aspectos sociográficos de la población del Pirineo Vasco," 3–26. In English, see Barandiaran, *Selected Writings of José Miguel de Barandiarán*.
3. Ibarra, *Erroibarko eta Esteribarko hizkera*, 244.
4. Camino, *Aezkoako euskararen azterketa dialektologikoa*, 55.
5. Fraile and Fraile, *Oiartzungo hizkera*, 63.
6. Bonaparte, *Le verbe basque en tableaux* (1869), rpt. in *Opera omnia vasconice*, vol. 1, 226.
7. See Lafitte, *Grammaire basque: Navarro-labourdin littéraire*.

Part 1. Basque Dialects: The Structure of Basque Dialects

1. Oihenart, *Notitia utriusque Vasconiae tum Ibericae tum Aquitanicae*, rpt. in the *Revista Internacional de Estudios Vascos*, 353. In English, parts of this text are reproduced in Madariaga Orbea, *Anthology of Apologists and Detractors of the Basque Language*, 292–305.
2. See Caro Baroja, *Los pueblos del norte de la Península ibérica* and *Materiales para una historia de la lengua vasca en su relación con la latina*. In English, see Caro Baroja, *The Basques*, 20–22 and 357–58.
3. Etxarri, *Euskaldunen Amerika: Bidaia bat EEBBetan zehar*, 8.

Chapter 2. Zuberoan Basque

1. Euskaltzaindia, *Euskal Herriko Hizkuntz Atlasa: Ohiko euskal mintzamoldeen antologia*, 175.
2. d'Abbadie and Chaho, *Études grammaticales sur la langue euskarienne*; Oihenart, *Notitia utriusque Vasconiae*.
3. Inchauspe, *Le verbe basque*; Gèze, *Éléments de grammaire basque*.
4. Archu, *Bi mihiren gramatika uskara eta franzesa*.
5. Oihenart, *Les proverbes basques recueillis par le S. d'Oihenart: Plus les poesies du mesme auteur*.
6. Peillen, "Bela-ko zaldunaren zuberotar hiztegia, XVIII. Mendean," 128.

7. For more detailed explanations about this, see Artola and Tellabide, "Euskararen muga 1980: Urtean," 247–60 and Etxegorri, "Jeruntzeko üskara: Ekialdeko Euskara," 247–86.
8. Belaipere, *Catechima laburra eta Jesus-Christ goure ginco jaunaren eçagutcia, salvatu içateco*, II 33, II 68.
9. Caro Baroja, "Dos notas descriptivas: La agricultura en Vera de Bidasoa y caza de palomas en Echalar," 111, and *The Basques*, 222.

Chapter 3. Western Basque

1. For further explanations, see Merino Urrutia, *La lengua vasca en La Rioja y Burgos*.
2. Kardaberatz, *Dotrina cristiana edo cristiñau dotrinea*, in *Obras completas*, vol. 1, 454.
3. For an example in Hondarribia (Gipuzkoa), see Sagarzazu, *Hondarribiko eta Irungo euskara*.
4. I discuss this subject in greater depth in *Euskara batua: Ezina ekinez egina*.
5. See Garibai, "Atsotitzak eta errefrauak," 76–78 and Lakarra, ed., *Refranes y sentencias 1596: Ikerketak eta edizioa*.
6. Joan Antonio Mogel, quoted in Villasante, "Texto de dos impresos sumamente raros de Juan Antonio de Moguel," 63.
7. Zabala, *El verbo regular vascongado del dialecto vizcaino*.
8. Ibid., 56.
9. Arana, *Lecciones de ortografía del euskera bizkaino* (1896), in *Obras completas de Sabino Arana Goiri*, vol. 2, 822.
10. Barrutia, *Bermeo eta Mundakako arrantzaleen hiztegia* and *Bizkaiko arrantzaleen hiztegia*.
11. Taken from Azketa, *Fikeko berbakera*.
12. Sagarzazu, *Hondarribiko eta Irungo Euskara*, 67.
13. See Martinez de la Cuadra, *Nabarniztarren berbakera*.
14. Errazti, *Iurreta Elizateko euskara eta toponimia*, 127.
15. Ormaetxea, *Aramaioko euskara*, 137.
16. Etxebarria, *Zeberio haraneko euskararen azterketa etno-linguistikoa*, 245.
17. Makazaga, *Elgoibarko euskara*, 143.
18. Errazti, *Iurreta Elizateko euskara eta toponimia*, 125.
19. Ormaetxea, *Aramaioko euskara*, 72, 86.
20. Gilisasti, *Urduliz aldeko berba lapikokoa*, 44, 108, 161, 195, 322.

Chapter 4. Navarrese Basque

1. For further information, see Descheemaeker, "La frontière dans les Pyrénées Basques." In English, see Bray, *Living Boundaries*, esp. chap. 4.
2. For further information, see Olano, "Gipuzkoa ondoko bi hizkera nafar: Areso eta Leitzako paradoxa."
3. Mitxelena, *Fonética Histórica Vasca*, 41.

4. Camino, *Aezkoako euskararen azterketa dialektologikoa.*
5. On this, see Montoya, *Urdazubi eta Zugarramurdiko Euskara* and "Urdazubi eta Zugarramurdiko euskararen norabidea."
6. Urquijo, "Cartas escritas por el príncipe L.-L. Bonaparte a algunos de sus colaboradores," 280.
7. On this, see Olano, *Areso eta Leitzako hizkerak* and *Aio, Leitze! Leitzako euskararen hiztegia*; and Zubiri and Perurena, *Goizueta eta Aranoko hizkerak.*
8. For a more detailed explanation of this topic, see Erdozia, *Sakana erdialdeko euskara* and *Sakanako hiztegi dialektologikoa*; and Zuazo, "Burundako hizkera."
9. Bonaparte, *Le verbe basque*, 226.
10. Azkue, *Diccionario vasco-español-francés* (1905), xxvi–xxvii.
11. For more on these issues, see Lakar and Iriarte, *Bortzirietan aditutakoak*, Lakar and Apalauza, *Malerreka solasean*, and Zelaieta, "Bortzerrietako euskara, herriz herri (ez)berdintasunetan barren."
12. Examples taken from Cabodevilla, *Aetzen uskara*, Camino, *Aezkoako euskararen azterketa dialektologikoa*, and Ibarra, *Erroibarko eta Esteribarko hizkera* and *Erroibarko eta Esteribarko hiztegia.*
13. For example, see Ibarra, *Ultzamako hizkera.*
14. Bonaparte, "Observaciones acerca del vascuence de Valcarlos."
15. Mitxelena, *Fonética Histórica Vasca.*
16. Yrizar, *Morfología del verbo auxiliar labortano.*
17. See N'Diaye, *Structure du dialecte basque de Maya*; Izeta, *Baztango hiztegia*; Lakar and Telletxea, *Baztan solasean*; and Salaburu, *Hizkuntz teoria eta Baztango euskalkia* and *Baztango mintzoa.*
18. Salaburu, *Baztango mintzoa*, 169.
19. On this, see Hualde, *Euskararen azentuerak.*
20. Taken from ibid.
21. Camino, *Aezkoako euskararen azterketa dialektologikoa*, 300.

Chapter 5. Central Basque

1. Munibe, *El borracho burlado*, 389–90.
2. Kardaberatz, *Eusqueraren berri onac*, 13.
3. In Ruiz de Larrinaga, "Cartas del P. Uriarte al Príncipe Luis Luciano Bonaparte," 276.
4. In ibid., 279.
5. Cited in Urquijo, "Cartas escritas por el príncipe L.-L. Bonaparte a algunos de sus colaboradores," 257.
6. Altube, "La unificación del euskera literario," 202.
7. Villasante, "Oñatiko euskera," 270.
8. For examples, see Zuazo, *Deba ibarreko Euskara.*
9. Larramendi, *Diccionario trilingüe del castellano, bascuence y latin*, xxx.
10. Bonaparte, *Carte des sept provinces basques* and *Observations sur le basque de Fontarabie, d'Irun, etc.*
11. Yrizar, *Morfología del verbo auxiliar alto navarro septentrional*, vol. 1.

12. Bonaparte, *Observations sur le basque de Fontarabie, d'Irun, etc.*, 150.
13. Bonaparte, *Observations sur le formulaire de prone*, 7.
14. Bonaparte, *Observations sur le basque de Fontarabie, d'Irun, etc.*
15. By, respectively, Agirretxe, Lersundi, and Olaetxea, *Pasaiako hizkera*; Agirretxe and Esnaola, *Lezoko euskararen azterketa*; Fraile and Fraile, *Oiartzungo hizkera*; and Sagarzazu, *Hondarribiko eta Irungo Euskara.*
16. Sagarzazu, *Hondarribiko eta Irungo Euskara*, 106.
17. Ibid., 81.
18. Fraile and Fraile, *Oiartzungo hizkera*, 135.
19. Ibid., 100.
20. Sagarzazu, *Hondarribiko eta Irungo Euskara*, 84.
21. Mitxelena, *Fonética Histórica Vasca*, 385.
22. Sagarzazu, *Hondarribiko eta Irungo Euskara*, 84.
23. Yrizar, *Contribución a la dialectología de la lengua vasca*, vol. 2, 44.
24. Mitxelena, "Arantzazutik Bergarara," 471; In English, "From Arantzazu to Bergara," 277.
25. Mitxelena, "En torno a algunos aspectos del habla de Rentería (Guipúzcoa)," 94.
26. Yrizar, *Morfología del verbo auxiliar alto navarro septentrional*, vol. 2, 386.
27. Sagarzazu, *Hondarribiko eta Irungo Euskara.*
28. Campión and Broussain, "Informe a la Academia de la Lengua Vasca sobre unificación del euskera," 9.
29. Yrizar, *Contribución a la dialectología de la lengua vasca*, vol. 2, 212.
30. Olano, "Gipuzkoa ondoko bi hizkera nafar: Areso eta Leitzako paradoxa," 141.
31. Bozas Urrutia, "Contribución al diccionario vasco," 213.
32. Artola, in Yrizar, *Morfología del verbo auxiliar alto navarro septentrional*, vol. 2, 587.
33. See Zubiri and Perurena, *Goizueta eta Aranoko hizkerak* and Olano, *Areso eta Leitzako hizkerak* and *Aio, Leitze! Leitzako euskararen hiztegia.*
34. Apalauza and Arraztio, *Araitz-Beteluko ahotsak.*
35. Apalauza, "Nafarroako ipar-mendebaleko euskara: Imotz, Basaburu Nagusia, Larraun eta Araitz-Betelu."
36. Ibarra, *Ultzamako hizkera*, 602.
37. Ibid., 227.
38. For examples, see Iturain and Loidi, *Orioko euskara*, Labaka, Azurza, and Bereziartua, *Lasarte-Oriako euskararen azterketa*, Furundarena, *Astigarragako hizkera*, and Pikabea, Aginaga, *Errioko jarduerak eta bertako hiztegia.*
39. For examples, see Azurmendi, *Ataungo euskara* and *Zegamako euskara*, Hurtado, *Goierriko eta Tolosalde hegoaldeko hizkerak*, Etxabe and Garmendia, *Zaldibiako euskara* and *Ordiziako euskara*, and Agirrebeña et al., *Beasaingo Euskara.*
40. For examples, see Lasa, *Urretxu eta Zumarragako Euskara.*
41. For examples, see Saiz and Serrano, *Getariako hitanoa*, Azkue, *Hitanoa Zumaian*, Castillo, Romo, and Giralt, *Azkoittiko euskerie*, Azpeitia, *Zestoarren erretolika*, Txurruka and Urbieta, *Debako euskara*, and Agirrebeña et al., *Zarautz hizketan.*

42. Etxabe and Garmendia, *Zaldibiako Euskara*, 78.
43. Ibid.
44. Quoted in Jauregi, *Correspondencia de Gerhard Bähr con R. M. Azkue, H. Schuchardt y J. Urquijo*, 200.
45. See Azpeitia, *Zestoarren erretolika*.
46. Ibid., 12, 74, 93.
47. Etxabe and Garmendia, *Zaldibiako Euskara*, 73.
48. Apalauza, "Nafarroako ipar-mendebaleko euskara," 80.
49. Zubiri and Perurena, *Goizueta eta Aranoko hizkerak*, 82.
50. Ibid., 80.
51. See Azkue, *Hitanoa Zumaian*.

Chapter 6. Navarrese-Lapurdian Basque

1. Oihenart, *Les proverbes basques recueillis par le S. d'Oihenart*.
2. Bonaparte, *Le verbe basque en tableaux*, 226.
3. Azkue, *Diccionario vasco-español-francés*, xxvi–xxvii.
4. Yrizar, *Contribución a la dialectología de la lengua vasca*, vol. 2, 329.
5. Allières, "Petit atlas linguistique basque français *Sacaze*."
6. Guiter, "Atlas et frontières linguistiques," 102–3.
7. For examples, see Alberdi, "Euskararen tratamenduak: bilakaera" and *Euskararen tratamenduak: erabilera*.
8. Bonaparte, *Observations sur le formulaire de prône conservé naguère dans l'église d'Arbonne*, 2–4.
9. Urte, *Grammaire cantabrique basque*, 5.
10. Etxeberri, *Laburdiri escuararen hatsapenac*, 156.
11. On this, see Pikabea, *Lapurtera idatzia (XVII–XIX)*.
12. The most important works are: Duhau, *Hasian hasi: Beskoitzeko Euskara*; Salaberri Zaratiegi, "Luzaideko euskara, Mezkirizkoaren eta Aezkoakoaren argitan"; Salaberri Zaratiegi and Kamino, "Hitz eratorriak Luzaideko hizkeran," "Aditz trinkoen orainaldiko formak Luzaideko euskaran," and *Luzaideko euskararen hiztegia*; Camino, "Nafarroa Behereko euskara"; and Epelde, "Lapurdiko hego-ekialdeko euskararen kokapenerantz" and "Larresoroko gaur egungo Euskara."
13. Epelde, "Lapurdiko hego-ekialdeko euskararen kokapenerantz," 276.
14. Montoya, *Urdazubi eta Zugarramurdiko Euskara*, 79.
15. Epelde, "Larresoroko gaur egungo Euskara," 669.
16. Montoya, *Urdazubi eta Zugarramurdiko Euskara*, 77.

Chapter 7. Basque in the Americas

1. The information in this section has been taken from William A. Douglass and Jon Bilbao's book *Amerikanuak: Basques in the New World*.
2. Arantzadi, "Congreso Internacional de Estudios Vascos," 402.
3. Lhande, *La emigración vasca*, vol. 2, 19.

4. Grandmontagne, *Los inmigrantes prósperos*, 385.
5. See Garate, "Segunda contribución al Diccionario Vasco," 104 and "La Historia y Geografía de España ilustradas por el Idioma Vascuence" (1935), 262; Ormaetxea, *Euskaldunak poema*, 10; and Labaien, "Euskera'ren batasuna," 28.
6. Douglass and Bilbao, *Amerikanuak*, 335.
7. Ibid., 330–35.
8. Etxaide, "Euskaldunak Ipar-Amerikan," 49.
9. [Castor Uriarte] in *Euskera* 1959: 254 and [Arrue] in *Euskera* 1973: 255–56., 254.
10. In *Euskera*, 1973: 255–56.
11. In *Euskalduna*, 1955, 7. No. 1.
12. See Wilbur, "The Phonemes of the Basque of Bakersfield, California."
13. Etxabe, "Estatu Batuetako Idaho estatuko euskararen azterketa," 380.
14. Aranzadi Zientzia Elkartea, *Euskalerriko Atlas Etnolinguistikoa*, Euskera, 30–2, 1985, 381–85.
15. Etxabe, "Estatu Batuetako Idaho estatuko euskararen azterketa."
16. Amorrortu, *Basque Sociolinguistics*, 134.
17. Douglass and Bilbao, *Amerikanuak*, 163.
18. Ibid., 163–64.
19. Ibid., 168.
20. Ibid., 384.
21. Gachiteguy, *Les basques dans l'ouest americain*, 105.
22. On the importance of the First National Basque Festival, see Douglass, "Inventing an Ethnic Identity: The First Basque Festival."
23. Mitxelena, *Sobre el pasado de la lengua vasca*, 19.
24. See Amorrortu, "Retention and Accommodation in the Basque of Elko, Nevada" and "Language Maintenance and Change: American Basque," in *Basque Sociolinguistics*, 130–35.
25. On this, see Garciarena, "Los campesinos vascos en América y sus descendientes argentines," Douglass and Bilbao, *Amerikanuak*, Agirre, "El euskera en la República Argentina," Decroos, *The Long Journey: Social Integration and Ethnicity Maintenance among Urban Basques in the San Francisco Bay Region*, Oiarzabal, *Gardeners of Identity*, and Camus, "A Historical Comparative Study of Basque Institutions in the United States."
26. Amorrortu, "Retention and Accommodation in the Basque of Elko, Nevada," 433.
27. Ibid., 451.

Chapter 8. The Main Features of Basque across Several Dialects

1. Hualde and Bilbao, *A Phonological Study of the Basque Dialect of Getxo*, 57.
2. Ibid.
3. Iturain and Loidi, *Orioko Euskara*, 9.
4. Yrizar, *Morfología del verbo auxiliar alto navarro septentrional*, vol. 2, 252.
5. See Erdozia, *Sakana erdialdeko Euskara*.

6. See Mallea, *Mendata, gure geurea danentzat.*
7. See Leizarraga, *Jesus Christ gure Jaunaren Testamentu Berria.*
8. Erdozia, *Sakana erdialdeko Euskara.*
9. Bonaparte, *Phonologie de la langue basque.*
10. For examples, see Hualde, "Arbizuko hizkeraren zenbait soinu bereizgarriz."
11. Salaburu, *Baztango mintzoa.*
12. Lasa, *Urretxu eta Zumarragako Euskara*, 162.
13. Montoya, *Urdazubi eta Zugarramurdiko Euskara*, 203.
14. Agirretxe and Esnaola, *Lezoko euskararen azterketa*, 73.
15. Montoya, *Urdazubi eta Zugarramurdiko Euskara*, 108.
16. Zubiri and Perurena, *Goizueta eta Aranoko hizkerak*, 123.
17. For examples, see Iñigo, Salaberri, and Zubiri, "-ki aditz-atzizkiaren gainean."
18. Sagarzazu, *Hondarribiko eta Irungo Euskara*, 81.
19. Yrizar, *Morfología del verbo auxiliar labortano*, 52.
20. Mitxelena, *Fonética Histórica Vasca*, 385, 578.
21. For information about words from the Deba Valley in Gipuzkoa, for example, see Zuazo, *Deba ibarreko Euskara*, 71–73.
22. Coyos, *Le parler basque souletin des Arbailles*, 86.
23. Mitxelena, *Sobre el pasado de la lengua vasca*, 47.
24. Salaburu, *Hizkuntz teoria eta Baztango euskalkia*, vol. 1, 174–75.
25. Salaburu, *Baztango mintzoa.*
26. Lekaroz, "Antzinako baztanera," 83.
27. N'Diaye, *Structure du dialecte basque de Maya*, 82, 106.
28. Olano, *Areso eta Leitzako hizkerak*, 262.
29. Fraile and Fraile, *Oiartzungo hizkera*, 148.
30. Epelde, "Larresoroko gaur egungo Euskara," 673.
31. Ibid.
32. Agirretxe and Esnaola, *Lezoko euskararen azterketa*, 135.
33. Salaburu, *Hizkuntz teoria eta Baztango euskalkia*, vol. 2, 180.
34. Epelde, "Larresoroko gaur egungo Euskara," 675.
35. Haase, *Sprachkontakt und Sprachwandel im Baskenland*, 146, 149.
36. Salaberri Zaratiegi and Kamino, "Hitz eratorriak Luzaideko hizkeran," 70, 73.
37. Duhau, *Hasian hasi*, 62, 185.
38. Epelde, "Lapurdiko hego-ekialdeko euskararen kokapenerantz," 296.
39. Camino, *Aezkoako euskararen azterketa dialektologikoa*, 98.
40. Epelde, "Larresoroko gaur egungo Euskara."
41. Gimet, "Le Kostatar: Dialecte basque de la région de St. Jean-de-Luz," 243.
42. Salaberri Zaratiegi and Kamino, "Hitz eratorriak Luzaideko hizkeran," 77.
43. Duhau, *Hasian hasi: Beskoitzeko Euskara*, 81.
44. Oyharçabal, "À propos d'un usage prédicatif particulier des pronoms personnels intensifs en basque."
45. Epelde, "Lapurdiko hego-ekialdeko euskararen kokapenerantz," 293.
46. Haase, *Sprachkontakt und Sprachwandel im Baskenland*, 148.
47. Duhau, *Hasian hasi: Beskoitzeko Euskara*, 171.
48. Ibid., 105.

49. Epelde, "Lapurdiko hego-ekialdeko euskararen kokapenerantz," 297.
50. For further explanation, see Rebuschi, "A Note on Focalization in Basque" and Oyharçabal, "ba- baiezko aurrizkia."
51. N'Diaye, *Structure du dialecte basque de Maya*, 51, 56, 103, 122, 130.
52. Txillardegi, "Zubererazko transkribaketa bat," 36.
53. For examples, see Hualde, *Basque Phonology*.
54. Bonaparte, *Le verbe basque en tableaux*, 434.
55. Agirretxe, Lersundi, and Olaetxea, *Pasaiako hizkera*, 122, 149.
56. For examples, see Oñederra, *Euskal fonologia: Palatalizazioa* and Hualde, *Basque Phonology*.
57. Salaburu, *Hizkuntz teoria eta Baztango euskalkia*, vol. 2, 158–59.
58. Ormaetxea, *Aramaioko Euskara*.
59. Yrizar, *Morfología del verbo auxiliar alto navarro septentrional*, vol. 1, 203.
60. Coyos, *Le parler basque souletin des Arbailles*, 142.
61. Epelde, "Lapurdiko hego-ekialdeko euskararen kokapenerantz," 284.

Bibliography

Abbadie, Antoine Thompson, and J. Augustin Chaho. *Études grammaticales sur la langue euskarienne*. Paris: Arthus Bertrand, 1836.

Agirre, Vicente. "El euskera en la República Argentina." *Boletín del Instituto Americano de Estudios Vascos* 33, no. 131 (1982): 126–30.

Agirrebeña, Aintzane, Itziar Alberdi, Xabier Mendiguren, and Asier Sarasua. *Beasaingo euskara*. Beasain: Beasaingo Udala, 2007.

Agirrebeña, Aintzane, Belen Maiz, Fernando Muniozguren, Asier Sarasua, and Miren Zabaleta. *Zarautz hizketan*. Zarautz: Zarauzko Udala, 2007.

Agirretxe, Joxe Luix, and Imanol Esnaola. *Lezoko euskararen azterketa*. Lezo: Lezoko Unibertsitateko Udala, 2000.

Agirretxe, Joxe Luix, Mikel Lersundi, and Ortzuri Olaetxea. *Pasaiako hizkera*. Pasaia: Pasaiako Udala, 2000.

Alberdi, Jabier. "Euskararen tratamenduak: bilakaera." *Fontes Linguae Vasconum* 26, no. 67 (1994): 401–33.

———. *Euskararen tratamenduak: Erabilera*. Iker-9 series. Bilbo: Euskaltzaindia, 1996.

Allières, Jacques. "Petit atlas linguistique basque français *Sacaze*." *Via Domitia* 7 and 8 (1960–1961): 205–19 and 81–125.

Altube, Seber. "La unificación del euskera literario." *Eusko-Jakintza* 3 (1949): 181–204.

Altuna, Patxi. "Bonapartek eta Aita Aranak elkarri egin kartak." *Fontes Linguae Vasconum* 17, no. 46 (1985): 305–341.

Amorrortu, Estibalitz. "Retention and Accommodation in the Basque of Elko, Nevada." *Anuario del Seminario de Filología Vasca "Julio de Urquijo"* 29, nos. 2–3 (1995): 407–54.

———. *Basque Sociolinguistics: Language, Society, and Culture*. Reno: Center for Basque Studies, University of Nevada, Reno, 2003.

Apalauza, Amaia. "Nafarroako ipar-mendebaleko euskara: Imotz, Basaburu Nagusia, Larraun eta Araitz-Betelu." *Fontes Linguae Vasconum* 40, no. 107 (2008): 63–104.

Apalauza, Amaia, and Kontxi Arraztio. *Araitz-Beteluko ahotsak: Ahozko tradizioaren bilduma*. Iruñea: Nafarroako Gobernua, Beteluko Udala, and Araizko Udala, 2007.

Arana, Sabino. *Lecciones de ortografía del euskera bizkaino* (1896). In *Obras completas de Sabino Arana Goiri*, edited by Martin Ugalde. Volume 2. Donostia: Sendoa, 1980.

Arantzadi, Telesforo. "Congreso Internacional de Estudios Vascos." *Euskalduna* 173 (October 28, 1900): 401–5.

Arantzadi Zientzia Elkartea. *Euskalerriko Atlas Etnolinguistikoa*. 2 Voumes. Donostia: Arantzadi Zientzia Elkartea, 1984–1990.

Archu, Jean-Baptiste. *Bi mihiren gramatika uskara eta franzesa*. 1852. Facsmile, Donostia: Hordago, 1979.

Artola, Koldo, and Josu Tellabide. "Euskararen muga 1980: Urtean." *Fontes Linguae Vasconum* 22, no. 56 (1990): 247–60.

Arxu. See Archu.

Azketa, Sorkunde. *Fikeko berbakera*. Bilbo: Gamiz-Fikako Udala and Bizkaiko Foru Aldundia, 2002.

Azkue, Resurrección Maria. *Euskal-Izkindea: Gramática eúscara*. Bilbo: Astuiko Jose-n Moldegintzan, 1891.

———. *Diccionario vasco-español-francés*. 1905–1906. Reprint, Bilbo: Euskaltzaindia, 1984.

Azkue, Xabier. *Hitanoa Zumaian: Egoera, erabilera, transmisioa eta formak*. Zumaia: Zumaiako Udala, 2000.

Azpeitia, Agurtzane. *Zestoarren erretolika*. Zestoa: Zestoako Udala, 2003.

Azurmendi, Joxe Migel. *Ataungo euskara*. Lazkao: Goiherriko Euskal Eskola; Maizpide Euskaltegia; and Lazkaoko Udaleko Kultur Batzordea, 1996.

———. *Zegamako euskara*. Lazkao: Goiherriko Euskal Eskola; Maizpide Euskaltegia; and Udaleko Kultur Batzordea, 1998.

Bähr, Gerard. "Estudio sobre el verbo guipuzcoano." *Revista Internacional de Estudios Vascos* (Series of eight articles published between 1926 and 1935).

Barandiaran, Jose Migel. "Aspectos sociográficos de la población del Pirineo Vasco." *Eusko-Jakintza* 7 (1953–1957): 3–26.

———. *Selected Writings of José Miguel de Barandiarán: Basque History and Prehistory*. Compiled and with an Introduction by Jesús Altuna. Translated by Frederick H. Fornoff, Linda White, and Carys Evans-Corrales. Reno: Center for Basque Studies, University of Nevada, Reno, 2007.

Barrutia, Eneko. *Bermeo eta Mundakako arrantzaleen hiztegia*. Bilbo: Udako Euskal Unibertsitatea, 1996.

———. *Bizkaiko arrantzaleen hiztegia*. Bilbo: Labayru Ikastegia; Bilbao Bizkaia Kutxa, 2000.

Belapeire, Athanase. *Catechima laburra eta Jesus-Christ goure ginco jaunaren eçagutcia, salvatu içateco*. Paue: Jérôme Dupoux, 1696. Facsimile, edited by Jean-Louis Davant. Bilbo: Euskaltzaindia, 1983.

Bonaparte, Louis-Lucien. *Carte des sept provinces basques, montrant la délimitation actuelle de l'euscara*. London: Stanford's Geographical

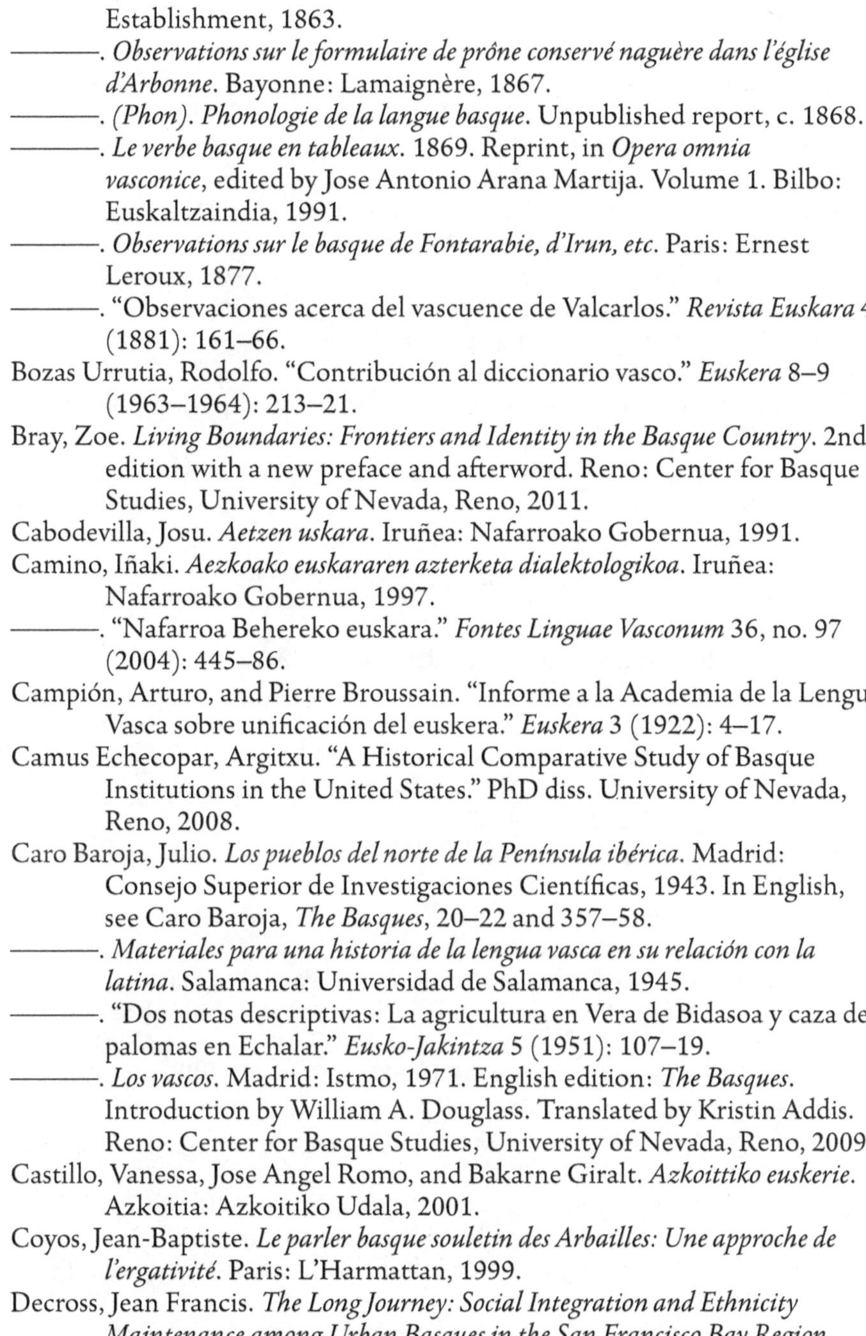

Establishment, 1863.

———. *Observations sur le formulaire de prône conservé naguère dans l'église d'Arbonne*. Bayonne: Lamaignère, 1867.

———. *(Phon). Phonologie de la langue basque*. Unpublished report, c. 1868.

———. *Le verbe basque en tableaux*. 1869. Reprint, in *Opera omnia vasconice*, edited by Jose Antonio Arana Martija. Volume 1. Bilbo: Euskaltzaindia, 1991.

———. *Observations sur le basque de Fontarabie, d'Irun, etc*. Paris: Ernest Leroux, 1877.

———. "Observaciones acerca del vascuence de Valcarlos." *Revista Euskara* 4 (1881): 161–66.

Bozas Urrutia, Rodolfo. "Contribución al diccionario vasco." *Euskera* 8–9 (1963–1964): 213–21.

Bray, Zoe. *Living Boundaries: Frontiers and Identity in the Basque Country*. 2nd edition with a new preface and afterword. Reno: Center for Basque Studies, University of Nevada, Reno, 2011.

Cabodevilla, Josu. *Aetzen uskara*. Iruñea: Nafarroako Gobernua, 1991.

Camino, Iñaki. *Aezkoako euskararen azterketa dialektologikoa*. Iruñea: Nafarroako Gobernua, 1997.

———. "Nafarroa Behereko euskara." *Fontes Linguae Vasconum* 36, no. 97 (2004): 445–86.

Campión, Arturo, and Pierre Broussain. "Informe a la Academia de la Lengua Vasca sobre unificación del euskera." *Euskera* 3 (1922): 4–17.

Camus Echecopar, Argitxu. "A Historical Comparative Study of Basque Institutions in the United States." PhD diss. University of Nevada, Reno, 2008.

Caro Baroja, Julio. *Los pueblos del norte de la Península ibérica*. Madrid: Consejo Superior de Investigaciones Científicas, 1943. In English, see Caro Baroja, *The Basques*, 20–22 and 357–58.

———. *Materiales para una historia de la lengua vasca en su relación con la latina*. Salamanca: Universidad de Salamanca, 1945.

———. "Dos notas descriptivas: La agricultura en Vera de Bidasoa y caza de palomas en Echalar." *Eusko-Jakintza* 5 (1951): 107–19.

———. *Los vascos*. Madrid: Istmo, 1971. English edition: *The Basques*. Introduction by William A. Douglass. Translated by Kristin Addis. Reno: Center for Basque Studies, University of Nevada, Reno, 2009.

Castillo, Vanessa, Jose Angel Romo, and Bakarne Giralt. *Azkoittiko euskerie*. Azkoitia: Azkoitiko Udala, 2001.

Coyos, Jean-Baptiste. *Le parler basque souletin des Arbailles: Une approche de l'ergativité*. Paris: L'Harmattan, 1999.

Decross, Jean Francis. *The Long Journey: Social Integration and Ethnicity Maintenance among Urban Basques in the San Francisco Bay Region*. Reno: Associated Faculty Press and Basque Studies Program, University of Nevada, 1983.

Descheemaeker, Jacques. "La frontière dans les Pyrénées Basques." *Eusko-*

Jakintza 4 (1950): 127–78.

Douglass, William A. "Inventing an Ethnic Identity: The First Basque Festival." Reprint, in *Global Vasconia: Essays on the Basque Diaspora*. Reno: Center for Basque Studies, University of Nevada, Reno, 2006.

Douglass, William A., and Jon Bilbao. *Amerikanuak: Basques in the New World*. Reno: University of Nevada Press, 1975.

Duhau, Henri. *Hasian hasi: Beskoitzeko euskara*. 2 Volumes. Donibane Lohizune: Alinea; Akoka, 1993–2003.

Epelde, Irantzu. "Lapurdiko hego-ekialdeko euskararen kokapenerantz." *Fontes Linguae Vasconum* 36, no. 96 (2004): 271–303.

———. "Larresoroko gaur egungo euskara." *Euskera* 49, no. 2 (2004): 663–77.

Erdozia, Jose Luis. *Sakana erdialdeko euskara*. Iruñea: Nafarroako Gobernua, 2001.

———. *Sakanako hiztegi dialektologikoa*. Iruñea: Nafarroako Gobernua; Euskaltzaindia, 2004.

Errazti, Alberto. *Iurreta Elizateko euskara eta toponimia*. Iurreta: Iurretako Udala, 1994.

Etxabe, Jon Joseba. "Estatu Batuetako Idaho estatuko euskararen azterketa." *Euskera* 30, no. 2 (1985): 377–87.

Etxabe, Karmele, and Larraitz Garmendia. *Zaldibiako euskara*. Zaldibia: Zaldibiako Udala, 2003.

———. *Ordiziako euskara: Garai bateko bizimodua eta gaurko hizkuntza-egoera*. Ordizia: Ordiziako Udala; Hitzaro Euskara Elkartea, 2004.

Etxaide, Jon. Pseudonym "Uarrain." "Euskaldunak Ipar-Amerikan." *Euzko-Gogoa* 3, nos. 1–2 (1952): 47–51.

Etxarri, Joseba. *Euskaldunen Amerika: Bidaia bat EEBBetan zehar*. Donostia: Elkar, 1994.

Etxebarria, Juan Manuel. *Zeberio haraneko euskararen azterketa etno-linguistikoa*. Zornotza: Ibaizabal, 1991.

Etxeberri, Joanes. *Laburdiri escuararen hatsapenac*. Paris, 1712 . Facsimile, edited by Julio Urquijo. Originally designed to be published in the *Revista Internacional de Estudios Vascos* 28 (1937) but unpublished due to the outbreak of the Spanish Civil War. Reprint, Bilbo: La Gran Enciclopedia Vasca, 1976, 85–201.

Etxegorri, Philippe. "Jeruntzeko üskara: Ekialdeko euskara." *Fontes Linguae Vasconum* 35, no. 93 (2003): 247–86.

Euskaltzaindia. *Euskal Herriko Hizkuntz Atlasa: Ohiko euskal mintzamoldeen antologia*. Book and four CDs. Bilbo: Euskaltzaindia, 1999.

Fagoaga, Isidoro de. "Printze euskaltzale bat: Luis Luziano Bonaparte." *Egan* 35 (1975): 3–12.

Fraile, Idoia, and Ainhoa Fraile. *Oiartzungo hizkera*. Oiartzun: Oiartzungo Udala, 1996.

Furundarena, Joxe Jabier. *Astigarragako hizkera*. Astigarraga: Astigarragako Udala, 1998.

Gachiteguy, Adrien. *Les basques dans l'ouest americain*. Bordeaux: Ezkila, 1955.
Garate, Justo. "Segunda contribución al Diccionario Vasco." *Revista Internacional de Estudios Vascos* 24 (1933): 94–104.
———. "La Historia y Geografía de España ilustradas por el Idioma Vascuence." *Euskera* 16, nos. 3–4 (1935): 187–354 and 18, nos. 1–2 (1937): 3–64.
Garciarena, José María. "Los campesinos vascos en América y sus descendientes argentinos." *Boletín del Instituto Americano de Estudios Vascos* 6, no. 22 (1955): 128–38.
Garibai, Esteban. "Atsotitzak eta errefrauak." Reproduced in *Egan*, supplement of the *Boletín de la Real Sociedad Vascongada de Amigos del País* 5–6 (1956): 76–78.
Garibai, Esteban. "Refranes en bascuençe." *Revista Internacional de Estudios Vascos* 27 (1936): 553–622.
Gèze, Louis. *Éléments de grammaire basque*. 1873. Facsimile. Donostia: Hordago, 1979.
Gilisasti, Iñaki. *Urduliz aldeko berba lapikokoa*. Urduliz: N.p., 2003.
Gimet, Roger. "Le Kostatar: Dialecte basque de la région de St. Jean-de-Luz." *Eusko-Jakintza* 5 (1950): 221–50 and 393–424.
Grandmontagne, Francisco. *Los inmigrantes prósperos*. 1933. Reprint, Madrid: Aguilar, 1960.
Guiter, Henri. "Atlas et frontières linguistiques." In *Les dialectes romans de France à la lumière des atlas régionaux*, edited by Georges Straka and Pierre Gardette. Paris: Éditions du C.N.R.S., 1973.
Haase, Martin. *Sprachkontakt und Sprachwandel im Baskenland*. Hamburg: Buske, 1992.
Hualde, Jose Ignazio. *Basque Phonology*. London and New York: Routledge, 1991.
———. "Arbizuko hizkeraren zenbait soinu bereizgarriz." *Uztaro* 18 (1996): 49–60.
———. *Euskararen azentuerak*. ASJU supplement 42. Donostia and Bilbo: Gipuzkoako Foru Aldundia; Euskal Herriko Unibertsitatea, 1997.
Hualde, Jose Ignazio, and Xabier Bilbao. 1992. *A Phonological Study of the Basque Dialect of Getxo*. ASJU supplement 29. Donostia: Gipuzkoako Foru Aldundia, 1992.
Hualde, Jose Ignazio, and Jon Ortiz de Urbina, eds. *A Grammar of Basque*. Berlin and New York: Mouton de Gruyter, 2003.
Hurtado, Irene. *Goierriko eta Tolosalde hegoaldeko hizkerak*. Lazkao: Goierriko Euskal Eskola Kultur Elkartea; Maizpide Euskaltegia; Lazkaoko Udala, 2001.
Ibarra, Orreaga. *Ultzamako hizkera: Inguruko euskalkiekiko harremanak*. Iruñea: Nafarroako Gobernua, 1995.
———. *Erroibarko eta Esteribarko hizkera*. Iruñea: Nafarroako Unibertsitate Publikoa, 2000.
———. *Erroibarko eta Esteribarko hiztegia*. Iruñea: Nafarroako Gobernua;

Euskaltzaindia, 2007.
Inchauspe, Emmanuel. *Le verbe basque*. 1858. Facsimile. Donostia: Hordago, 1979.
Intxauspe. See Inchauspe.
Iñigo, Patxi, Patxi Salaberri Zaratiegi, and Juan Joxe Zubiri. "-*ki* aditz-atzizkiaren gainean." *Fontes Linguae Vasconum* 27, no. 69 (1995): 243–95.
Irizar. See Yrizar.
Iturain, Iñaki, and Loren Loidi. *Orioko euskara*. Orio: Orioko Udala, 1995.
Izeta, Mariano. *Baztango hiztegia*. Iruñea: Nafarroako Gobernua, 1996.
Jauregi, Oroitz, ed. *Correspondencia de Gerhard Bähr con R. M. Azkue, H. Schuchardt y J. Urquijo*. ASJU supplement 36/2. Donostia: Gipuzkoako Foru Aldundia, 2005.
Kardaberatz, Agustin. *Dotrina cristiana edo cristiñau dotrinea*. In *Obras completas*, edited by León Lopetegui. Volume 1. Bilbao: La Gran Enciclopedia Vasca, 1973.
———. *Eusqueraren berri onac*. In *Obras completas*, edited by León Lopetegui. Volume 1. Bilbao: La Gran Enciclopedia Vasca, 1973.
Labaien, Antonio M. Pseudonym, "Ibalan." "Euskera'ren batasuna." *Euzko-Gogoa* 3, nos. 1–2 (1952): 26–28.
Labaka, Ana, M. Eugenia Azurza, and Juan Ignazio Bereziartua. *Lasarte-Oriako euskararen azterketa*. Lasarte-Oria: Lasarte-Oriako Udala, 1996.
Lafitte, Pierre. *Grammaire basque: Navarro-labourdin littéraire*. 1944. 2nd expanded edition. Donostia: Elkar, 1979.
Lakar, Maite, and Nora Iriarte. *Bortzirietan aditutakoak. Ahozko tradizioaren bilduma*. Iruñea: Nafarroako Gobernua, 2003.
Lakar, Maite, and Amaia Apalauza. *Malerreka solasean: Ahozko tradizioaren bilduma*. Iruñea: Nafarroako Gobernua, 2005.
Lakar, Maite, and Ana Telletxea. *Baztan solasean: Ahozko tradizioaren bilduma*. Iruñea: Nafarroako Gobernua and Baztango Udala, 2006.
Lakarra, Joseba, ed. *Refranes y sentencias 1596: Ikerketak eta edizioa*. Bilbao: Academia de la Lengua Vasca, 1996.
Larramendi, Manuel. *El imposible vencido: Arte de la Lengua Bascongada*. 1729. Facsimile. Donostia, Hordago, 1979.
———. *Diccionario trilingüe del castellano, bascuence y latin*. 2 volumes. San Sebastián: Bartholomè Riesgo y Montero, 1745.
Lasa, Xabier. *Urretxu eta Zumarragako euskara*. Urretxu-Zumarraga: Zintzo-Mintzo euskaltzale elkartea, 2004.
Leizarraga, Joanes. *Jesus Christ gure Jaunaren Testamentu Berria*. La Rochelle: Pierre Hautin, 1571.
Lekaroz, Gorka. "Antzinako baztanera: XVIII mendeko prediku argitaragabe bat." *Fontes Linguae Vasconum* 38, no. 101 (2006): 69–94.
Lhande, Pierre. *La emigración vasca*. 2 volumes. Translated by Ignacio Basurko Berroa. San Sebastián: Auñamendi, 1971.

Madariaga Orbea, Juan. *Anthology of Apologists and Detractors of the Basque Language*. Translated by Frederick H. Fornoff, María Cristina Saavedra, Amaia Gabantxo, and Cameron J. Watson. Reno: Center for Basque Studies, University of Nevada, Reno, 2006.

Makazaga, Jesus Mari. *Elgoibarko euskara*. Elgoibar: Elgoibarko Udala; Elgoibarko Izarra Kultur Elkartea; Badihardugu Deba Ibarreko Euskara Elkartea, 2007.

Mallea, Idoia. *Mendata, gure geurea danentzat*. Mendata: Mendatako Udala, 2002.

Martinez de la Cuadra, Alberto. *Nabarniztarren berbakera*. Nabarniz: Nabarnizko Udala, 2006.

Merino Urrutia, Jose J. Bautista. *La lengua vasca en La Rioja y Burgos*. Logroño: Servicio de Cultura de la Excma. Diputación Provincial de Logroño, 1978.

Mitxelena, Koldo. "Arantzazutik Bergarara." *Euskera* 24 (1978): 467–77. In English, see "From Arantzazu to Bergara." In Koldo Mitxelena, *Koldo Mitxelena: Selected Writings of a Basque Scholar*. Compiled with an introduction by Pello Salaburu. Translated by Linda White and M. Dean Johnson. Reno: Center for Basque Studies, University of Nevada, Reno, 2008.

———. "En torno a algunos aspectos del habla de Rentería (Guipúzcoa)." *Boletín de la Real Sociedad Vascongada de los Amigos del País* 6 (1950): 89–94.

———. *Fonética Histórica Vasca*. 1961. 2nd expanded edition. ASJU supplement 4. Donostia: Gipuzkoako Foru Aldundia, 1976.

———. *Sobre el pasado de la lengua vasca*. Donostia: Auñamendi, 1964.

———. *Sobre historia de la lengua vasca*. 2 volumes. ASJU Supplement 10. Donostia: Gipuzkoako Foru Aldundia, 1998.

Mogel, Joan Antonio. *Confesio eta comunioco sacramentuen gañean eracasteac*. Iruñea: Libruguille Ezquerrorem Alargunaren Echean, 1800.

———. "Texto de dos impresos sumamente raros de Juan Antonio de Moguel." Edited by Luis Villasante. *Boletín de la Real Sociedad Vascongada de los Amigos del País* 20 (1964): 61–73.

Montoya, Estibalitz. *Urdazubi eta Zugarramurdiko euskara*. Iruñea: Nafarroako Gobernua, 2004.

———. "Urdazubi eta Zugarramurdiko euskararen norabidea." *Fontes Linguae Vasconum* 36, no. 96 (2004): 249–69.

Munibe, Xabier. *El borracho burlado*. 1764. Facsimile. *Revista Internacional de Estudios Vascos*. Published in installments betwen 1907 and 1909.

N'Diaye, Geneviève. *Structure du dialecte basque de Maya*. Paris and The Hague: Mouton, 1970.

Oiarzabal, Pedro J. *Gardeners of Identity: Basques in the San Francisco Bay Area*. Reno: Center for Basque Studies, University of Nevada, Reno, 2009.

Oihartzabal. See Oyharçabal.

Oihenart, Arnaut. *Notitia utriusque Vasconiae tum Ibericae tum Aquitanicae*.

Paris: S. Cramoisy, 1638. 2nd expaned edition, 1656. Translated into Spanish by Javier Gorosterratzu in the *Revista Internacional de Estudios Vascos*, 1926–1928. Facsimile. Vitoria-Gasteiz: Eusko Legebiltzarra, 1992. In English, parts of this text are reproduced in Madariaga Orbea, *Anthology of Apologists and Detractors of the Basque Language*, 292–305.

———. *Les proverbes basques recueillis par le S. d'Oihenart, plus les poesies du mesme auteur*. Paris, 1657.

Olano, Mikel. *Areso eta Leitzako hizkerak*. Leitza: Nafarroako Gobernua; Leitzako Udala; Aresoko Udala, 1998.

———. "Gipuzkoa ondoko bi hizkera nafar: Areso eta Leitzako paradoxa." In *Dialektologia gaiak*, edited by Koldo Zuazo. Vitoria-Gasteiz: Arabako Foru Aldundia; Euskal Herriko Unibertsitatea, 2000.

———. *Aio, Leitze! Leitzako euskararen hiztegia: Etnografia, corpusa, dialektologia*. Leitza: Nafarroako Iparraldeko Euskara Mankomunitatea, 2005.

Oñederra, M. Lourdes. *Euskal fonologia: Palatalizazioa*. Leioa: Euskal Herriko Unibertsitatea, 1990.

Ormaetxea, Nikolas. Pseudonym "Orixe." *Euskaldunak poema*. Zarautz: Itxaropena, 1950.

Ormaetxea, Txipi. *Aramaioko euskara*. Aramaio: Aramaioko Udala, 2002.

Oyharçabal, Beñat. "*ba-* baiezko aurrizkia." *Euskera* 29, no. 1 (1984): 351–71.

———. "À propos d'un usage prédicatif particulier des pronoms personnels intensifs en basque." In *Hommage à Jacques Allières (I): Domaine basque et pyrènèen*, edited by Michel Aurnage and Michel Roché. Angelu: Atlantica, 2002.

Peillen, Txomin. "Bela-ko zaldunaren zuberotar hiztegia, XVIII. Mendean." *Fontes Linguae Vasconum* 15, nos. 41–42 (1983): 127–46.

Pikabea, Jabier. *Aginaga, Errioko jarduerak eta bertako hiztegia*. Lankidetzan collection. Donostia: Eusko Ikaskuntza, 2005.

Pikabea, Josu. *Lapurtera idatzia (XVII–XIX): Bilakaera baten urratsak*. Donostia: Euskal Herriko Unibertsitatea; Kutxa Fundazioa, 1993.

Rebuschi, Georges. "A Note on Focalization in Basque." *Journal of Basque Studies* 4, no. 2 (1983): 29–42.

Ruiz de Larrinaga, Juan. "Cartas del P. Uriarte al Príncipe Luis Luciano Bonaparte." *Boletín de la Real Sociedad Vascongada de los Amigos del País* 10 (1954–1958): 231–302, 13: 220–239, 330–348, 429–452 and 14: 397–443.

Sagarzazu, Txomin. *Hondarribiko eta Irungo euskara*. Irun: Alberdania, 2005.

Saiz, Ainhoa, and Gurenda Serrano. *Getariako hitanoa*. Getaria: Getariako Udala, 1999.

Salaberri Zaratiegi, Patxi. "Luzaideko euskara, Mezkirizkoaren eta Aezkoakoaren argitan." In *Dialektologia gaiak*, edited by Koldo Zuazo. Vitoria-Gasteiz: Arabako Foru Aldundia; Euskal Herriko Unibertsitatea, 2000.

Salaberri Zaratiegi, Patxi, and Peio Kamino. "Hitz eratorriak Luzaideko hizkeran." *Fontes Linguae Vasconum* 33, no. 86 (2001): 67–86.

———. "Aditz trinkoen orainaldiko formak Luzaideko euskaran." *Fontes Linguae Vasconum* 33, no. 87 (2001): 193–202.

———. *Luzaideko euskararen hiztegia*. Iruñea: Nafarroako Gobernua; Euskaltzaindia, 2007.

Salaburu, Pello. *Hizkuntz teoria eta Baztango euskalkia: Fonetika eta fonologia*. 2 Volumes. Leioa: Euskal Herriko Unibertsitatea, 1984.

———. *Baztango mintzoa: Gramatika eta Hiztegia*. Iruñea: Nafarroako Gobernua; Euskaltzaindia, 2005.

Saussure, Ferdinand de. *Cours de Linguistique générale*. Edited by Charles Bally and Albert Sechehaye. Lausanne and Paris: Librairie Payot, 1916.

Txillardegi. Pseudonym for Jose Luis Alvarez Enparanza. "Zubererazko transkribaketa bat." *Fontes Linguae Vasconum* 12, no. 34 (1980): 29–36.

Txurruka, Alazne, and Josune Urbieta. *Debako euskara*. Deba: Ostolaza Kultur Elkartea, 2003.

Urquijo, Julio. "Cartas escritas por el príncipe L.-L. Bonaparte a algunos de sus colaboradores." *Revista Internacional de Estudios Vascos* 4 (1910): 233–97.

Urkixo. See Urquijo.

Urte, Pierre. *Grammaire cantabrique basque*. Edited by Wentworth Webster. Bagnères-de-Bigorre: Imprimerie D. Berot, 1900.

Villasante, Luis. "Oñatiko euskera." *Egan* 27 (1968): 80–94.

Wilbur, Terence H. "The Phonemes of the Basque of Bakersfield, California." *Anthropological Linguistics* 3, no. 8 (1961): 1–12.

Yrizar, Pedro. *Contribución a la dialectología de la lengua vasca*. 2 Volumes. Donostia: Gipuzkoako Aurrezki Kutxa Probintziala, 1981.

———. *Morfología del verbo auxiliar alto navarro septentrional* (2 liburuki). Iruñea: Nafarroako Gobernua; Euskaltzaindia, 1992.

———. *Morfología del verbo auxiliar labortano*. Iruñea: Euskaltzaindia; Euskal Herriko Unibertsitatea, 1997.

Zabala, Joan Mateo. *El verbo regular vascongado del dialecto vizcaino*. San Sebastián: Ignacio Ramón Baroja, 1848.

Zelaieta, Edu. "Bortzerrietako euskara, herriz herri (ez)berdintasunetan barrena." *Fontes Linguae Vasconum* 36, no. 96. (2004): 223–48 and 37, no. 99 (2005): 287–306.

Zuazo, Koldo. "Burundako hizkera." In *Euskal Dialektologiako Kongresua*, edited by Ricardo Gómez and Joseba A. Lakarra. ASJU supplement 28. Donostia: Gipuzkoako Foru Aldundia, 1994.

———. *Euskara batua: Ezina ekinez egina*. Donostia: Elkar, 2005.

———. *Deba ibarreko euskara: Dialektologia eta Tokiko batua*. Eibar: Badihardugu Euskara Elkartea, 2006.

Zubiri, Juan Joxe, and Patziku Perurena. *Goizueta eta Aranoko hizkerak*. Leitza: Nafarroako Gobernua; Goizuetako Udala; Aranoko Udala, 1998.

Index

Place names in the Basque Country are followed by parenthetical references to the province in which they are located: Araba (A), Bizkaia (B), Gipuzkoa (G), Lapurdi (L), Lower Navarre (LN), Navarre (N), or Zuberoa (Z)

About the Author

Koldo Zuazo (Eibar, Gipuzkoa, 1956) is a Basque linguist, professor at the University of the Basque Country, and specialist in Basque language dialectology and sociolinguistics. His work on the Basque dialects has reshaped the field of Basque dialectology. His new classification and new maps of Basque dialects have been a revolution in a field where few changes were made since the Louis Lucien Bonaparte's mid-nineteenth-century works.

About the Translator

Aritz Branton (Chester, UK, 1964) is a translator specialized in literature, linguistics and general humanities. He translates between English and Basque and, occasionally, from Romance languages to the former. Aritz writes for *the-balde* and *Entzun!* magazines about literature and music and is also involved in various publishing projects.

www.ingramcontent.com/pod-product-compliance
Lightning Source LLC
LaVergne TN
LVHW091054080826
845145LV00002B/746

* 9 7 8 1 9 3 5 7 0 9 4 2 8 *